Management, Information and Power

Information Systems Series
Series Editor: Professor I.O. Angell

Management, Information and Power

A narrative of the involved manager

Lucas D. Introna

Department of Information Systems
London School of Economics and Political Science

MACMILLAN

First published 1997 by
MACMILLAN PRESS LTD
Houndmills, Basingstoke, Hampshire RG21 6XS
and London
Companies and representatives
throughout the world

ISBN 0–333–69870–3

A catalogue record for this book is available
from the British Library.

This book is printed on paper suitable for recycling and
made from fully managed and sustained forest sources.

10 9 8 7 6 5 4 3 2 1
06 05 04 03 02 01 00 99 98 97

Printed and bound in Great Britain by
Antony Rowe Ltd, Chippenham, Wiltshire

Dedicated to my mother
with gratitude and fondness

The desire to know and the craving for explanations will never bring us to thoughtful questioning. Invariably the desire to know is already the concealed arrogance of self-consciousness which relies on fabricated reason and its reasonableness. Wanting to know does not want to relinquish hope in the face of that which is worthy of thought

Martin Heidegger

It is of cardinal importance that one should abolish the true world. It is the great inspirer of doubt and devaluator in respect of the world we are: it has been our most dangerous attempt yet to assassinate life.

Friedrich Nietzsche

Contents

Preface

This book started more than a decade ago. While working as a systems analyst, trying to develop management information systems, I became aware of the difficulty of answering seemingly obvious questions such as: "What is management information?"; "How do managers actually use it in doing whatever they do?". The world of management theory seemed so obvious and clear cut. I remember distinctly how excited I was on completing my MBA and having this sense of now knowing it. I could analyze, articulate, describe, suggest, solve, and a lot more. Yet, my everyday work seemed messy, unanalyzable, unarticulatable, unsolvable, and so on. No matter how hard one tried to be the manager that the theory said one ought to be, these eloquent models seemed to crumble in the face of the everyday 'getting the job done'. Getting the job done seemed to make the ideal increasingly elusive. Not only this, most of the managers for whom I tried to develop management information systems, talked about this sense of elusiveness in getting 'it' all together. Buried in the concerns of getting the everyday job done, absorbed in pushing it through, the world seemed to resemble a brawl in the bar rather than a chess game.

My initial reaction was that there seems to be a need to expand, or alter, our understanding of the nature of the everyday world of the manager in the organization. The more I immersed myself in a diverse body of literature, the more it became clear to me that there was a particular world view that informed the majority of management thinking; a world view deeply rooted in the Enlightenment, especially in the Descartes dualism. At the centre of this world view seemed to be the idea of the *thinking, rational, purposive manager*. Looking back at this realization, it is now apparent to me that this phenomenon of a particular world view dominating the discourse in a particular field is clearly not unique to management thought. However, what is unique, in my opinion, is the degree to which this world view seems to dominate in spite of numerous challenges, and in spite of an extensive and sustained deconstruction of the Enlightenment project that forms its basis. Why is this so?

Is it the pervasive *moral* legitimacy that this idea of a thinking, rational, purposive manager has? Is it that the alternative of an 'unthinking', 'irrational', 'purposeless' manager is just too ghastly to contemplate? Would managers lose their good name if they were to acknowledge that they are not the skilful planners and decision makers which they are made out to be, and which they, from time to time, believe themselves to be. To acknowledge that they are rather skilful opportunists that mostly depend on gut feel, that collude, coerce, and do whatever is necessary to get-the-job-done. Would it be too dangerous to contemplate this possibility? Is the image of a thinking, rational and purposive manager more true because it is more virtuous? Surely this cannot be an argument as Nietzsche (1973, p.39) aptly points out:

> No one is likely to consider a doctrine true merely because it makes happy or makes virtuous.... Happiness and virtue are no arguments.... Something might be true although harmful and dangerous in the highest degree; indeed, it could pertain to the very fundamental nature of existence that a complete knowledge of it would destroy one – so that the strength of a spirit could be measured by how much truth it could take, more clearly, to what degree it needed, it attenuated, veiled, sweetened, blunted, and falsified.

What is the alternative then? This book is an attempt rearticulate the idea of the manager; the manager *in* the world; not as the thinking, rational and purposive manager but as the *involved* manager. The manager that is always already *in*-the-world. The manager that cannot escape the messyness, the ambiguity, the play of force, in a world that cannot be un-entangled. Everything is already caught up, and tied to a whole, that has no logical beginning, no obvious logic, no simply present solutions, or ways out. There is no striating it out, or shaking it out, once and for all. The straightening it out and the shaking it out will itself become caught up, tied to, in many unexpected ways – where untying at one end may be tying at a whole lot of other ends. This is a world of *being-in*, of gut feel and thinking on your feet – in this world success is defined by your ability to see the gaps, grasp the opportunities and translate them into possibilities. This is the world of the *involved* manager; this is the image I will seek to present. It is not a neat and eloquent story; it is not a prescriptive story; but hopefully it is a real story – and this is why it is worth telling.

Heidegger will help us think through what it means to be an involved manager in-the-world. We are not *in* the world in a way a table is *in* the world. We are *involved* in a world that is present even *before* we think of it, plan it, or decide it. Gadamer, Wittgenstein and Heidegger will help us think through how this involved manager understands the world and acts in this world already known. They will help us understand what it means to make sense of the world. They will show us that the involved manager understands the world and knows how to act in it even before thinking, even before reasoning, and deciding. It may even be that what we call deciding, are merely acts of reifying what was already known in doing in the world. Ashby will help us to argue that control based on representational knowing will always lead to a zero-sum game; that every layer of externally located control will have to be paid for with a loss of flexibility in the lower level. Varela will help us think through what it means to get the job done in-the-world where we have collapsed the Taylor dualism, the layers; when we reunite thinking and doing. Foucault and Glegg will help us think through the network of power relations that are always already present in understanding and doing in the world. We will see that power cannot be escaped; that it is always already present. Finally, we will see how these concepts of the involved manager, information as understanding, and power, provide us with a useful framework to think through what management information means in-the-world of the involved manager.

This book is not finished. It is a rough draft. However, it needs to get out now. I suspect that many of the ideas in this book will relate to things currently being said by others – if the ideas, arguments and remarks in this book do not bear 'a stamp which mark them as mine', I do not wish to lay any further claim to them. Let me conclude this preface with some thoughts from Wittgenstein. His concluding paragraphs in the preface of his *Philosophical Investigations* is a clear reflection of how I feel about this book: "I should not like my writing to spare other people the trouble of thinking. But, if possible, to stimulate someone to thoughts of their own. I should have liked to produce a good book. This has not come about, but the time is past in which I could improve it."

Lucas Introna
London, 1997

Acknowledgements

I would like to acknowledge all who have aided me in writing this book, many more than listed below. I know that as time goes by others will be remembered, others who should be mentioned by name, and to them I apologise for not giving them the credit they so richly deserve.

There are many persons who contributed to the initial forming of the ideas in this book; Dewald Roode for his patience as an initial sounding board for many of the ideas in this book. Also the staff of the Philosophy Department at the University of Pretoria who endured my enquiries and who listened to my ideas, in particular, Pieter Du Toit, Alex Antonites and Marius Schoeman. I hope I have done justice to the thoughts of the great thinkers they have aided me to understand. Various persons read the initial draft manuscript and provided excellent comments, I want to particularly mention Edgar Whitley, Rodrigo Magalhaes and Julika Siemer. I believe it would also be appropriate to explicitly acknowledge the extensive review done by Matthew Jones from the University of Cambridge who acted as reviewer for Macmillan. His comments vastly improved the final product.

For his collaboration on Chapter 5 I would like to acknowledge Leiser Silva. His intellectual contribution to this important chapter significantly enhanced it. Writing does not come easily to me. For his excellent job of taking my twisted prose and turning it into readable and enjoyable English I want to acknowledge Mike Cushman. Mike not only edited the book but made many invaluable comments on structure, logic, and flow. His contribution to this book has been significant in style and content.

There are always those who support your ideas and believe in your work in spite of your doubts. They inspire by always being there for you as mentor, friend, listener, and supporter. In this capacity I want to acknowledge the contributions made by Henry Lederle, Dewald Roode, Nick Du Plooy, Edgar Whitley, Dick Boland, Heinz Klein, Duane Truex, Kalle Lyytinen and Ian Angell. It is their belief in me that sustained me in moments of grave doubt. In particular I want to acknowledge the support of Ian Angell for getting this book into print. Many colleagues and friends listened to my ideas and tolerated my moments of joy and despair. They are: my colleagues at the University of Pretoria, my colleagues at The London School of Economics and Political Science, my brother Lorenzo and my friend Danie Le Roux.

Finally, I want to acknowledge the many sacrifices made by my family. My parents, brothers and sisters who *always* encouraged me. I sincerely thank my wife and friend Georgie, for her critique and encouragement. She listened, always with interest, to these ideas for many years, at appropriate and inappropriate times, whether she felt like it or not. In conclusion, I would like to thank Georgie and my children Thomas and Isabelle who had to experience my absence, in mind and body, in the many hours that went into this work.

Lucas Introna

1 Introduction: why and how to think?

- *Introduction*
- *The philosophy of this book*
- *Review of the structure and content of the book*

Introduction

Everything here is the path of a responding that examines as it listens. Any path always risks going astray, leading astray. To follow such paths takes practice in going. Practice needs craft. Stay on the path, in genuine need, and learn the craft of thinking, unswerving, yet erring.

Heidegger

The purpose of this book

This book is about responding to a different path; about thinking and listening differently, but why? I will argue that the techno-functionalist paradigm (Burrell & Morgan, 1979), the current archetype for the information systems discipline, is exhausted. In applying this paradigm to everyday world problems, anomalies are being generated and are rapidly accumulating, to the point where a serious question of legitimacy now confronts the discipline. Senior executives are questioning the return on massive investments in information technology (Strassman, 1990). Critical sociologists are questioning the ethics and efficacy of the *new fordism* embodied in functionally inspired interventions such as business process re-engineering (Mumford, 1996). The failure of information technology projects seems to be as pervasive as ever (Duffy, 1993; Page *et al.*, 1993). A general uneasiness seems to prevail in many areas of the discipline.

Many in the current techno-functionalist paradigm may acknowledge the current 'crisis'; however, for them it is clear evidence that there is still much work to be done in articulating it, and making more precise, the tools at their disposal. In some sense they may be right. I would rather argue with Kuhn (1970; 1977) that it is a revolution and not just a revival that is needed to move the discipline out of the current 'crisis'– undoubtedly the first of many.

1

Notwithstanding this, it has to be acknowledged that there have been various attempts to revolutionize the discipline by expanding its theoretical foundations: through the use of critical theory (Hirschheim & Klein, 1994; Lyytinen, 1986); hermeneutics (Boland, 1983; Introna, 1993); and structuration theory (Orlikowski & Gash, 1992; Walsham, 1993); to name but a few. However, these efforts seem to be continually marginalized into isolated pockets away from the mainstream. They are often discarded as philosophical endeavours with very limited practical benefit. Yet, the very community who dismisses these efforts does not question the *implicit* assumptions of their own ontological and epistemological position, holding it as self-evident. This state of affairs must not prevail. As researchers try to understand and explain these anomalies they will, eventually, have also to question the assumptions that define the paradigm itself (Kuhn, 1970).

Such efforts, however, can easily become insignificant in a discipline like information systems, where real world problems weigh heavily on practitioners and researchers alike and the need to serve the interests of major sponsors constrains. The demand to produce neatly packaged answers to messy real world problems, that spiral in complexity, threatens to engulf all of us. Ironically, though, the assumptions that drive this demand for solutions are exactly those that are now in crisis.

If there is a way out of this dilemma, it is not through more positivist research, in spite of the massive institutional legitimacy of such work. Generating more data, be it through more rigour or precision, using the same assumptions will just add to the confusion. I believe that it is time for a *new story*; we need thinking that consciously attempts to change the very basis of the story.

The law of requisite variety (Ashby, 1957) demands more variety in our thinking and in our theories, to match the complexity of the world we study. The off-the-shelf techno-functionalist solutions of the 1970s and 1980s may have been suitable as a first stab; however, we can no longer afford to present them, uncritically, to our students and to practitioners. The world view that underpins these answers has been under severe and sustained criticism for a hundred years and more (Feyerabend, 1993; Foucault, 1983; Heidegger, 1962; Heidegger, 1984; Nietzsche, 1967; Wittgenstein, 1956). It is now becoming imperative for the information systems discipline to expand its theoretical base, if it wants to learn from and contribute to the discourse of related disciplines. This expansion means being prepared to 'listen' to alternative narratives about the phenomena before us. The logic of these narratives may not be immediately obvious, since they may not resonate with our long held beliefs. However, the lack of immediate resonance does not make them less 'true', less powerful, explanations; it merely indicates that they are based on a new world view based on new assumptions about the world. In fact, we should expect an alternative story to seem, at first, to be obscure and rather unconvincing. This should not, however, prevent us from staying open to the challenges and possibilities that such an alternative narrative may hold.

This book, therefore, is not merely about new frameworks, models and checklists to perpetuate, and further legitimate, the existing story. It is, first and foremost, about thinking differently. It risks telling a new story; a new story but a well-known theme, *the manager and information in the organization*. The theme itself is interesting but not paramount, it is the context to draw upon in organizing the story as it unfolds. The way the narrative is told is paramount. Consequently, this new narrative is not located in the discourse of Science; it is located in the everyday world, the world we are always already *in* even before the narrative itself begins. It is the narrative of the *involved manager in-the-world*.

Where are we now?

Today there is more confusion than ever before about what information 'is' or 'is not'. This is despite information seeming to be, at least in some sense, a rudimentary element of what society is about. The British Computer Society, in *The Computer Journal,* in 1985, and again in 1989, attempted to initiate a debate on the issue of a theory of information by making it the subject of a special issue. Both times, the response was so limited that the editor had to fill the journal with papers on other matters. Most textbooks on information systems contain such definitions as: "[d]ata consists of facts and figures that are relatively meaningless to the user. Information is processed data, or meaningful data" (McLeod, 1995). What does this definition mean? Is it information just because it has been processed? What are facts and figures? What does 'meaningful' mean? Maybe, by referring to the meaning of these words in the Oxford dictionary, these definitions could be deconstructed?

Data consists of facts and figures that are relatively meaningless to the user. Information is processed data, or meaningful data

- *facts*: "things that are known to have occurred, to exist, or to be true."
- *meaningless*: "have no meaning or significance."
- *meaning*: "what is meant by a word, action, idea, etc."
  these definitions in turn lead to:

- *known*: "have in mind; have learnt; be able to recall."
- *mean*: "have as one's purpose or intention" or "intent to convey or indicate or refer to a particular thing or notion."
- *significance*: "importance; noteworthiness"

Thus we can conclude that data are things that are known (we have in mind, have learnt or can recall) but are relatively unimportant (refers to something unimportant). Information is processed data that is important (or refers to something important). If we exclude the notion of processing, with the assumption that its purpose is to make the 'things' important, then we can conclude that *information is things that we know and are of importance or noteworthy*. If we accept this idea then we ought again to ask the question again: "What does it mean to *know*?", for without an answer to this, there is not even a beginning of an adequate understanding of a system that is for or about information. The answer to this question will depend on a whole set of assumptions that we may bring to the discussion. There is a whole branch of philosophy, epistemology, which has as its purpose to answer this, seemingly innocuous, question. We could continue to deconstruct many of the typical definitions of information in this way and discover that they do not make much sense, or are circular.

Management, as with information, is a concept fraught with vagueness and ambiguity. There are as many definitions of what management is as there are managers or academics writing about management. Even a synthesis of more than one of these vague definitions creates no clearer concept of what management is. There are definitions such as: "getting things done through others" (Holt, 1987). Or, by way of example, take the following passage from the management classic *Management: Tasks, Responsibilities, Practices*, by Peter Drucker (1974, p.12):

> *Management and managers are the specific need of all institutions, from the smallest to the largest. They are the specific organ of every institution. They are what holds it together and makes it work. None of our institutions could function without managers.*

From this passage, we could conclude that management is those activities that hold institutions together and make them work. Is there anything that happens in organizations that we can directly or indirectly exclude from this category? This leads to equating management with the organization.

Adding computing technology to this, already confusing, situation seems merely to compound the problem and, thus, management information systems are seen by many managers as an imposed evil. They seem to be systems for legitimizing the idea that information is equal to rational and that rational is equal to good. Managers can often be heard bewailing that information technology is absorbing their ever-shrinking budget and then drowning them in irrelevant data.

I have tried to show that the issue of management information in the organization is not a matter of simply stapling a couple of well understood and unambiguous concepts (management and information) together. It is definitely not merely a matter of automating facts-processing to make them useful. Furthermore, notions such as 'know', 'facts' and 'importance' should indicate that management information (and systems) is first and foremost a *social* phenomenon and not a purely technological one.

I will argue that the only way to make sense of these phenomena is to return to the *things themselves*; to think through and understand the most fundamental unit, *the manager*, in the world of everyday doing. The manager is the 'place' where management and information originate and have their *being*. We should, however, not be interested in the manager of science, the thinking, rational and purposive manager, but rather the manager concernfully *involved in-the-world*, the living manager, the manager as *is*. Accordingly, the purpose of this book is to explore the notions of management, information and power from the perspective of the manager who is *always already involved in* the organization.

Why management information?

There has been much research on the concept of management and information (including management information systems). This research has, however, for the most part, been limited to *observer* based scientific constructions, projected onto *decontextualized* empirical data, in such a way that our understanding of the manager and information has become abstract, lifeless, and artificial. Take, for example, the following text from the seminal work by Gordon Davis (1974, p.32, p.140-147):

> *The value of information is related to decisions. If there were no choices or decisions, information would be unnecessary.*
>
> *...Another way to explain the process of decision making is in terms of a continuous activity motivated by an objective of transforming the system (business, department, family, etc.) from its current state to a desired state. The desired state causes a search for the means to achieve it.*
>
> *...[T]he computer acts as an adjunct to the human decision maker in computing, storing, retrieving, analysing, etc., data. The design allows the human decision maker to allocate tasks to himself or to the computer.*

> *...The limits of human decision makers in organizations plus the relative efficiency of human processing of decisions mean that the MIS should program as many decisions as possible.*
>
> *...For these [non-programmed decisions], the MIS provides, where possible, a set of tools by which the decision maker can structure the decision-making process.... the MIS may be designed with partial structuring to speed up the remaining human processing.*

The logic and assumptions of this piece can be summarized as follows:

- Making decisions is what managers do.
- Decisions are directed towards, and emanate from, objectives.
- Decisions need and define facts.
- Information consists of facts that describe the current state of affairs.
- Computers are very efficient at making decisions, applying facts to rules.
- The task of decision making is best divided between the manager and the computer, with the computer being preferred.
- The human manager and the electronic computer are both, essentially, computing systems for rational decision making.

Although this book was published in 1974, it is my contention that this line of thinking about managers, decision making, and information is still the prevalent archetype, albeit in a much more subtle form. Especially, there is still a strong emphasis on the link between information and rational decision making. Olson and Courtney (1992, p.21) argued that: "Decision making is one of the important elements in business success, and it is what executives are hired to do." This is obviously, in a superficial way 'true'. Yet it does not stand up to our primordial and tacit knowledge of what we actually do in our everyday lives. Day to day, it appears, we act out what we already know and then, in observing ourselves, conclude that what we have done was to 'make a decision'. There may be those times when we explicitly attend to decisions. However, I will argue, these are better understood as derivatives of a more primordial decision: the acting out of an understanding which we *always already have* because we are concernedly involved *in-our-world*. Once we start thinking through alternative interpretations for the story of the manager and decision making in everyday organizational life, then the obviousness of the prevailing fades.

Much information systems research has been severely limited by the assumption that management information systems are principally a technological phenomenon. Although many information systems researchers seem to be aware of this assumption, and the incorrect technological bias in it, they still opt to make these assumptions anyway. I will argue that this technological bias is the logical consequence of a story that began with a tool, the computer, as its main (and unchallenged) character. By positing this main character, the story was kept coherent by always returning to it. Hence, the story of information systems is, and stays, first and foremost, the story of the computer.

Traditionally, management information systems are described as those systems that support management in the execution of such management tasks as planning, controlling, problem-solving and decision-making. Under this broad concept can be placed functional (marketing, manufacturing, financial, etc.) information systems, decision support systems, group decision support systems, expert systems, executive information systems, and so forth. Although many authors would acknowledge in their introductions that information systems refer to *more* than the computerized information systems, the vast majority only discuss and deal with such systems in their treatment of the subject.

The *raison d'être* of management information systems, as a tale within the history of the computer in business, evolved in a seemingly logical and obvious manner. The narrative of this history is often told as a logical unfolding of three epochs: the data processing era, the management information era, and the strategic information systems era (Earl, 1989; Ward et al., 1990; Wiseman, 1985). Since this story is well known I will only mention the first two here. Initially, computing technology was used for *data processing*; that is to automate basic business processes (transactions). Instead of writing out and calculating the total of an invoice by hand, for example, the process can be done much more efficiently by a computer. The computer stores certain customer data in a data store and standard product data in another data store. All the clerk has to do is to select the customer (by a customer number) and select the products (by a product code) and tell the computer how much of each the customer has ordered. The computer then compiles, calculates and prints the invoice in seconds, a task that would have taken the clerk 10 to 15 minutes. This automation represents a vast improvement in efficiency and it is no wonder that the business community were genuinely pleased with this new invention. There was a euphoric sense of wonder and excitement about the efficiency improvements that this new invention could bring.

This era was followed by the *management information era*. Managers realized that there were now masses of data stored in data stores all over the organization. Some of this data was about entities, such as customers or suppliers, and some of this data reflected transactions between the entities; and transactions that reflected the utilization (movement, consumption, etc.) of resources (people, money, material). Managers could now get direct answers to specific questions by using the 'information system'; questions such as: How many customers do we have? How many customers buy more than X of products from us in a year? Who is our biggest customer? How much of product Y do we have in our store?

The computer used a program to read the data and process it, by selecting, sorting, comparing or doing some arithmetic calculation with it. The result of this process was *information* and the person interested in the answers was the *'manager'*. Thus was *management information* produced. By means of this management information, management was now to be informed. Also, with this management information, managers could now make more effective decisions. This appears to be logical and fairly simple, but somehow things did not quite work that way; the enormous success of the data processing era has not been duplicated in the management information era. Instead of managers praising the computer and its capabilities, there is growing discontent with the high cost of computer technology and its poor value for money. When it dawned in the late 1970s, the management information system era was meant to lead to a new and exciting age when all sorts of 'information' would be available at the touch of a button, but it has not lived up to expectations. In spite of huge investments in information technology the average manager is still "drowning in ever-increasing irrelevant data and starving for relevant information". Making sense of the everyday landscape of getting the job done is as difficult as ever.

This book will endeavour to provide an insight into what went wrong. It will argue that the core of the problem is a lack of understanding of the assumptions that currently inform our concepts of the manager, information, management and power. Management information, as articulated in the techno-functionalist paradigm (Burrell & Morgan, 1979), was largely based on a common-sense idea of information and its role in everyday organizations. Its explicit development was largely the incidental result of developing computerized data processing systems. Management information systems emerged into industry, without any fundamental thinking to direct or shape them. It is only when things started breaking down, that academics woke up to the problem of *information*.

From this technologically inspired base, management information systems evolved. The manager, under the influence of Taylorism (Taylor, 1914), was viewed as a decision-making black box – merely the recipient of a stream of information from the system (Davis & Olsen, 1985; Simon,

1977). It all looked so obvious and simple that it could not possibly fail; yet it did. For example, one of the issues that the pioneers neglected to comprehend was the relationship between *representation* and *reality*, the map and the territory. How does the map relate to the territory? What assumptions does *this* mapping the territory imply (what is included, what excluded and who decides this)? What can we, and what can we not, 'know' from the map? Is there more than one way to read the map? Whose interests does a particular mapping and interpretation serve and at whose expense?

The problem of representation and reality had been (and still is) at the centre of central philosophical themes for many decades; themes in epistemology, such as the language and doing of science; in ontology, such as the question of the status of representations; in ethics, such as the question of legitimacy in the use and interpretation of representations; and so forth. The philosophy of language has for many decades grappled with the issues that we in the information systems discipline have treated, and still treat, as almost trivial problems; problems such as the relationship between symbols and that which they stand for. This is not an attack on the discipline. It is a serious reflection on the past and, hopefully, a beginning of the appreciation of the richness and subtlety of the problems that we discard as theoretical distractions.

These, then, are the issues that this book will endeavour to include in the articulation of an alternative narrative:

- *What is a manager?* What does a manager do? How does the manager do what he does? How does the manager exist in the organization on a daily basis?
- *What is information?* What are its characteristics? How does it come into existence? What is, or is not, an information system?
- *What is management?* How does a manager manage? What is the process of management? What must the manager do in order to manage successfully?
- *What is power?* How does it come about? How is it utilized? How does it influence managers, their actions and decisions?
- *What is management information?* What are the characteristics of management information? How and where does management inform-ation come about? How does it relate to management?

Each of the questions above could be the subject of a book in its own right. Nevertheless, this book will develop a platform from which all these questions can be discussed. It can by no means answer them in any amount of detail; it can, however, suggest ways of thinking and point out possible directions towards answers. Even though conclusive answers cannot in any way be provided, useful insights and new understanding may flow from the attempt to 'muddle' through these questions.

The philosophy of this book
On the general design

When writing a book it is always difficult to decide what must be included and what left out; also the level of detail for each topic. Much of this book is dedicated to developing and exploring ideas outside the mainstream paradigm, to making them come alive, to telling an anti-story. Yet these ideas need to be located in some way in relation to the current paradigm. This locating, however, is not intended as a detailed deconstruction of the current paradigm. Such a deconstruction is not within the scope of this book and has been done, to varying degrees, elsewhere, including (Avgerou & Cornford, 1995; Boland, 1983; Capra, 1982; Ciborra, 1994; Derrida, 1982; Dreyfus & Dreyfus, 1986; Feyerabend, 1975; Foucault, 1977; Heidegger, 1962; Heidegger, 1984; Lyotard, 1986; Lyytinen, 1986; Maturana & Varela, 1987; Nietzsche, 1967; Rorty, 1982; Stamper, 1988; Winograd & Flores, 1987). Therefore, in each case I will present only a sort of archetype of what can be seen as the salient features of the techno-functionalist paradigm. In many cases these archetypes are nearer to sketches and are not intended to be complete. The intention is to create contrast, while acknowledging that there are many possibilities in between. Furthermore, I am making the assumption that most readers do have a reasonably clear picture of the prevailing archetype; hence a few broad strokes will suffice. If this assumption is not made the book would become unmanageable and the coherency of this anti-story would be lost.

From epistemology to ontology: the involved manager

The central figure in this anti-story will be the *involved manager*, the *manager in-the-world*, as opposed to the paradigmatic *rational purposive manager*. In order to explain the significance of what this means we need to step back and look, in more general terms, at the ways in which we tend to view and investigate phenomena.

Normally there is a dialectical relationship between our ontology and our epistemology. Or, to put it more simply: the things we find and the ways we explain them are determined by the way we look (epistemology), and by the things we expect to find (ontology). Generally, the results of our research, our science, are *constructions* (models, theories, perspectives, descriptions) made by *observers* (researchers, participants, participant observers). The degree to which these constructions are valid, legitimate, or deemed to be true, is the degree to which they correspond to, reflect, or mirror the reality which they are supposed to model or describe. The data collected by objective measurement or subjective interpretation are used to construct or re-construct models, theories, interpretations and so forth. The intention is for a positivist to make them more predictive, or for an interpretivist, to add to a more comprehensive understanding.

It is the picture, the representation, and the way it is constructed, by and for the researcher that is important. As Heidegger (1977, p127) points out: "We first arrive at science as research when and only when truth has been transformed into the certainty of representation." If this picture is more predictive, or provides clearer, or alternative, perspectives on the problem at hand then the science is succeeding. This mode of enquiry is almost exclusively *observer-centric*, and operates *within* the subject/object dualism of Descartes. In the case of positivism this dualism is very strong and explicit as part of the ground rules of the game. In interpretivism this dualism is weak and implicit and is seen as a barrier to utilize and overcome. Yet, even in all but the most extreme variants of interpretivism it is assumed that the observer *qua* observer can gain access to reality in some way.

Polanyi (1973) argues that there are many things that we do not know that we 'know'; we know more than we can say. Hence, there is a knowing *before* any representation. Even when a manager is asked what she normally does, or is doing, the response will merely be her interpretation of what she 'thinks' she is doing. This is also true in the case of a participant observer; they may be 'closer' to the reality, but will also merely end up with a description of what they 'think' they are doing and observing. It does not matter how ethnographic or participative, or non-intrusive our investigations are, we still end up with representations (pictures, descriptions, theories and the like) by *observers* about the reality they 'think' they observed, measured or experienced. Hence, we have the postmodern claim that everything is *always already interpretation* (Foucault, 1984).

In the observer-centric mode of enquiry we can only investigate the world through representations; "the Being of whatever *is*, is sought and found in the representedness of the latter" (Heidegger, 1977, p131). What about the world *before* representation, before epistemology? Is the world only true if we (humans) can describe it? Does that mean that we can only know to a degree what we can represent? Surely the world is more than can show up on the horizon of our reason and of our senses? If this is true, we should not only try and understand the world as observers (as traditional science forces us to do). We should instead return to 'the things themselves' – on their own home ground, as it were. We should *think through* the world even before the maps, the theories, etc. – the world before thinking itself (Heidegger, 1968). It is the world of the *always already involved* human being (*Dasein*). Human beings do not act in the way observers think they act and *this includes them as observers of themselves*. Instead, they act in ways that make sense *in* the situation. And, because they are concernedly involved in a world which they always already understand (Heidegger, 1962), they 'know' what makes sense in the situation even *before* thinking about it, before representation. They act, not because they know and have thought about it, but because *being-in* the world implies 'always already knowing' how to act in that world. The world is always already present. This may all sound very abstract and peculiar, yet I am convinced that by the end of our journey the validity and importance of this alternative story will be evident.

This book is the narrative of the *always already involved manager*. Specifically, I want to think through the way this involved manager makes sense of the world (information); I want to think through how this involved manager gets the job done (management); and we want to think through how this involved manager exploits moments of *force* to get to whatever makes sense and to what gets the job done (power). In thinking through we should continually resist the observer temptation to attribute to this manager plans, intentions, decisions, models and representations. These notions are neat and tidy concepts with which researchers can build theories, models, descriptions and interpretations. They have no onto-logical reality outside the minds of the observers. We *are* before we think, not, as Descartes argued, because we think. Creating representations only arrives after we have already existed in-the-world. It is our *being-in* that is the rudimentary basis of what we are and what we do.

Heidegger (1962) argues that we need a shift from epistemology to ontology. This provides a way to 'think' about the manager in-the-world without first making models and constructing theories. We need to stop doing Science and return to the most fundamental question of all "the Being of being", the *real* of the real, the *is* of is-ness. The real is not, as Descartes argued, what we can think; the *real* is in the things themselves, in their own suchness. The most profound problem is not the epistem-ological problem of explaining how the ideas in our minds can be true, or correspond with, the external world. For even this subject/object epistemology "presupposes a background of everyday practices into which we are socialized but that we do not represent in our minds" (Dreyfus, 1991, p.3). Therefore this book, taking seriously the argument of Heidegger, will not enquire about the being (manager) that we *know*, that we picture in our head as corresponding to the world. It will enquire about the manager that simply *is*, the involved manager. We cannot do this by imposing our constructions on the world. As Heidegger (1962, pp.37-8, emphasis added) explains:

> *[W]e have no right to resort to dogmatic constructions and apply just any idea of Being and actuality to this entity [Dasein: the manager], no matter how 'self-evident' that idea may be; nor may any of the 'categories' which such an idea prescribes be forced upon Dasein without proper ontological consideration. We must rather choose such a way of access and such a kind of interpretation that this entity can show itself in itself and from itself. And this means that it is to be shown as it is proximally and for the most part – in its average everydayness.*

Post-modernists would object and say that even this phenomenological access is mere speculation by a different type of observer. This may be true. If so, my only defence for the narrative that will unfold in the coming chapters, is that it is at least as legitimate as that which was produced by observer-constructed observation and theory. In the final analysis every reader should individually decide whether this story is more or less convincing than the others available to him or her. It is my conjecture that this alternative story of the *always already involved manager* is a viable alternative narrative that provides a way to understand many of the anomalies generated by the functionalist paradigm. This alternative story demands to be accounted for.

To summarize: the general theme of the book will consist of the juxta-position of two *Weltanschauungen* based on two fundamentally different ontological and epistemological positions. The first is the primordial notion of the management world, based on being-in, with its core concept of the *always already involved manager*. The second, a derivative of the first, is the traditional observer-based, scientific notion, of the management world with its core concept of the *thinking, rational and purposive manager*. The two positions are summarized in Table 1.1.

I will endeavour to develop this dual theme in the chapters to follow, without trying to force it to much. Hopefully readers will also develop this distinction in their own reading of the book.

Table 1.1: The manager: two ontological positions

	Manager	Information	Management	Power
Primordial notion based on being-in	involved manager	hermeneutic understandin g	Manus – the present hand	local network of force relations
Derivative notion based on observation	rational manager	representation al knowing (episteme)	Taylorist dualism	Located source of action

Given that the story of the rational manager is reasonably well understood, the emphasis in the book will be on the alternative story. In the narrative, the always already involved manager will hold centre stage.

Review of the structure and content of the book

The important elements of the structure of the book and of the individual chapters are depicted in Figure 1.1. Outlined below are the main arguments of each chapter.

1. Introduction: why and how to think? This chapter explains the need for fundamental thinking in management and information, in-the-world of management. It argues for an ontological shift from the rational and purposive manager to the involved manager; from the 'ought' to the 'is'. The rest of the book will show that this shift will result in a fundamentally different interpretation of such phenomena as decision making, information, understanding and planning. The chapter also outlines the central issues that this book will attempt to think through.

2. The manager: involved in-the-world. Chapter 2 develops the notion of the involved manager. It starts with the archetype of the manager as a perfectly rational and purposive being; a character with moral standing; a noble professional achieving noble ends. The discussion then moves to a more realistic picture of the manager, as depicted by Mintzberg and Sayles, amongst others. It is a picture of the manager who is forced to superficiality by fragmented, discontinuous events occurring throughout the organization. It is this in-the-world messy-ness that is at the heart of the manager's being in-the-world. Using the work of Martin Heidegger, the manager as *Dasein* is understood as always already in-the-world.

This being-in-the-world nature of the manager challenges many of the traditional assumptions about the manager's world and work. In addition Polanyi argues, with Heidegger, that much of the manager's knowledge about this being-in-the-world is tacit and personal. This tacit and personal source of know-how is always the default already present basis of management action. Hence, the central argument of the chapter is that the involved manager, tacitly understanding and acting in-the-world, is a more appropriate archetype for thinking about management and information than the notion of a rational and purposive manager.

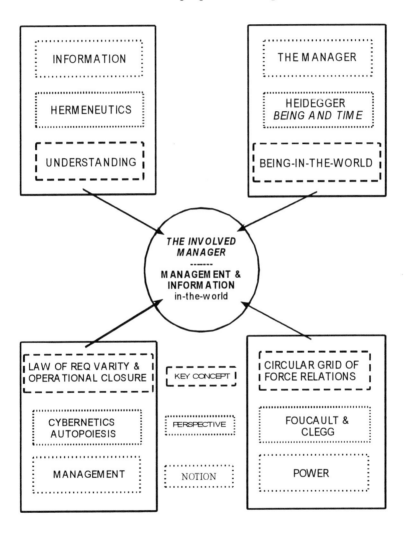

Figure 1.1: Conceptual structure of the book

3. Information: as understanding. The purpose of Chapter 3 is to develop the notion of information as hermeneutic understanding. The chapter starts with a brief review of the current archetypes of information. It argues that most current definitions use terms such as 'meaningful' and 'understanding' but neglect to make explicit how these concepts should be understood. The hermeneutic paradigm, as a theory of interpretation and understanding, provides a point of departure for thinking through information in-the-world of the involved manager. The chapter argues that understanding is always situated, part of a form of life. Not only is understanding situated it is always already present as part of being-in-the-word. The sense, or significance, of language (and information) is not in-the-language but is in-the-form-of-life that the participants share. Hence, the kernel of the chapter is that understanding, present as part of being-in-the-world, is the primordial basis of information. Any other form of understanding will ultimately have to be anchored on this primal basis.

4. Management: and *manus*. Chapter 4 develops the notion of management as *manus*. The chapter presents the prevailing concept of management through the paradigmatic idea of scientific management as put forward by Taylor. The chapter argues that Taylor, as the Descartes of management thought, articulated management as the *thinking* separate from the doing. With this separation, the Taylorist dualism emerged as the paradigmatic concept of the modern management idea. The chapter argues, using first-order cybernetics and systems theory, in particular the law of requisite variety, that the Taylorist dualism creates a control paradox that cannot be solved within first-order cybernetics. It is essentially a zero sum game where variety in the management system must be paid for by loss of variety in the organization; this in turn limits the ability of the organization to participate in the environment. The solution to this dilemma is to relocate control back in the system, to reintegrate thinking and doing as proposed by autopoetic theory. The chapter therefore continues to articulate management as located in-the-world. This shift leads to a reinterpretation of what managers do and why they do it. In particular the important role of language again emerges.

5. Power: the network of force relations. Chapter 5 develops the notion of power as a network of force relations. The chapter argues that the traditional idea of power as *located* in an agent is not very useful to understand the dynamics of power in-the-world of the involved manager. The chapter draws on Foucault's definition of power as a grid of circular force relations that are both medium and outcome of itself. From this perspective every relation is always already a power relation; a relation that is dynamic, diffused, and unstable. Power engenders as much as it restricts. Every act, event, interpretation is always already mediated by power; there is no 'outside' of power. With this notion of power in mind the chapter continues to discuss the circuits of power framework proposed by Clegg. This framework provides a set of concepts that allows for a more detailed appraisal of the role and dynamics of power in-the-world. The usefulness of the framework is demonstrated using a case study of a failed information systems implementation project in the London Ambulance Service. The essential argument of the chapter is that the involved manager is always already involved in power. It is in, and through, this involvement that the involved manager must get the job done.

6. Management information: knowing, explaining and arguing. Chapter 6 is the central component of the book. The purpose of this chapter is to integrate the insights of the previous chapters into a framework for understanding management information in-the-world. The chapter argues that management information is best understood within the three modes of being of *Dasein*. At the most primal level management information is understanding as *know-how*. In this available, ready-to-hand mode the involved manager in-the-world always already knows what to do. In this mode decisions are actions that show up as sensible next steps. In the unavailable mode the manager must *appropriate* the world already understood. In moments of dislocation the startled manager needs to restore the sense or significance through hermeneutic interpretation. In this mode representations are *used* as available tools in-the-world already understood. In the occurrent, present-at-hand mode understanding becomes entangled in the circuits of power. Understanding emerges as arguments about the world. Knowledge and power fuse to create regimes of truth. The chapter presents a short case study to demonstrate how management information functions in these different yet tightly integrated modes of being. The essential argument is that the most primordial basis of management information will always be involvement in-the-world.

7. Implications: so what and what now? Chapter 7 attempts to draw some conclusions and implications from the narrative of the involved manager. Some counter-arguments are considered, such as why formal management information systems are still such pervasive phenomena. It is argued that the significance of formal management information systems is not so much hermeneutic as political; not sense making but truth making. The chapter also suggests some broader interpretations of the ideas espoused by reflecting on a variety of issues such as planning, virtual organizations and decision support systems.

A final comment on the structure of each chapter and the book as a whole. In each chapter I start off by briefly articulating the techno-functional archetype of the concept under discussion. In each case, the purpose is not to give a full account of the current 'state of the art' of the notion involved. The purpose is merely to outline what I believe to be the central notions of thought as embodied in this thinking. Thereafter, the chapter will be followed by a more radical interpretation and discussion on the very nature of the concept itself. This design tends to make the later part of each chapter more challenging.

As for the book as a whole; all the chapters 'pour into' Chapter 6 where management and information are completely re-articulated and re-interpreted. As such I expect that Chapter 6 will make little sense if the arguments in the preceding chapters are not followed through. Since this book is an attempt to re-articulate our understanding of management and information in-the-world comprehensively, I would expect it to raise more questions than it will answers. However, it is my belief that as Churchill said: *this is not the end. It is not even the beginning of the end. But it is, perhaps, the end of the beginning.*

References

Ashby, W.R. (1957), *An Introduction to Cybernetics*, New York, John Wiley & Sons.

Avgerou, C. and Cornford, T. (1995), 'Limitations of Information Systems Theory and Practice: A Case for Pluralism', in Falkenberg, E. (ed.), *Information Systems Concepts: Towards a consolidation of views*, London, Chapman & Hall.

Boland, R.J. (1983), 'The In-Formation of Information Systems', in Boland, R.J. and Hirschheim, R.A. (eds.), *Critical Issues in Information Systems Research*, New York, John Wiley & Sons.

Burrell, G. and Morgan, G. (1979), *Sociological Paradigms and Organizational Analysis*, Portsmouth, New Hampshire, Heinemann.

Capra, F. (1982), *The Turning Point: Science, Society and the Rising Culture*, London, Fontana Paperbacks.

Ciborra, C.U. (1994), 'The Grassroots of IT and Strategy', in Ciborra, C. and Jelassi, T. (eds), *Strategic Information Systems: A European Perspective*, Chichester, Wiley.

Davis, G.B. (1974), *Management Information Systems: Conceptual Foundations, Structure and Development* (2nd Edition), London, McGraw-Hill.

Davis, G.B. and Olsen, M.H. (1985), *Management Information Systems: Conceptual Foundations, Structure and Development* (2nd Edition), London, McGraw-Hill.

Derrida, J. (1982), *"Differance,"* *Margins of Philosophy*, Chicago, University of Chicago Press.

Dreyfus, H.L. (1991), *Being-in-the-world: a Commentary on Heideggers Being and time, Division I*, Cambridge, Mass, MIT Press.

Dreyfus, H.L. and Dreyfus, S.E. (1986), *Mind over Machine: The Power of Human Intuition and Expertise in the Era of the Computer* (Paperback edition, with Tom Athanasiou Edition), New York, The Free Press.

Drucker, P.F. (1974), *Management: Tasks, Responsibilities and Practices*, London, Heinemann.

Duffy, M. (1993), 'Londons Embarrassing Mistake', *Journal*.

Earl, M. (1989), *Management Strategies for Information Technology*, New York, Prentice Hall (UK).

Feyerabend, P. (1975), *Against Method*, London, Verso.

Feyerabend, P. (1993), *Against method* (3rd edition), London, Verso.

Foucault, M. (1977), 'Truth and Power', Gordon, C. (ed.), *Power / Knowledge: Selected Interviews & Other Writings 1972-1977*, New York, Pantheon Books.

Foucault, M. (1983), 'The Subject and Power', Dreyfus, H.L. and Rabinow, P. (eds.), *Michel Foucault: Beyond Structuralism and Hermeneutics*, Chicago, The University of Chicago Press.

Foucault, M. (1984), 'Nietzsche, Genealogy, History', Rabinow, P. (ed.), *The Foucault Reader*, Middlesex, England, Penguin Books.

Heidegger, M. (1962), *Being and time*, Oxford, Basil Blackwell.

Heidegger, M. (1968), *What is Called Thinking*, New York, Harper & Row.

Heidegger, M. (1977), 'The Age of the World Picture', *in* Lovitt, W. (ed.), *The Question Concerning Technology and Other Essays*, New York, Harper & Row.

Heidegger, M. (1984), *The Metaphysical Foundations of Logic*, Bloomington, Indiana University Press.

Hirschheim, R. and Klein, H. (1994), 'Realizing Emancipatory Principles in Information Systems Development: The Case for ETHICS', *MIS Quarterly*, 18, 1, 83-109.

Holt, D.H. (1987), *Management: Principles and Practices*, Englewood Cliffs, New Jersey., Prentice-Hall International.

Introna, L.D. (1993), 'Information: A Hermeneutic Perspective', *The First European Conference on Information systems*, Henley on Thames, England.

Kuhn, T.S. (1970), *The Structure of Scientific Revolutions* (2nd Edition), Chicago, Ill., The University of Chicago Press.

Kuhn, T.S. (1977), *The Essential Tension: Selected Studies in Scientific Tradition and Change.*, Chicago, Ill., The University of Chicago Press.

Lyotard, J.-F. (1986), *The Postmodern Condition: A Report on Knowledge*, Manchester, Manchester University Press.

Lyytinen, K. (1986), *Information Systems Development as Social Action: Framework and critical implications*, University of Jyvaskyla., Unpublished Ph.D. Thesis.

Maturana, H. and Varela, F. (1987), *The Tree of Knowledge: The Biological Roots of Human Understanding*, Boston, Shambhala.

McLeod, R. (1995), *Management Information Systems: A study of computer based information systems*, Englewoods Cliffs, NJ, Prentice Hall.

Mumford, E. (1996), *Systems Design: Ethical Tools for Ethical Change*, Basingstoke, Macmilllan.

Nietzsche, F. (1967), *The Will to Power*, New York, Vintage Books.

Olson, D. and Courtney, J. (1992), *Decision Support Models and Expert Systems*, New York, Macmillan Publishing Company.

Orlikowski, W.J. and Gash, D.C. (1992), 'Changing frames: Understanding Technological Change in Organizations', *Center for Information Technology Research Working Paper*, Cambridge, MA, MIT Sloan School of Management.

Page, D., Williams, P. and Boyd, D. (1993), "Report of the Public Inquiry into the London Ambulance Service", London, HMSO.

Polanyi, M. (1973), *Personal Knowledge: Towards a Post-critical Philosophy* (1st pbk edition), London, Routledge & Kegan Paul.

Rorty, R. (1982), *Consequences of Pragmatism*, Minneapolis, University of Minnesota Press.

Simon, H.A. (1977), *The New Science of Management Decision* (2nd Edition), Englewood Cliffs, N.J., Prentice Hall.

Stamper, R. (1988), 'Pathologies of AI', *AI & Society*, 2, 1, 3-16.

Strassman, P. (1990), *The Business Value of Computers*, New Canaan, The Information Economics Press.

Taylor, F.W. (1914), *The Principles of Scientific Management*, London/New York, Harper & Row.

Walsham, G. (1993), *Interpreting Information Systems in Organizations*, Chichester, John Wiley.

Ward, J., Griffiths, P. and Whitmore, P. (1990), *Strategic Planning for Information Systems*, New York, John Wiley & Sons.

Winograd, T. and Flores, F. (1987), *Understanding Computers and Cognition*, Massachusetts, Addison-Wesley.

Wiseman, C. (1985), *Strategy and Computers*, New York, Dow Jones-Irwin.

Wittgenstein, L. (1956), *Philosophical investigations*, Oxford, Basil Blackwell.

2 The manager: involved in-the-world

- *Introduction*
- *Some current archetypes of the manager*
- *The manager in-the-world*
- *The manager and management skill*
- *Management and social construction of rationality*
- *Conclusions about the manager*

Introduction

Dasein, in its familiarity with significance, is the ontical condition for the possibility of discovering entities which are encountered in a world with involvement (readyness-to-hand) as their kind of Being, and which can thus make themselves known as they are in themselves.

Martin Heidegger in *Being and Time*

In chapter one it was argued that a particular ontological view of the manager and the manager's role in the enterprise leads to a particular interpretation of the 'what' and 'why' of the management and information in the organization. The purpose of this chapter is to explore the ontological position of the *involved manager*.

The discussion will start with the archetypal, but mythical, modern manager, the perfect, rational and purposive being who is the expert of technology; *the* engineer of industrial and commercial society; the 'master of the ship' who efficiently and effectively pursues goals and objectives, always striving to do better, to achieve more with less; a character with moral standing; a noble professional achieving noble ends. The discussion will then move to a more realistic picture of the manager, as depicted by Mintzberg and Sayles: the manager who is forced to superficiality by fragmented, discontinuous events occurring throughout the organization; the manager who must be a master politician, master negotiator, expert psychologist and counsellor, expert communicator, and much more.

This manager does not exist in a vacuum but is very much *in*, and part of, the world. Next, the chapter will apply an even more fundamental thinking process, using the work of Martin Heidegger (1962; 1988; 1992) to develop an understanding of the *involved manager*, the manager as a being-in-the-world. From this analysis the manager emerges as a being struggling with 'every-day-ness', thrown into-the-world. This being in-the-world allows the manager to understand this world. A world that is for the most part always already present and available. In understanding the world the involved manager always already knows what to do in-order-to get the job done.

This will be followed by a section on management skills applying the work of Polanyi. Using Polanyi, it will be argued that managers will mostly base their action on that knowledge which is personal or embodied. This notion of *tacit* knowing links very closely with the analysis of Heidegger. The chapter will conclude with an interpretation that shows the manager itself in itself and from itself – in its average every-day-ness. This is the manager for whom the information system must be available.

Some current archetypes of the manager
The manager as stock character

To a large extent, the manager has become a stock character of our time – a "folk hero of contemporary society" (Mintzberg, 1980). The manager is seen as someone who represents what society believes in and whose behaviour is regarded to be, in principle, morally correct. In this sense, the manager is not only a social role model but is much more besides. As MacIntyre (1981, p.29) explains: "A (stock) character is an object of regard by the members of the culture generally or by some significant segment of them. He furnishes them with a cultural and moral ideal. ... The character morally legitimates a mode of social existence." What then is this morally legitimate mode of existence? The stock character, manager, can best be described by the following traits:

- The manager is a rationally motivated and purposive individual.
- The manager efficiently and effectively transforms: unskilled labour into skilled labour; raw material into products; investments into profits.
- Measurable economic performance is the only benchmark for the manager.
- The manager is the master of technique and technology.
- The manager is the creator and sustainer of economic wealth and well-being.

The description as given above is implicitly the prevalent perception of the manager in society as a whole. This is evident from the following description of a manager by Strong (1965, p.5): the manager "adds foresight, order, purpose, integration of effort, and effectiveness to the contribution of others." This implicit view of the manager can also be seen in the descriptions of the manager and management by Peter Drucker (1974, p.12 my emphasis): "Management and managers are the specific need of all institutions, from the smallest to the largest. They are the specific organ of every institution. *They are what holds it together and makes it work.* None of our institutions could function without managers." Also: "Management is the organ of institutions, the organ that *converts a mob into an organization,* and human efforts into performance" (Drucker, 1980).

This type of manager is beyond reproach and is morally justified. But are these the managers that occupy the factories, and the shops, and the businesses of everyday life – it this stock character real? Is this stock character image of the manager consistent with the everyday 'getting the job done' that managers seem to face? What are the assumptions of this view of the manager and management? This view assumes that the manager can *separate* herself from the 'mob' (Taylorist dualism). It assumes that the manager is present, but not always already involved, always already entangled. It would seem that it is not possible to be involved and separate. This image of the manager is too 'removed', to separate from, the messy and entangled reality. In the following section Mintzberg paints a more realistic picture of a manager caught up in the everyday; in a world that is fragmented, superficial and *ad hoc.*

Managers at work

The manager, according to the principles of management specified by Fayol (1949), is seen as the master of the ship. The person who must effectively and efficiently turn investments into profits for the owners of the business. How should this be done? Fayol (1949, p.43) describes managerial work as executed by way of the activities of management namely: planning, organizing, staffing, co-ordinating, controlling and leading. In spite of the obvious logic inherent in the Fayolian management activities, managers on the job still seem to grapple with the every-day-ness of management tasks. Somehow, their activities get so diffused into the everyday coping that it is difficult for them to say when and how they actually perform the management activities, if at all. As Carlson (1951) concluded: "If we ask a managing director when he is co-ordinating, or how much co-ordination he has been doing during a day he would not know, and even the most skilled observer would not know either" (p. 24). Many academics and practitioners alike have been puzzled by this phenomenon – what do managers actually do? Mintzberg (1980, p.7) in his book *The Nature of Managerial Work* makes the following statement: "Although an enormous amount of material has been published on the manager's job, we continue to know very little about it."

The first major work that studied what managers actually did was published in 1951 by Sune Carlson (1951). He studied the daily events of nine Swedish directors, over a period of thirty five days, using a diary method. He found that the managers had very limited *alone* time. For example, one director only managed 12 periods of more than 22 minutes alone in the 35 days of the study. The average alone times for the executives were as little as one hour per day. The picture painted by Carlson is one of fragmentation, brevity, *ad hoc*ness and an emphasis on face-to-face interaction. These same results were found by Rosemary Stewart (1967) in her study of 160 British managers and, again, by Mintzberg in his 1973 study. Mintzberg (1980, p.173) identifies the following five characteristics of managerial work:

- Managers typically spend brief periods of time on fragmented activities, and are frequently interrupted.
- Managers tend to direct their attention to concrete issues and to the most current information, rather than to reflective planning.
- Managers spend one-third of their total time communicating with outsiders and one-third to a half of their time communicating with subordinates.
- Managers conduct two-thirds of their communication orally, mostly by telephone or unscheduled meetings. (This preference for interpersonal dialogue will be discussed in Chapter 3 on information.)

He summarizes the plight of the manager as follows: "We find the manager, particularly at senior levels, is overburdened with work. With the increasing complexity of modern organizations and their problems, he is destined to become more so. *He is driven to brevity, fragmentation, and superficiality in his tasks, yet he cannot easily delegate them because of the nature of his information.* And he can do little to increase his available time or significantly enhance his power to manage. Furthermore, he is driven to focus on that which is current and tangible in his work, even though the complex problems facing many organizations call for reflection and a far-sighted perspective" (my emphasis).

Sayles (1979, p.12) confirms much of what Mintzberg says about the characteristics of managerial work:

- Most of the working day is devoted to interaction with people.

- There is sporadic, impromptu and unplanned contact, jumping from issue to issue and between different people.
- Decisions are often the product of complex negotiations, extending over time and involving many interested parties.
- The multiplicity of goals identified by different groups and people are often conflicting, even contradictory, and priorities often vary.
- Results are often the product of many uncontrolled variables which are slow to emerge and difficult to predict.
- Problems and activities of the manager are often discontinuous and fragmented with no clear beginning or end.

All the studies of managers, irrespective of country or level, seem to produce the same answers. In order to make sense of the managers' activities Mintzberg makes use of the notion of *roles*, instead of Fayol's classical model of *activities*. Mintzberg (1980, p169) summarizes these roles as follows: "The manager must design the work of his organization, monitor its internal and external environment, initiate change when desirable, and renew stability when faced with disturbances. The manager must lead his subordinates to work effectively for the organization, and he must provide them with special information, some of which he gains through the network of contacts that he developed. In addition, the manager must perform a number of 'housekeeping' duties, including informing outsiders, serving as figurehead, and leading in major negotiations." The large variety of roles that a manager must contend with emphasizes the variety, and thus the complexity, of the managerial job. Ambiguity and uncertainty are the rule rather than the exception. This complexity and ambiguity defies simplistic approaches and theories. Although these role definitions do provide us with a sense of the complexity of the manager's world, they do not help us to understand the way in which the manager actually copes with it. What is clear, however, is that there is more to the managerial job than the stock character manager archetype suggests.

A seemingly more realistic picture of the manager emerges: the image of a white water canoeist seems relevant. There is the sense of being in the midst of a force that is continually and ambiguously dragging the boat forward. The only option is to keep the canoe stable and prevent it from tipping over; there are only occasional fleeting chances to glance up to scan the rapid ahead.

Is this a better picture of the world of the manager? In order to understand the manager's being and interaction with the world better, one needs to take a more fundamental step and examine the manager as an existing being-in-the-world. One must understand the way humans interact with the world, in more general terms, before one can really understand a human as a manager managing an organization.

The manager in-the-world

This section will use the work of Martin Heidegger (1962; 1988; 1992), to gain insight into the manager's interaction with their world. The manager is a conscious being who cannot escape the reality of being-in-the-world. This section will explain what it means to be-in-the-world. This insight will be used to construct a realistic image of the manager that can be used as a basis for understanding the 'who' for which management information has its being.

Heidegger's fundamental argument, as was outlined in Chapter 1, is that our search for the real (the Being of being) was wrong in that it was based on the metaphysics of humanism; it had an anthropocentric basis. Humanity through Descartes' *cogito ergo sum* ordained itself as *the* foundation that defines *what is* and *what is not*. Heidegger sees this humanistic perspective as an inauthentic mode of understanding. Being-the manager in this case needs to be understood in its own 'suchness'; on its own home-ground as being-in-the-world.

Being-in-the-world

This section discusses a series of ideas that lead towards a sense of what it means to be-in-the-world. The discussion may be technical at some points but the picture as a whole will emerge in a comprehensible way.

Dasein

The manager is primordially *Dasein*. What does this mean? In order to understand what it means to *be* Heidegger uses the notion of *Dasein* (*Da* – there; *Sein* – being). *Dasein* is what we may think of as being human, in the sense of being able to be aware of our own existence in a world where others exist. *Dasein* understands *being* in that it already understands itself. *Dasein*'s suchness is to *be-in*. Heidegger (1962) explains: "Its ownmost being is such that it has an understanding of that being, and already maintains itself in each case in a certain interpretedness of its being" (p.36). However, *Dasein* is not a self-conscious subject. It understands itself only in the sense of knowing what it means to be-in. Therefore "the 'essence' of *Dasein* lies in its existence" (Heidegger, 1962, p.67). Only *Dasein* can stand back from or *out* from its own occurrence in the world and observe itself. Its being is, for itself, always already available; it is *ready-to-hand*.

This rather complex argument can be put more simply in the following manner – although with a loss of richness. Heidegger argues that we, as human beings, know what it means to *be* since we *know*, in some vague, but very real sense, that we *are*. Nobody can seriously say that they doubt the reality of their own existence. All human beings have, therefore, as a basic constitutive element, this *is-ness*. Even before the manager is a rational purposive being, the manager is a *Dasein* that is always already involved in the world. *Dasein* is not a subject, or *res cogitans*, before which things appear: it is rather a clearing where beings in their beingness can appear. This is why *Dasein* is the 'there' of 'being'; and therefore the starting point from which to understand what it means for anything to 'be'. Before the manager is a rational purposive being, the manager is a *Dasein* that is *in*volved in the world.

Being-in

We can only really understand what *Dasein* is when we consider *Dasein* as being-in-the-world. *Dasein is* only in its being-in-the-world. What does it mean to be-in something? Clearly we are in the world in a different way than a table is in a room. Heidegger argues that we normally use the concept of *inclusion* when we use 'in': such as 'she is in the house'. This ontic use of 'in' is, however, dependent on a more primordial (and forgotten) sense of 'in'; such as 'he is in love' or 'she is in thought'. This is not mere metaphorical language, Heidegger argues, it refers to an existential sense of 'in'. In this ontological form of 'in' the sense of *involvement*, or concerned absorption, is implied. Table 2.1 contrasts the ontological and ontic senses of 'in'.

In the most primordial ontological mode of existence *Dasein* is always already involved (concernedly absorbed) in the world. The ontic mode of existence is a derived mode that presupposes the former. It is therefore not a mode of existence that *Dasein* sometimes selects, and sometimes not. *Dasein* "is never 'primarily' a being which is, so to speak, free from being-in, but which sometimes has the inclination to take up a 'relationship' toward the world. Taking up relationships toward the world is possible only *because Dasein*, as being-in-the-world, is as it is" (Heidegger, 1962, p.84).

Dasein exists in the world by dwelling in it. Our immersion in the world is due to the fact that we are concernedly involved in the world. When we "inhabit or dwell in something it is no longer an object for us but becomes part of us and pervades our relation to other objects in the world." (Dreyfus, 1991, p.45). Maybe an analogy, though rather simplistic, may make the relationship between *Dasein* and its being in the world clear. *Dasein* is in-the-world as a fish is in the water. As the fish dwells in the water its immersion becomes so complete that the water seems to 'disappear'. In everything that the fish does the water is always already present. If the fish were asked the question, if it were at all possible, "Do you know that you are in water?", it would be quite startled by this, unimaginable question. With this in mind we can better understand the following concise summary by Heidegger: "The statement, '*Dasein* has, as the basic constitution of its being, a being-in-the-world' is thus supposed to be a statement of essence. It implies that *Dasein* 'has' in its essence, something like world, and does not obtain a world by the fact that it exists" (Heidegger, 1984, p.170).

Table 2.1: The ontological and ontic senses of being 'in'.

[Adapted from Dreyfus (1991, p.43)]

	Existential Sense (Ontological)	**Categorical Sense (Ontic)**
In	In-volvement, being-in Personal involvement He is in love	In-clusion, being in Spatial inclusion She is in the office
At	She is at work (absorbed in it)	He is at work (place of work)
By	She stood by (remained faithful to) her friend	He stood by (beside) his friend

The manager as *Dasein* is in-the-world. This means that the manager cannot 'step back', get 'out' or look at things or situations from the 'outside' as is often referred to. The manager must be thought of ontologically as a being always already involved in the world.

Intentionality

Dasein does not merely float around in-the-world (in a way that it might appear to an observer that a fish does). *Dasein* is '*intentionally*' involved in the world. It is, however, not a detached contemplation based on some mental model of essences. Detached contemplation is always already rooted in a *doing* that is a knowing. "(Heidegger) sees detached contemplation as a privative modification of everyday involvement. He seems to be saying that the detached, meaning-giving, knowing subject that is at the centre of Husserlian phenomenology must be replaced by an embodied, meaning-giving, *doing* subject" (Dreyfus, 1991, p.47). It was maintained, in phenomenology and in other modern consciousness philosophies, that we *know* (i.e. have a theory or model) and then we act based on this knowledge. Heidegger (1988) argues, however, that we act because we always already know, because *Dasein* is a being-in-the-world. Therefore, the traditional ontic concept of intentionality as the directedness of the mind through various states, activities or attitudes must be abandoned.

We are, however *directed* in our being-in-the-world; we *comport* (*Verhalten*) ourselves towards beings. "Comportments have the structure of directing-oneself-toward, of being directed-toward" (Heidegger, 1988, p.58). Thus every comportment-towards has a specific 'towards' as its directedness. *Dasein* does not go about selecting its comportments, or selecting not to be comported at all. Intentionality as comportments "belongs to the existence of *Dasein*.... To exist then means among other things, to be as relating to oneself by comporting with beings. It belongs to the nature of *Dasein* to exist in such a way that it is always already with other beings" (Heidegger, 1988, p.157). Thus, in doing – or rather comporting – *Dasein* knows the world because it is already in it. Hence, "every act of directing oneself toward something receives the characteristic of knowing.... In whatever way we conceive of knowing, it is ...a comportment toward beings" (Dreyfus, 1991, p.53). This view is also strongly supported by Varela (1987), a biologist, who argues : "we admit knowledge whenever we observe an effective (or adequate) behaviour in a given context... In the same way, the fact of living – of conserving structural coupling uninterruptedly as a living being – is to know in the realm of existence. In a nutshell: to live is to know" (p. 174).

This difference between the traditional intentionality concept and the notion of comportment can be summarized as in Table 2.2. This dist-inction will become clearer as the discussion proceeds. Nevertheless, it can already be seen that comportment is the concerned involvement of an immersed *Dasein* interacting with an always already present whole; a whole that has significance only in its whole-ness. The manager does not think about the world and then formulate objectives (intentions) to direct action in that world. The manager is always already 'directed' in the world because the manager is involved in the world. In this involvement the manager always already knows and is therefore always already directed. We can therefore conclude that the notion of objectives, so prevalent in management discourse, is merely a *post facto* construction to articulate those comportments which already exist in action.

Table2.2: Intentionality and comportment

	Intentionality	Comportment
Based on	Mental content (models)	Being-in (world)
Directed towards	Objects (ontic world)	Equipment (tools)
Relationship	Models —Intention— Objects	Being-in —Comportment— Equipment

Dasein's relationship to beings (things)

The world as available or ready-to-hand

How do we interact with the world in our directedness or comportment? We interact with that which is nearest; the things of our everyday. The way we interact with them is in using them. Thus "our primordial relationship with the world is to use it: i.e., the world, for us, is available (zuhanden)" (Heidegger, 1962, p.56). *Zuhanden* is often also translated as ready-to-hand.

Heidegger calls these near things which we use in our concerned and comported involvement in the world, equipment (Zeug). "(Heidegger)... proposes to demonstrate that the situated use of equipment is in some sense prior to just looking at things and that what is revealed by use is ontologically more fundamental than the substances with determinate, context-free properties revealed by detached contemplation" (Dreyfus, 1991, p.61). In our everyday dealings, our concerned involvements with the things around us we create the possible clearing within which the things reveal themselves to us in their use. Therefore the being of those beings which we encounter as closest to us can be exhibited not as "bare perceptual cognition" but rather through "that kind of concern which manipulates things and puts them to use" (Heidegger, 1962, p.95). This is explored further in Chapter 3.

In our dealings in-the-world "we come across equipment for writing, sewing, working.... Equipment is essentially 'something-in-order-to'" (Heidegger, 1962, p.97). But it is not merely an isolated in-order-to, it is part of a field or nexus of concerned equipmentality. Equipment is that which is available; but only available because of *Dasein*'s involvement in the world and only as part of an equipmental whole. Thus, equipment only makes sense in terms of its reference to other equipment: "Equipment – in accordance with its equipmentality – always is in terms of its belonging to other equipment: inkstand, pen, ink, paper, blotting pad, table lamp, furniture, windows, doors, room" (Heidegger, 1962, p.97). We may view the equipment whole as an extending field of equipment that we are familiar with and in which specific equipment, from time to time emerges, becomes available, in order to function as part of our involvement in the world.

How do we, in our involvement, discern specific items of equipment? The "specific *thisness* of the equipment, its individuation ... is not determined primarily by space and time in the sense that it appears in a determinate space-and-time position. Instead, what determines a piece of equipment as an individual is its equipmental character and the equip-mental nexus" (Heidegger, 1988, p.292). Thus, "no matter how sharp we just look at the 'outward appearance' of things in whatever form this takes, we cannot discover anything available" (Heidegger, 1962, p.98). Where something is put to use, "our concern subordinates itself to the 'in-order-to' which is constitutive for the equipment we are employing at the time: the less we just stare at the hammer-thing, and the more we seize hold of it and use it, the more primordial does our relationship to it become, and the more unveiledly it is encountered as that which it is – equipment" (Heidegger, 1962, p.98). The everyday example of working on a computer will illustrate this. The user knows what a keyboard is by using it to type; but typing makes sense only in the process of doing something on the computer such as writing a letter; in turn, writing a letter only makes sense in sending a message to somebody, and so on. On the other hand, a person can stare at the keyboard, we could count the keys, we could even comment on the layout. However, all this will tell the user nothing about what a keyboard 'is'. It is when someone uses a keyboard in order to type, in order to write a letter, in order to send a message, that they know, ontologically, what a keyboard is.

It is in the act of seizing hold of the equipment, that the equipment will, as it were, *withdraw*. Only when equipment has *withdrawn* will it be available authentically (Heidegger, 1962, p.99). Hence our primordial relationship with equipment is in using it in everyday involvements to the point that it becomes unthought. Heidegger calls this unthought involvement practical circumspection: "The view in which the equipmental nexus stands at first, completely unobtrusive and unthought, is the view and sight of practical circumspection, of our practical everyday orientation." (Heidegger, 1988, p.163). However, we do find that sometimes equipment does seem to jump out of its equipmental whole so that we become explicitly confronted with it. It seems to become objects placed before our consciousness. We become explicitly aware of them. How should we understand this?

The world as occurrent (present-at-hand)

The previous section characterized, being-in-the-world as absorbed involvement, however, when the referential whole fragments, things become occurrent (*vorhanden*) (Heidegger, 1962, p.107). *Vorhanden* is also, at times, translated as present-at-hand. It is at this point where traditional intentionality comes into play. When the referential whole is broken the equipment leaps out and becomes an object placed in front of a subject. In the computer example: when a particular key gets stuck (or produces an out of ordinary character on the screen) the individual key becomes an object of reflection.

Table 2.3: The world as occurrent (breakdown)

Mode of being	What happens	Dasein's stance
Unavailableness	(1) Equipment Malfunction (conspicuous: mistyped a key)	Get going again (backspace and restrike the key)
	(2) Temporary breakdown (obstinate: key repeatedly gets stuck)	Practical deliberation. Eliminating the disturbance (treat it with some lubricating agent)
	(3) Permanent breakdown (obtrusive: unable to get a key to produce a character on the screen)	Hopeless standing before but still concerned
Occurrentness	Everyday practical activity stops.	Detached standing before. Theoretical reflection Skilled scientific activity. Observation and experimentation
Pure occurrentness	Rest. Getting finished	Pure contemplation. Just looking at something. (Curiosity)

In dealing with this occurrent nature of breakdowns Heidegger distinguishes three different modes of being. This is summarized in Table

2.3. This table is adapted to the computer example from Dreyfus (1991, p.124). The table shows that when equipment becomes unavailable, although there is a level of *objectification* (some mental content in the mind of a subject), there is still active involvement. It is only where there is permanent breakdown to the point that the involvement in the everyday activity is stopped that the equipment is severed from its equipmental nexus and decontextualized as an object with certain features and properties. In such a case the object can be recontextualized into formal models and scientific theories so as to 'solve' the problem. Alternatively, what is now an object can become pure occurrentness; the pursuit of a solution is altogether abandoned and the user now just stares at the keyboard and reflects on this as a phenomenon. Maybe the user reflects on some questions such as: "what sort of a device is this?"; "why do we use keyboards to enter data into the computer?"; "what is it about typing that make keyboards appropriate to use?".

Structure of the world

Building on the above discussion on being-in, equipment, and avail-ableness the broader context of the nature of *Dasein*'s involvement in the world can be explored. Several questions need to be answered. What world is this, and what does it mean? Is it the sum of all entities in three-dimensional space that we sense with our senses and then add together? Or is the world more existential, so that it is experienced as the "business world" or the "fashion world"? Heidegger argues that it is more ontological than any of these: "(the) world is not something subsequent that we calculate as the result from the sum of all beings. The world comes not afterward but beforehand, in the strict sense of the word. Beforehand: that which is unveiled and understood already in advance in every existent *Dasein* before any apprehending of this or that being, beforehand as that which stands forth as always already unveiled to us" (Heidegger, 1988). Thus if anything is *available* then the world is already in place, though not intentionally or thematically (Heidegger, 1962, p.114).

How does our concerned use of equipment fit into the world. Heidegger argues that to function, equipment must fit into a context of meaningful everyday activity. Heidegger calls this fitting in *involvement*. As with equipment, involvement makes only sense in an involvement whole: "With any such (available) entity as entity, there is an involvement....That in which it is involved is the 'towards-which' of serviceability, and the 'for-which' of usability. With the 'towards-which' of serviceability there can again be an involvement: *with* this thing, for instance, which is available, and which we accordingly call a 'hammer', there is an involvement in hammering, there is an involvement in making something fast; with making something fast, there is an involvement in..." (Heidegger, 1962, p.116). The specific involvement (such as writing a letter) has in "each case been outlined in advance in term of the totality of such involvements... In a workshop, for example, the totality of involvements which is constitutive for the available in its availability, is 'earlier' than any single item of equipment;..." (Heidegger, 1962, p.116). The fact that I am an administrator who communicates with customers through the use of letters is prior to my typing a letter which is prior to my constructing my comportments through sentences which is prior to my striking the keys....

This chain of involvements does not merely circulate randomly and haphazardly. Since the "totality of involvements itself goes back ultimately to a towards-which in which there is no further involvement: ... This primary towards-which is not just another towards which as something in which an involvement is possible. The primary towards-which is a for-the-sake-of-which" (Heidegger, 1962, p.116). We can see in Heidegger's term "for-the-sake-of-which" a use that calls our attention to the way human activity makes long term sense without suggesting the idea of some final goal intentionally formulated and kept in the head. *Dasein* does know, in the sense of having a plan in its head, where-it-is-going for in it is already part of an involvement whole that has a for-the-sake-of-which implicitly there.

We may view the involvement whole in terms of a set of already there relationships which refer to each other and this set of relationships makes any specific involvement significant: "for-the-sake-of-which signifies an in-order-to; this, in turn, a towards-this; the latter, an in-which of an involvement. These relationships are bound up with one another as a primordial whole; ... The relational whole of this signifying we call 'significance'. This is what makes up the structure of the world – the structure of that wherein *Dasein*, as *Dasein*, already is." (Heidegger, 1962, p.120). Using this, the previous example could be reformulated follows:

> *In* attending to my administration I type on the keyboard *in-order-to* write letters *towards* communicating with my customers *for-the-sake-of* being successful in business.

The relationships 'in', 'in-order-to', 'towards', and 'for-the-sake-of' all indicate the nature of the involvement whole. It is their togetherness that make things and actions significant.

This discussion has described concerned involvement in the practical everyday. It shows that the worldliness of the world cannot be separated from *Dasein*'s way of being. *Dasein* projects forth its world in an involvement whole. *Dasein is* in as much as it is involved in the world. For *Dasein*, to *be* is to be-in-the-world.

Dasein and thrownness

In the discussion of the concept of the world it was indicated that man (and woman) is always already in the world. This relationship leads to what Heidegger calls *thrownness*. Man is thrown into the world;. not choosing to be born, not choosing the circumstances into which to be he is born. As Gelven (1970, p.78) explains: "There is much that is unalterable about my existence; and I can, in certain moods, either overlook it or meet it in one of many ways; but it is always there." There is often the perception that the individual is a free ahistorical agent who can select ends and means and achieve rationally selected goals and objectives. The concept of thrownness refutes this conception.

The previous canoeist example may make this notion of thrownness more explicit. The canoeist in a rapid can ensure that she does not overturn or that she does not hit a rock, but she cannot alter the fact that she is being swept forward by the rushing water. In thrownness, as in the rapid, not to take action is to take action, not to decide is to decide. Thrownness will turn indecision into decision and inaction into action. A belief that to achieve one's purposes it is only necessary to make the *right* decisions at the *right* time, is often mistaken belief. No action is action, as one is always already in an inescapable relationship with the world. This does not, however, mean that we are completely in the hands of some sort of power beyond our control, that fate has taken hold of us in such a way that, irrespective of our decisions and actions, 'what will be will be'. This is not the Heideggerian concept of thrownness.

Thrownness is that always already involvement whole which compels *Dasein* to act, to be. Thrownness is not teleological, it is not designed or willed; it just is. People one often find themselves in a position or situation, not because of their choices or decisions but by default? – because they are involved in a world. This is thrownness. The concept of thrownness contradicts the conception that with all the right information the rational manager will make the right decisions and will be ensured of success and will be effective. The consequence for the general view of the manager as a user of information of accepting Heidegger's analysis that thrownness is an inherent part of *Dasein*'s existence are profound. It now makes sense to look again at the manager and consolidate some of the insights gained from Heidegger's analysis of *Dasein*.

The involved manager (in-the-world)

The previous sections have provided an overview of *Dasein* as being-in-the-world. The next task is apply this perspective to the manager as being-in-the-world. In general it should be that the commonly held view of managers is extremely limited, and may well be completely devoid of real significance.

The manager is involved in the world. The manager's actions and decisions cannot be understood by isolating them. This may be useful for analysis, but it would have little bearing on what managers actually do (or decide), and why they actually so do or so decide. Whenever a manager does or decides something it will always already be based on the prior involvement whole. The manager's being-in (involvement) means that the manager cannot step back, get out or look at things or situations from the outside as is often suggested. Any effort to get distance between the manager and the problem situation is artificial since the only authentic basis for understanding the world is being involved in the world. This involvement is not something the manager selects or not; the manager is always already involved.

In dwelling in the world the specific decisions and actions of the manager disappear into the involvement whole as being available (ready-to-hand). Managers, therefore, when questioned afterwards, cannot always say why they have selected a specific course of action rather than another. They must often try to reconstruct their actions and decisions to try and explain their rationality. Within the world, and as part of the involvement whole, that specific decision or action seemed available and significant (i.e. related to the toward-which). Thus managers do not intentionally select decisions or actions according to some blueprint, model, or theory in their heads; rather these flow from the fact that the manager is always already involved in the world. Actions and decisions do not derive their rationality from detached reflection or rationalization. The manager *knows* what to do or decide by virtue of being always already involved the world. Hence being-in-the-world is the manager's most primordial sense of knowing and is the default source for actions and decisions. One conclusion that can be drawn from this discussion is that managers' decisions and actions do not have a global rationality only a local, or situated, rationality. Managers make decisions and take actions that seem to make sense within their involvement whole. From outside or from above these actions and decisions may even look irrational.

Managers use data, from the information system and various other sources, as equipment in-order-to make judgements or take actions. It should be noted, however, that the daily production report is not equipment as such, it is only equipment within a equipment whole. The daily production report only makes sense because it refers to other equipment such as machines, production schedules, production meetings, production targets, actual production units and factory floors. The manager only understands the report in *using* it: in discussion at the production meeting; in setting up targets; in developing production schedules; or in negotiating with the trade union. In using it, the report will withdraw. Detached reflection on the report would not make the report available. It is only as part of the involvement whole (meetings, negotiations, requests) that it will become significant and available.

If the report ceases to be part of the equipment whole then it will stand out as occurrent (present-at-hand). This breakdown will make the manager aware of the report as an object. This will happen if, for example, the report is late, too faint to read, changed in layout, or obviously incorrect. Therefore, contrary to the common wisdom managers do not become aware of reports as objects or inputs into their decisions when they are available, it is only when there is a breakdown that the reports jump out at them. This is why managers have difficulty in explaining which data is used when and for which decisions it is used. This type of analysis assumes an occurrent mode of being that is not the default mode of the manager in-the-world.

This discussion has indicated the need for a more fundamental understanding of the manager in order to succeed in providing information systems that are available.

The manager and management skill

The work of Polanyi (1973) provides another perspective on the manager in-the-world. Managers frequently accept that, in practice management is an art or a skill. Accepting this claim requires exploring the notion of *tacit knowledge*. Tacit knowledge is knowledge that the manager will draw upon when performing a management act, such as making a decision or making a judgement, but would not be able to articulate when asked to make it explicit. In Polanyi's words: "we know more than we can say." It is this tacit dimension that is the driving force behind the practice of a skill.

In order to make this notion of tacit knowledge explicit Polanyi uses the idea of *subsidiary* and *focal* awareness. It can be imagined in terms of the classical foreground and background distinction. In performing a task, there are certain aspects of the task that are in the focal awareness (foreground) and others in the subsidiary awareness (background). For example, if I want to enter a room, the room and my purpose for entering would be in the focal awareness. The door and its opening mechanism that I need to operate in order to enter will be in the subsidiary awareness. I would not attend to these particulars in the act of entering the room. They are mere tools in my subsidiary awareness that I draw upon in the act of entering, like mere 'tools'. However, for something to become a tool to be drawn upon in the focal act, it must become part of my body, like fingers in the act of touching, or like feet in the act of walking or standing. I can be subsidiarily aware of something only when it is *part of me* – when it is embodied – as Polanyi (1973) explains: "Our subsidiary awareness of tools etc. can be regarded now as the act of making them form a part of our own body. ... We pour ourselves out into them and assimilate them as parts of our existence" (p. 59). This is not only true for such concrete artefacts as door handles, hammers, staples or pens, but also for such conceptual tools as presuppositions. We assimilate most of our presuppositions by "learning to speak of things in a certain language ... we have no clear knowledge of what our presuppositions are and when we try to formulate them they appear quite unconvincing" (p. 59). When we accept a certain set of presuppositions and use them as our interpretative framework, we may be said to "dwell in them as we do in our body" (p. 60).

The notion of *embodiment* of tools that is drawn upon in the focal act is clearly of paramount importance in the understanding of management as a skill. The art of knowing, of personal knowledge, is not a rational act of building models that can be employed as procedures for actions, decisions and judgements. It is more than this; it is the attempt to assimilate certain particulars as extensions of our body. In this way, by becoming imbued with our subsidiary awareness, they can form a coherent focal entity. This conclusion is completely in line with the result that Heidegger provided in his analysis. As equipment becomes available it withdraws. In the equipment whole it becomes part of our bodies; it becomes the way we do things.

Subsidiary awareness and focal awareness are *mutually exclusive*. Our attention can hold only one focus at a time. It would be self-contradictory to be both subsidiarily and focally aware of the particulars at the same time (p. 56-57). We can, and will, only attend to one focus at a time. In a Heideggerian sense we will only become focally aware of our tools – or our body in Polanyi's argument – if there is a *breakdown*. We only become aware of the opening mechanism if the door does not open or the pen does not write. This aspect combined with the notion of embodiment is a powerful argument against organizational learning theories that argue for detached reflection as a mode for eliciting knowledge. If a manager reflects on his presuppositions (thinking tools) then he is not able to articulate, in any convincing way, what role they play in his focal actions (decisions, judgements, etc.). If he draws upon them in a focal act he again is not able to make explicit which ones are employed and when.

Thus personal knowledge, or tacit knowledge has its roots in the subsidiary awareness of our body as merged in our focal awareness of external objects. In this sense an object is transformed into a tool by a "purposive effort envisaging an operational field in respect of which the object guided by our efforts shall function as an extension of our body" (p. 60). This implies that there is a reliance on a *personal commitment* involved in all acts of intelligence. Through this personal commitment we integrate into ourselves some things which, at that time, are part of our subsidiary awareness. As Polanyi explains: "Every act of personal assimilation by which we make a thing form an extension of ourselves through our subsidiary awareness of it, is a commitment of ourselves; a manner of disposing of ourselves." (p. 61)

This notion of personal knowledge is at the heart of what managers do. Until this is addressed information systems will never become part of the manager's body. And thus they will not become part of the focal acts of judgements and other management action.

The arguments of Heidegger and Polanyi are powerful and seem to have an intuitive truth; this is especially so for people with some years of experience in management. However, there are many managers who use information in what purports to be detached rational decision-making. The next stage is to examine why managers act out these detached rational roles when the analysis of Heidegger and Polanyi seems to suggest that they are inauthentic.

Management and social construction of rationality

In the decision-making metaphor, the manager is seen as a rational being looking for, and desiring information to make rational decisions based on fact and fact alone. This picture of the detached rational manager was effectively challenged by Feldman and March in their innovative article

Information in Organizations as Signal and Symbol (Feldman & March, 1981, p.175).

Feldman and March described numerous examples of where information was available, or where information was requested, for decision-making, but where the decisions taken did not at all reflect the use of the information. Some of the decisions taken were radically opposed to the decisions that would have been expected with the information that was available to the decision makers. Maybe, it could be argued, the information was used to *construct* an idea of rationality in a *post hoc* way since the managers believed that rationality is a highly desired trait and that it would legitimate their decisions. From the discussion of Polanyi and Heidegger above it seems conceivable that the decisions may have been based on tacit (involvement) knowledge that the manager drew upon but was not able to articulate. The manager might then construct the rationality by looking for data to reproduce the decision or act so that it could be seen to be rational from the outside.

Feldman and March do not believe that organizations or individuals are primordially irrational. They argue that there are various reasons (other than decision-making) why information is gathered, produced and utilized:

• *Incentives for information production.* Organizations provide many incentives for information production. Information production is seen as inherently good and indicative of rational activity, however this does not necessarily mean that the information is used. The possession of information gives a sense of security. There is the general conviction that a decision with explicit information is better than a decision without explicit information and this may lead to the erroneous assumption that the more the information, the better the decision. Thus information becomes the way to bridge the gap between the rational manager and the manager in-the-world.

• *Information as surveillance.* There is a continuous scanning of the environment just in case. There is the expectation that if the manager scans the environment sufficiently, then there will be no surprises. When or if the manager needs to make a decision, then all the relevant information will be available to make it quickly. The problem is that relevance is determined by the application context. Consequently, because the application context is not known in advance, all possible data is gathered, even gossip. When the decision time comes, the manager is overloaded and finds it difficult to link the information with the decisions. From a Heideggerian point of view non-specific surveillance does not make much sense since it would imply an occurrent mode of reflection. Surveillance *within* the involvement whole does make sense. Heidegger calls this *circumspection*. This is done continuously as part of a set of comportments; it is this absorbed looking around that establishes the basis for the next comportment.

• *Strategic information.* The deployment of information is often used as a method to persuade someone or some group. Information becomes a basis upon which conflicts are resolved. In such cases, information is interpreted and reconstructed to serve the purpose of each party. The legitimacy granted to, so regarded, objective facts provides a resource that the parties can draw on to capture the moral high ground to justify their actions or decisions.

All these instances suggest that information in many cases can be seen as a social symbol in the same way that a certain suburb, club, or make of car indicates that a person has a particular social status. Information becomes a symbol, a symbol especially of rationality, of competence as decision-maker and manager. As Feldman and Marsh (1981) explain: "The gathering of information provides a ritualistic assurance that the appropriate attitude about decision-making exists. Within such a scenario of performance, information is not simply the basis for action. It is a representation of competence and a reaffirmation of social virtue. Command of information and information sources enhances perceived competence and inspires confidence."

The reasons put forward by Feldman and Marsh are interesting and informative. What is clear, however, is that there is a social dimension to information use or utilization that has nothing to do with rational decision-making. This conclusion supports the analysis of Heidegger and makes sense of many cases of so-called rational decision-making that can be seen in industry. An obvious question, flowing from this conclusion, is to what extent the social construction of rationality can justify the very large investments in information technology. This type of use may be inevitable until the myths of objectivity and rationality are dispelled. On the other hand, the ambiguous option of living without these islands of certainty may not be an option for mere mortal managers absorbed in coping with the everyday.

Conclusions about the manager

This section will draw some of the major conclusions and implications arising from the discussion: it will provide a synopsis of the manager as being, the manager's job, and the manager as information user.

The manager is in-the-world

The concept of the manager in-the-world implies that the manager cannot escape the following:

• *Being in-the-world*: The manager cannot isolate herself from the world. Thus it is impossible or at least highly artificial for her to try to remove herself from the world in order to make objective and rational decisions, to undertake reflective planning, or to attempt problem solving. Where the manager is, there the world is. Any attempt to separate the manager from the world would be to no avail. Managers cannot select to be, or not to be, involved in the world. They always already are.

• *Being thrown into the world*. Part of being in-the-world is being subjected to thrownness. Not everything is subject to the manager's choice; she is thrown into situations, decisions, problems and even, sometimes, solutions. Only in very few and limited cases can the manager choose the plan, the structures, the people, the equipment, the procedures, or the systems. More importantly, she cannot choose the culture, the values, or the tradition of the organization. More often than not, she is given these variables and must perform in spite of them and not because of them. She can, indeed, change them over time, but usually only with difficulty (especially in the case of such things as organizational culture). This reality has made good managers fail and allowed bad managers to succeed. The logic of mathematics is not the logic of being-in-the-world.

It is clear that the manager in-the-world cannot be, in the traditional sense of the words, an objective and rational decision maker and problem solver, for it is not a true, real, or actual mode of existence. This does not mean that managers are irrational. It merely means that the logic of the actions and decisions are themselves *bound in* the logic of the local involvement whole and can only be understood as such. Furthermore, the whole space of local logics may combine into a global logic that may or may not seem rational either to the manager or to an observer.

The manager's *a priori* mode of existence is ready-to-hand

The manager uses equipment in-order-to do the things managers do. Only if there is a breakdown will the equipment emerge as objects – as things severed from their context. That which is available to the manager will be used. The manager in concerned involvement does not contemplate and reflect, the manager applies and uses tools. There are some important conclusions that flow from this ready-to-hand mode of existence :

- *Getting-the-job-done.* Managers are not primarily preoccupied with plans, goals and objectives. They are involved in the daily task of getting-the-job-done. It is only in situations of breakdown that managers may reflect on what they call the larger picture. Goals and plans must be situated in the world, within the involvement whole, as part of the body, if they are to become part of the local logic.

- *Applying available equipment.* Unless there is a breakdown, the manager actively applies the equipment as available, without considering them as objects, in using them in-order-to achieve goals or purposes. This implies that the manager does not actively think of machines as 'machines', or of plans as 'plans', or of time as 'time' or of information as 'information'. They are all merely available tools that link together as part of the equipment and involvement whole.

- *Information as available equipment.* The information must be available to the manager as available equipment for it to be used (in the manner that a hammer is available to the carpenter). It must be an inseparable part of the total managerial involvement whole; not objectified or isolated, only available. If it is there, and it functions as the equipment that the manager requires, it will be used.

The manager's work is complex, fragmented and *ad hoc*

The manager's job is characterized by the following traits, indicated in the work Mintzberg and Sayles cited previously:

- *Increased complexity.* The manager is faced with ever-increasing complexity, discontinuity and unpredictability. This was noted Peter Drucker in 1978 in his book *The Age of Discontinuity* (Drucker, 1978) and has been confirmed by many other authors since. Society has not yet recognized this and still tries to use simple models to explain complex reality. This aspect will be dealt with further in the chapter on management.

- *The here and now.* In dealing with the complexity in-the-world, the manager is absorbed in the here-and-now. It was shown above that this flows from her being thrown into-the-world where the manager must dwell in the everyday doing.

- *Fragmentation.* The manager's task is fragmented. She is often interrupted and forced into superficiality. The fragmentation is the result of thrownness and the complexity that the manager must cope with. It was shown above that the manager has many roles to fulfil as part of a daily set of activities. Time to engage in any worthwhile reflection is very limited and Mintzberg believes a form of superficiality must ensue.

Ironically it is not reflection but involvement that is needed. If the manager is not concernedly involved in her domain of authority then the fragment-ation will break the referential whole and lead to a sense of unfamiliarity that will render any representation (data from the information systems) insignificant, merely occurrent objects before a detached manager, senseless. No amount of reflection, if possible at all, will make the occurrent world significant.

• *Complex, multi-dimensional involvements.* The majority of the man-ager's involvements are complex, involving many interests that must be reconciled by means of negotiation. This is a result of the manager being embedded in the world. There are many parameters already determined and there are many stakeholders. Most of these factors are intangible and informal, since they emerge as part of the manager's involvement, and as such they are not covered by the typical information system. The formal, computerized or computerizable, data system cannot, and should not, try and mirror this complexity. The manager needs understanding that can *only* be gained through involvement in the world.

• *Communication.* The manager spends most of his time in interpersonal communication. The manager usually prefers interpersonal communic-ation, as it is true dialogue and has the potential of creating true understanding. Face-to-face communication has an *involvement dimen-sion*, contextual dimension that is not present in human–computer interaction. This may be one of the major reasons why management information systems have been so unsuccessful.

• *Information, to become part of the manager's focal acts, must become extensions of his body (ready-to-hand).* The manager will use information if, and only if, it is available tools for working out of her understanding. Information must be available or ready-to-hand to her. This implies that it must form an integral part of the context of her managerial life. Every act of personal assimilation of data by which managers make that data form an extension of themselves through their subsidiary awareness of it (as extensions of their bodies) is a commitment of themselves; a manner of disposing of themselves.

Clearly the issue of information for the manager in-the-world is not a simple one, as many system developers have discovered. There are no simple models, theories, methodologies, or information technologies that can just make it work. There are no simple answers to be found. We need to comprehend the intuitive understanding that many managers have that allow their organizations to function effectively despite the lack of academic understanding of what they actually do. To continue to proclaim the myth of the rational manager, and all other notions tied to it, is no longer justified.

References

Carlson, S. (1951), *Executive Behaviour: A Study of the Work Load and Working Methods of Managing Directors*, Stockholm, Strombergs.

Dreyfus, H.L. (1991), *Being-in-the-world: a Commentary on Heidegger's Being and time, Division I*, Cambridge, Mass, MIT Press.

Drucker, P.F. (1974), *Management: Tasks, Responsibilities and Practices*, London, Heinemann.

Drucker, P.F. (1978), *The Age of Discontinuity: Guidelines to our Changing Society*, New York, Harper and Row.

Drucker, P.F. (1980), *Managing in Turbulent Times*, Oxford, Butterworth-Heinemann.

Fayol, H. (1949), *General and Industrial Management*, London, Pitman Publ.

Feldman, M.S. and March, J.G. (1981), 'Information in Organizations as Signal and Symbol', Administrative Science Quarterly, 26, 171-186.

Gelven, M. (1970), *A Commentary on Heidegger's "Being and Time"*, New York, Harper & Row.

Heidegger, M. (1962), *Being and Time*, Oxford, Basil Blackwell.

Heidegger, M. (1984), *The Metaphysical Foundations of Logic*, Bloomington, Indiana University Press.

Heidegger, M. (1988), *The Basic Problems of Phenomenology*, Bloomington, Indiana University Press.

Heidegger, M. (1992), *History of the Concept of Time*, Bloomington, Indiana University Press.

MacIntyre, A. (1981), *After Virtue: A Study in Moral Theory*, Notre Dame, Ind., University of Notre Dame Press.

Maturana, H. and Varela, F. (1987), *The Tree of Knowledge: The Biological Roots of Human Understanding*, Boston, Shambhala.

Mintzberg, H. (1980), *The Nature of Managerial Work*, Englewood Cliffs, New Jersey, Prentice-Hall Inc.

Polanyi, M. (1973), *Personal Knowledge: Towards a Post-critical Philosophy* (1st pbk Edition), London, Routledge & Kegan Paul.

Sayles, L.R. (1979), *Leadership: What Effective Managers Really Do and How They Do It*, New York, McGraw-Hill Book Company.

Steward, R. (1967), *Managers and Their Jobs*, London, Macmillan.

Strong, E.P. (1965), *The Management of Business: An Introduction*, New York, Harper & Row.

3 Information: as understanding

- *Introduction*
- *Some current archetypes of information*
- *Hermeneutics and the notion of understanding*
- *Gadamer and hermeneutic understanding*
- *Heidegger on understanding and interpretation*
- *Understanding and the information concept*
- *Hermeneutic conclusions about information*

Introduction

Each information systems design must have the quality of organizational dialogue and the quality of each individual's hermeneutic search for meaning as its ethical standard of success.

R.J. Boland Jr

A clear understanding of information is essential in order to comprehend management information fully. Information is an elusive and complex concept for the study of management as it is for all those disciplines which depend on it. Historically, there are many reasons why the concept of information is so elusive The current preoccupation with information *technology* and the propensity to identify the products of IT as information has further obscured the basic concept which should underlie the whole field.

In this chapter, information will be examined in a new and probably unexpected way. To start with some elements of the current body of knowledge on information will be reviewed. Next, the philosophy of hermeneutics will be discussed as a potentially suitable paradigm for understanding information. This will allow information to be related to data, knowledge and wisdom in order for it to be understood as part of a larger picture. The final part of the chapter suggests that the focus should be on sense making rather than on gathering and presenting information as usually defined.

Some current archetypes of information

The purpose of this discussion is to provide a backdrop and logical starting point for hermeneutics which is the main subject of the chapter. The intention is *not* to provide a comprehensive survey of the literature or to provide some sort of general taxonomy. This brief survey of some of the current views explains why hermeneutics is the most powerful paradigm for thinking through an understanding of what information is.

This section will distinguish two major information archetypes: the information archetype and the communication archetype. The first archetype was developed mainly due to advent of the computer. It has as its main concern the development of information 'producing' systems. The rapid development of computing technology and its application in most human institutions has made the information archetype predominant in mainstream thought. The second, the communication archetype, is based on the mathematical theory of information presented by Claude Shannon and Warren Weaver in their 1949 work *The Mathematical Theory of Communication* (Shannon & Weaver, 1949). This archetype has had less success in establishing itself in the mainstream of academic and commercial life, although communication theorists have tried, to a lesser or greater extent, to incorporate it into a more general theory of communication.

The information archetype

Two major academic disciplines have the information archetype as their central field of study, information systems and information science; outside of these there are some other general views to consider.

Information systems

A review of the definitions of information given in a selection of widely used teaching texts on information systems, or on data processing, which define a powerful orthodoxy within the information systems field, provides an idea of the connotations that mainstream information systems theorists attach to their concept of information.

> *Information usually implies data that is organized and meaningful to the person receiving it. Data is therefore raw material that is transformed into information by data processing. Information can be defined in terms of its surprise value. It tells the recipient something he did not know* (Davis & Olsen, 1985, p.30).

> *By themselves, data are meaningless; they must be changed to a usable*
> *form and placed in a context to have value. Data become*
> *information when they are transformed to communicate meaning or*
> *knowledge, ideas or conclusions* (Senn, 1990, p.58).

> *The recorded transactions are called data. This raw data can be*
> *analyzed in various ways to meet the unique information needs of*
> *the organization. Virtually any type of information can be produced*
> *from data. The data, however, represents thousands of facts, which,*
> *presented separately, would only confuse. The data must be*
> *processed to convert it into information. This is the task of the*
> *transaction processing system* (Ahituv & Neumann, 1990, p.147).

> *Information is data that have been put into a meaningful and useful*
> *context and communicated to the recipient who uses it to make*
> *decisions...Data are processed through models to create*
> *information...* (Burch & Grudnitski, 1989, p.4).

> *By information we mean data that have been shaped into a form that is*
> *meaningful and useful to human beings.*
> (Laudon & Laudon, 1996, p.9)

> *Data may be defined as any bit, from the dust in the air to the flecks in*
> *the carpet to the latest laundry list. Information is here considered*
> *to be data ordered to affect choice* (Wildavsky, 1983, p.30).

An analysis of these definitions reveals some notions common to them all.
Information is seen as the result of a *transformation, conversion or*
encoding process; data, as the raw material, must be transformed into
information. Information always has a *recipient* or user; the recipient must
experience that which is received as *meaningful* or of *value* (even if that
meaning or value is perceived solely by the user). And finally, information
may *effect change* in the receiving system.

   The conclusion that the only condition for data to become information is
that it must be *meaningful to the recipient* follows from these two
assumptions: that the conversion or transformation of data makes it more
meaningful to the recipient; and that meaningful data should have an effect
on the recipient. The *meaningful to the recipient* condition is necessary
and sufficient. In the texts cited, this condition often appears to be ignored
at the expense of conversion and transformation.

Information science

Two definitions give an idea of the connotations that information scientists
attach to the concept of information:

After a person has received and understood the content of a message, in ordinary speech we say that he has become informed about the matter at hand. This is a surprisingly precise and accurate statement. He has been 'in-formed' (Latin. in = in; within; formere = to shape or form). He has been inwardly shaped or formed; his image has been affected. Information is the alteration of the image which occurs when it receives the message.

Information is thus an event – an event which occurs at some unique point in time and space, to some particular individual. More precisely, 'information' is the name of a class of events, like the word 'explosion'. Every explosion is unique; no two are identical. .... Further, explosions cannot be stored or retrieved. One may of course, store and retrieve potentially explosive substances, or potential explosions, just as one may store and retrieve potentially informative substances-artefacts which under appropriate conditions may cause an 'information' to occur (Pratt, 1982, p.35).

'Data', as distinct to information, simply means something is given. It is assumed to be fact. The fact is not necessarily accurate or inaccurate; it is simply a given. Information assumes a level of understanding and interpretation with respect to that fact or those facts. .... Human interaction with the data system, as I'll call it, is significant in determining whether the result is information or data (Wurman, 1989, p.36).

Thus the information scientist is concerned with the effect or result of information. Information must *change* the recipient; it must lead to a level of interpretation and *understanding*. The key question to ask is what type, what sort, or which attributes of information would lead to a change in the recipient or would lead to some form of understanding.

Wurman (1989, p.38) further argues that: "Information must be that which leads to understanding. Everyone needs a personal measure against which to define the word. What constitutes information to one person may be data to another." Paul Kaufman (in Wurman, 1989), an information theorist, claims that "our society has an image of information which, although alluring, is very counterproductive". Kaufman calls for creating a new image of information that departs from the current view that confuses the capacity to transmit raw signals with the capacity to create meaningful messages: "One reason is that too much attention has been focused on computers and hardware and too little on the people who actually use information in order to make sense of the world and do useful things for each other" (p.40). Gregory Bateson, from the perspective of anthropology, defines information as follows: "Information is a difference that makes a difference" (Bateson, 1972).

There is no doubt from the above that the authors favour the view that information must be *meaningful to the recipient* in such a way that it leads to greater *understanding*.

The archetype summarized

- Within the mainstream information systems model, there has been too great an emphasis on the technology and too little emphasis on the true purpose of information – its meaning to the user or recipient.
- From the information science perspective information is about meaning and understanding.
- The degree to which information is meaningful and understood by the recipient is the degree to which it will effect change in the recipient.

The communication archetype

The concept of information theory (or communications theory) was developed by Shannon in 1949 in his work *The Mathematical Theory of Communication*. This theory of information has been widely applied, especially in the design of communication systems. In its simplest form, the theory defines information as follows:

The information content of a code, symbol, or sign is equal to the probability, when using this code to select the message (from a set of possible messages) sent by a sender, of selecting the correct message.

As Singh (1966, p.12) puts it: "Information in this context is merely a measure of one's freedom of choice when one selects a message from the available set, many of which may well be devoid of meaning." Wilden (1980, p.233) defines it as follows: "Strictly speaking it [information] is a measure of the degree of (semiotic) freedom, in a given situation, to choose among the available signals, signs, messages, or patterns to be transmitted (the repertoire), many of which may be entirely devoid of meaning. The smaller the freedom of choice from the given repertoire, the lower the possible information." Stamper (1985, p.169) compares information to size as follows: "Information applied to signs is like the term 'size' applied to physical bodies."

Thus, if one only uses the provided code (without any reference to any context whatsoever) to select the message (from a possible set of messages), then the *information content* of the code increases as the probability of selecting the correct message increases. From this it follows, as Shannon amply demonstrates in his theory, that if the code provides more information than is required to select the correct message, then there is a degree of *redundancy* in the code.

An important corollary of this definition of information is that as information increases uncertainty decreases. Uncertainty, in this sense, is uncertainty about the whether the message selected by the receiver is the one that the sender intended the receiver to select. To have complete information is to be 100% certain of selecting the right message and, therefore, to have no uncertainty. It is important to realize that the reduction of uncertainty refers to the selection of the correct message and has nothing to do with the content of the selected message. A person can select correct messages that have no meaning or relevance, not being able to place the message in a larger context in order to make it meaningful. Thus the notion, which the management and information systems theorists are so fond of, that "more information implies less uncertainty" is only true in the limited sense of message selection, not in terms of relevance or meaningfulness.

Wilden (1980) explains the difference between meaning and information (as defined by information theorists) as follows: "Meaning, more accurately here, signification, can be defined as the significance of the information to the system processing it. The more any given repertoire is analysed atomistically, and non-contextually, the more information, and the less signification [or meaning] the repertoire has. Individual letters in linguistic messages carry high information content, for instance, but practically no signification, for signification, like meaning, depends upon context, and the more context there is, the more there is redundancy (low information content) in the use of the repertoire" (p.235). Weaver (in Roszak, 1986, p.14) states: "It is surprising but true that, from the present viewpoint, two messages, one heavily loaded with meaning and the other pure nonsense, can be equivalent as regards information." It is clear from the above quotes that the concept of information, as seen by information theorists, has a very specific meaning that should not be confused with the more common use of the word.

There are some important concepts to be gained from information theory. The most important is in the area of redundancy. Redundancy can place an information overload on the receiver. However, redundancy also serves the purpose of creating the context for the information. Therefore it is neither easy, nor necessarily desirable, to eliminate it; it may not even be possible.

The concepts of information theory, although interesting, are not widely applicable, especially not in the area of management information. The assumption message selection as opposed to message meaning severely limits the usefulness of these ideas for our purposes.

Some conclusions about information

This section has reviewed the two most widely held archetypes of information. A number of issues arose of which three are significant for the themes that this book is discussing:

- Because information has been an integral part of our lives for centuries, information is still an ambiguous *concept* with a wide range of connotations attached to it. It has become a word to be used for anything that is communicated, either in written (encoded) or verbal form. This wider use makes precision in understanding it more difficult and more important.
- Information is not about processing or conversion but about its *meaning* to a recipient and its *understanding* by a recipient.
- The purpose of information is to *effect change* in the recipient.

All the definitions examined seem to indicate that understanding is integral to whatever constitutes information. The definitions logically imply that processing is neither a necessary nor sufficient requirement for something to constitute information; in contrast, it is understanding that is both necessary and sufficient. In spite of this very little, if any, attention is given by the proponents of either archetypes to the understanding of 'understanding' itself. It is this strange anomaly that we will now attend to.

The sections that follow will discuss two alternative perspectives on understanding. The first will be the hermeneutic perspective as presented in the work of Gadamer and the second will be the notion of understanding in the work of Heidegger. Both of these perspectives will assist us to develop notions of understanding that take as its foundation the *always already involved* manager.

Hermeneutics and the notion of understanding

The previous section has shown that information has, in some still unclear way or another, something to do with the concepts of meaning, understanding and interpretation. It seems pertinent, therefore, to get some basis of thinking through these notions of meaning, understanding, and interpretation, in order to gain insight into the nature of information. This section will use the theory of *hermeneutics* as a baseline to start elaborating these notions.

It can be said, although this may be an oversimplification, that hermeneutics is a theory of interpretation and understanding. Hermeneutic theory is not completely new to the field of management information. It has, to some degree, been developed by Richard Boland since 1983 (Boland, 1983; Boland, 1993; Boland & Tenkasi, 1993). However, this work has had rather limited impact in the community at large. This is despite hermeneutic theory aiming to strike at the heart of the information; identified by most of the writers within the orthodox perspectives as: "that which is meaningful to the user".

Hermeneutics, it can be argued, especially philosophical hermeneutics as developed by Hans-Georg Gadamer (1989), provides a frame for gaining insight into the nature of information. The previous chapter indicated that the involved manager in the available world always already understands that world. In this context Gadamer would argue that, in these moments of breakdown when this world becomes unavailable, the manager is distanced from the being-in. In such moments of estrangement hermeneutic interpretation can become the bridge to render the world *available* again. If this is true, then hermeneutics would seem to be the absent component that would address the notions of understanding and meaningfulness that are to be part of more recent definitions of information.

A brief history of hermeneutics

The origin of the word hermeneutics lies in the Greek verb *hermeneuein*, generally translated as 'to interpret'. Palmer (1969, p.13) explains that the verb *hermeneuein* and the noun *hermeneia* are derived from the name of the wing-footed messenger-god Hermes. Hermes is associated with the task of transmuting that which is beyond human understanding into a form that human intelligence can grasp. The word hermeneutics suggests the process of bringing a thing, a situation or a concept from unintelligibility to intelligibility. Initially, it referred to a set of principles used to interpret the Bible and other sacred texts. Later, the use of the word broadened to refer to non-biblical texts where the meaning was hidden and not apparent.

Schleiermacher (1799-1834*)*, a philosopher, conceived hermeneutics as being the science or art of understanding. Schleiermacher contended that the principles of understanding remain the same, whether the aim is to understand a legal document, religious scriptures or a work of literature. As Palmer (1969, p.86) points out, for Schleiermacher understanding, as an art, is the re-experiencing of the mental processes of the text's author. It is the reverse of composition, for it starts with the fixed and finished expression and goes back to the mental life from which it arose. The interpretation is the result of two interacting processes of interpretation: a grammatical interpretation of the text and its structure; and a psychological interpretation of the author. The psychological interpretation is a reconstruction of the thinking processes of the author within the author's own total life-context.

The philosopher and literary historian Wilhelm Dilthey (1833-1911) saw hermeneutics as a foundation for the *Geisteswissenschaften* (humanities and social sciences). Dilthey believed that it was invalid to use of the techniques of the natural sciences or *positivistic* techniques to study humanity. He sought a way to use concrete, historical and lived experience as the basis for understanding the *Geisteswissenschaften*. Although he rejected positivistic techniques, he still believed the requirement of objectivity to be of paramount importance. In hermeneutics he saw the methodological basis for understanding humanity. As Palmer (1969) explains: "The problem of understanding humanity was for Dilthey one of recovering a consciousness of the *historicality* of our own existence which is lost in the static categories of science. We experience life not in the mechanical categories of 'power' but in complex, individual moments of 'meaning,' of direct experience of life as a totality and in loving grasp of the particular. These units of meaning require the context of the past and the horizon of the future expectations; they are intrinsically temporal and finite, and they are to be understood in terms of these dimensions that is, historically" (p.101).

Dilthey believed the key word for human studies was *understanding*. Natural sciences must *explain* nature, human studies must understand humanity in its expression of life, in its creation of meaning and in its complete experience of life within a comprehensive historical context. For Dilthey *experience,* and the understanding of it, is the basic unit of meaning in the methodology of human studies. When referring to the concept 'experience', Dilthey uses the German word *Erlebnis* which can be more accurately translated as "immediate lived experience". Palmer (1969) explains it in the following manner: "In other words, a meaningful experience of a painting, for instance, may involve many encounters separated by time and still be called an 'experience' (Erlebnis)" (p.107). Erlebnis may not be seen as the *content* of a reflexive act of consciousness, for then it would be something of which one is conscious. *Erlebnis* is the act of experiencing, it is the direct contact with life which we call *lived experience*. It is clear from the above that Dilthey saw the *text* to be interpreted as the *Erlebnis* of humanity. If one is to succeed in understanding this text, one would understand humanity, which is the task of *Geisteswissenschaften*. Dilthey's contribution, focusing on life (via *Erlebnis*) as a text to be interpreted, prepared the way for Heidegger and Gadamer, whose views will be discussed in the next section on hermeneutic concepts.

The need for interpretation?

From the above discussion on the historical development of hermeneutics it seems as if the idea of interpretation comes into play when a situation of distance, or confusion is present. This idea of a rupture in the flow of understanding will now be further explored; first with the exploration of the need for interpretation, then of the result that may be expected from such a process.

Interpretation and breakdown

Why is interpretation necessary? One could start with a traditional functionalist model of communication. Put simply, a sender encodes a message in symbols, words, or signs to communicate to the receiver some meaning which the sender feels the receiver should know. The receiver must now unlock or interpret the symbols, words, or signs so as to attribute the 'correct' meaning to the communicated symbols, words, or signs. (The concept of meaning is purposefully left open at this stage of the discussion.) This communication process is subject to many sources of 'disturbance' that undermine its success. Some of the sources of disturbances could be:

- a limited set of symbols to communicate an unlimited set of meanings. There may not be a word, symbol, or sign available to which both the sender and receiver would attach the same meaning to encode a meaning that they wish to communicate;
- a time lapse between sending and receiving. The elapsed time may be from seconds to centuries (as is the case in the Bible or the Koran);
- a changing (evolving) set of relationships between words, symbols, or signs and the meanings they refer to;
- different frames of reference or contexts used by sender and receiver in the communication process.

These disturbances can cause the communication process to *break down*. It is in such instances that one could argue for some sort of interpretation to correct the 'failed' communication process. This seems sensible, yet it could also be argued that all communication is inherently 'failed' communication and thus in need of interpretation. This may be why Gadamer (1989) claims that "all understanding is interpretation" (p.350). For Gadamer, it is quite artificial to think of interpretation as separate from the act of understanding. As Hoy (1978) points out: "Because an understanding is rooted in a situation, it represents a point of view, a perspective, on what it represents. There is no absolute, aperspectual standpoint from which to see all possible perspectives. Interpretation is necessarily a historical process, continuously elaborating on the meaning grasped in an understanding and on the meaning of this understanding for itself. In this respect understanding is not a mere repetition of the past but participates in the present meaning" (p.52).

How does this interpretation in moments of distancing or breakdown happen? What is the 'it' that is understood? Is understanding, in some way, the recovery of meaning? In the discussion that follows, the symbol(s), word(s), or sign(s) involved process will be referred to as the 'text' that is in need of interpretation. The text could be a spoken text, a written text or even an enacted text. It may be true that there are definite differences involved in the interpretation of these different types of texts. It is also true, however, Gadamer argues, that there is always a common set of principles involved, namely hermeneutics.

Before thinking through the interpretation process it may be useful to step back and highlight a more fundamental, and often implicit point, namely, the continuing debate between objectivism and relativism. Objectivism is the basic conviction that there is some form of permanent, ahistorical matrix or framework to which one can ultimately appeal in order to determine truth or reality. Relativism is the basic conviction that the determination of truth or reality is always relative to some conceptual scheme, theoretical framework, society or culture.

Based on these definitions, the objectivist would claim that when a text is interpreted, the text will have an intrinsically constant, ahistorical meaning. Thus, when two individuals from different historical periods attempt to understand the same text, they should both strive to unlock the same, true, objective, inherently there, meaning of the text. If they understand the text differently, one or both of them were unsuccessful in understanding and relativism the true, objective meaning of the text.

Furthermore, the objectivist would claim that an interpretation is correct or true if, and only if, the meaning that the interpreter attributes to the text is indeed the same, or corresponds to, the meaning that the author of the text intended in the creation of the text (the question whether it is possible for the author to know what he intended, or whether he must also interpret it, will be discussed again later).

The relativist would contend that the meaning of a text evolves or changes as the historical, social, political, or moral context in which it is interpreted adapts and changes. Thus, in different historical contexts, different interpretations can be made. Ricoeur (1979) describes interpretation as a process of *appropriation*: "The term 'appropriation' underlines two additional features (of interpretation). One of the aims of all hermeneutics is to struggle against cultural (or any other contextual) *distance*. This struggle can be understood in purely temporal terms as a struggle against secular estrangement, or in more genuinely hermeneutical terms as a struggle against the estrangement of meaning itself, that is, from the system of values upon which the text is based. In this sense, interpretation 'brings together', 'equalizes', renders 'contemporary and similar', thus genuinely making one's own what was initially alien. Above all, the characterization of interpretation as appropriation is meant to underline the 'present' character of interpretation" (p.159). Through appropriation the interpreter renders the text relevant to the local, here and now, involvement whole.

In the section to follow this objectivist/relativist dichotomy will always be implicitly or explicitly present in the discussion. The argument will, nevertheless, be based on the belief that the work of Heidegger and Wittgenstein, which will emerge in the discussion, does offer some guidance on ways to transcend this proverbial knot.

From the discussion of the communication process above, it seems that interpretation comes into play in moments of breakdown when the involved actor gets distanced from the involvement whole – the world shifts from being ready-to-hand to being unavailable. *Dasein* is, for a moment, brought up short as the world leaps forth in its unavailableness. How should we think about this?

Interpretation and the 'recovery of meaning'?

It may be concluded, from the discussion of the communication process above, that the purpose of interpretation is to *recover* the *disturbed* meaning that was transmitted from the mind of the originator to the mind of the receiver. Hence interpretation can be viewed as a process of recovering this meaning, and understanding is the moment when the recovery is complete.

In order to think through this notion of the *recovery of meaning* it may be helpful to start by examining some obvious examples of interpretative situations. A simple example is the interpretation of a work of art. When a painter paints a canvas, she is encoding meaning or expressing meaning through the lines, texture and colours (or signs) that she uses. If a person is confronted with this work of art, should he *only* strive to interpret or decode the meaning that the painter intended? Maybe not. It would be a pity if the only possible meaning that can be construed from a work of art is that which the creator intended at the time of creation. That would assume that it possible for the creator to determine the intended meaning; however, she too must interpret or discover what she intended, as she is also alienated from the work as she completes it and must now understand this work which is outside herself.

This suggests that the artist merely creates a platform from which many meanings can evolve or jump to life as each individual interprets the work of art for himself. Even the creator can, at different times, interpret different meanings emanating from the work of art, and can in doing so, possibly discover more of herself, or of the subject of the work of art. Often one hears an artist say of another's interpretation of their work, 'after hearing this interpretation I think I now have another, or even a better understanding of what I meant when I created the work of art'. This implies that artists in fact discover more of themselves (or their subjects) through the interpretations of others. This seems intelligible since most of the skills involved in creating the work of art, as well as the knowledge of the subject matter, are tacit by nature.

It could be argued that this could be true for paintings, as paintings are a unique type of communication where the signs (colour, texture and lines) are very ambiguous and open to many different interpretations, but not so much for a musical manuscript, where the signs (notes, tempo and rhythm) are not as ambiguous. However, there is still talk of different interpretations of the same piece of music, even talk of a 'good' or a 'better' interpretation. Because of the tacit nature of creativity, the composer, in producing the music, merely creates a spectrum of possibilities, some of which he may, and some of which he may not, have been consciously aware of. It then follows that there can, indeed, be no one 'right' interpretation. Hoy (1978) explains Gadamer's position *vis-à-vis* the possibility of a 'right' interpretation as follows: "Furthermore, there is no 'one right interpretation'. Interpretation involves the continual mediation of the past and the present" (p.52).

From the discussion we can conclude that interpretation is not simply a recovery of lost meaning (due to disturbance). Rather, interpretation is the *making alive* of the text (art, music) in which the interpreter is actively involved. It may, therefore, be argued that art and music are obviously tacit or elusive by nature and therefore require interpretation. However, everyday language may appear to be much more clear-cut than art and music.

Interpretation and language

In language, it appears there is a relatively clear-cut relation between the word (the signifier or the sign) and that which it signifies or stands for (the signified). Hence it may seem that interpretation of everyday language should pose much less of a problem than the interpretation of art or music.

Wittgenstein (1956) argues that this view of language is only correct for a very primitive *language-game*. If language were to function merely as a set of clear and unambiguous pointers to objects (things, situations) in the world it would almost certainly break down in everyday use. Everyday language is not primitive – it is rich and subtle. It is intrinsically *constructed* as part of *what we do*. Language is a game in which the "language and the actions into which it is woven" are fused together (p.23). To speak a language is not to construct and utter grammatically good sentences. We always speak in a situation as part of doing whatever we are doing – speaking, like doing, is always already in the world. We have lawyer-speak, nurse-speak, shopping-speak, fishing-speak and so forth. These are *forms of life*, each with its own language-game. In the form of life called 'nursing', a theatre nurse may say "prep her!". This is a way (comprising words and rules for using these words) within that form of life, which is equivalent to "prepare this patient for the operating theatre" in the form of life called 'lay-person'. Everyday language is an accumulation of the various language-games we participate in as part of our everyday being in the world.

In speaking, in the course of doing in-the-world, we do not sit down and consider the words and rules for their application. We always already know it because we participate in the different forms of life as part of being-in-the-world. As Wittgenstein explains: "So you are saying that human agreements decide what is true and what is false? It is what human beings say that is true and false; and they agree in the language they use. That is not agreement in opinions but in form of life" (p.241). When, as part of the doing (forms of life) the language-game breaks down, language will become occurrent and require clarification or interpretation. In these situations language becomes a *text* in need of interpretation. The important point is, however, that the interpretation process cannot be severed from the form of life within which the language-game is always already embedded.

Gadamer (1989), using different terminology, argues the same point: "The difference between a literary work of art and any other text is not so fundamental. It is true that there is a difference between the language of poetry and the language of prose, and again between the language of poetic prose and of 'scientific' prose. These differences can certainly also be considered from the point of view of literary form. But the essential difference of these various 'languages' obviously lies elsewhere: namely, in the distinction between the claims of truth that each makes (the rules of the game). All literary works *have a profound community* (forms of life) in that the linguistic form makes effective the significance of the contents to be expressed. In this light, the understanding of texts by, say, a historian is not so very different from the experience of art. And it is not mere chance that the concept of literature embraces not only works of literary art, but everything that has been transmitted in writing" (p.145).

Taking what is said above and applying it to the theme of the book it becomes clear that the management information situation is also an instance that requires interpretation. The manager is to a greater or lesser extent *distanced* from the form of life from where the text originates (the 'shopfloor'). These *facts* are decontextualized through computer processing or through other forms of reporting. The manager must now try and understand it. The manager must try and translate it, as it were, from shopfloor-speak into management-speak. This will clearly be very difficult (if not impossible). This problem of incommensurability language-games of language-games, due to their rootedness in forms of life incommensurability, will be a theme that will permeate all the discussions, in some way or another, throughout the rest of the book. It will be argued that this is at the heart of the problem faced by all computerized management support systems: a problem that may be, of its nature, unsolvable.

To sum up: we understand our actions and we understand our language because we 'share' a life-world; we are always already in it. Interpretation becomes necessary in moments of breakdown, when, as part of speaking and doing, this tacit understanding breaks down. Interpretation, as with speaking, is part of the doing. They are both rooted in forms of life, in being-in-the-world.

Gadamer and hermeneutic understanding

In the discussion on the interpretive situation it was argued that interpretation comes into play when a *breakdown* occurs. It was suggested that in interpretive situations such as trying to understand art or music these breakdowns seems to be relatively self-evident. It was also argued, with reference to the work of Wittgenstein on language, that even the meaning of everyday language is not as self-evident as it seems. It was asserted that even everyday language is always rooted in forms of life, and therefore creates points of breakdown as individuals participate in the multiplicity of language games that make up their everyday existence.

Now that we have a sense of the interpretive situation we can turn more specifically to the idea of interpretation, and the 'process' of interpretation, as articulated by Gadamer.

Interpretation as the appropriation of meaning

In interpreting a *text* the interpreter must *re-root* it in the world, in a form of life. Since the text is just a series of movements, sounds, or patterns of ink on paper it has no intrinsic 'already present' context attached to it. The meaning of a text is therefore, in principle, *always ambivalent or incomplete*. The meaning of the text comes into being or is constituted by every act of interpretation or understanding by the different interpreters as they bring to bear their own perspectives, points of view, or forms of life on the text. Gadamer (1989) explains it as follows: "As we were able to show that the being of the work of art is play which needs to be perceived by the spectator in order to be completed, so it is universally true of texts that only in the process of understanding is the *dead trace of meaning* transformed back into living meaning. We must ask whether what was seen to be true of the experience of art is also true of texts as a whole, including those that are not works of art. We saw that the work of art is fully realized only when it is 'presented', and were forced to the conclusion that all literary works of art can achieve completion only when they are read. Is this true also of the understanding of any text? Is the meaning of all texts realized only when they are understood? In other words, does understanding belong to the meaning of a text just as being heard belongs to the meaning of music? Understanding must be conceived as part of the process of coming into being of meaning, in which the significance of all statements – those of art and those of everything else that has been transmitted – is formed and made complete" (p.146).

What is the role of *prejudice* or pre-judgement in understanding? The word prejudice here must not be seen in its normal negative sense. Gadamer uses it merely to describe the first stab, or initial understanding or interpretation, that the interpreter must necessarily make due to the lack of sufficient context or dialogue. This first stab understanding, or prejudice, will become negative only if the interpreter is not continually open to the potentiality of new understanding that may emerge.

Does this mean that Gadamer is proclaiming a subjectivist or a relativist approach to understanding? As Bernstein (1983) concludes: "For it would seem that if the meaning of a work of art or text is affected by, or conditioned by, the understanding of its meaning, then there does not seem to be any meaning that has 'objective' integrity, that is 'there' in the work of art or text to be understood" (p.125). This is, however, not true. What Gadamer is saying is that we cannot escape from our prejudices (a better translation of the German word *Vorurteil* would be 'pre-judgement', the anticipation of meaning which may or may not be substantiated by further experience). Gadamer's point would seem to be that anything new can *only* be understood in terms of what we already *know*. The first stab understanding is based on what Dasein always already understands as its being in-the-world: what one already knows or the tradition within which we find ourselves. If the process of understanding stops after this first step then, yes, it is subjective. But if we continually open ourselves to the text and continually re-evaluate our understanding against the text and the world in which the text is now located, we will be able to complete the meaning through the process of understanding. How then will we know that we are not misunderstanding the text? Gadamer (1989) argues that we cannot continually misunderstand the use of a word "without its affecting the meaning of the whole, so we cannot hold blindly to our own fore-meanings [and pre-judgements] of the thing if we would understand the meaning of another." However, we cannot simply forget our fore-meanings concerning the possibilities of the text or dialogue at hand. What we ought to do however is to "remain open to the meaning of the other person or text. But this openness always includes our placing the other meaning in a relation with the whole of our own meanings or ourselves in relation to it. ... Thus there is a criterion here also. The hermeneutic task becomes automatically a questioning of things and is always in part determined by this" (p.238). The hermeneutic task therefore is a delicate process of using our own bias (fore-meanings) yet anticipating the possibility that the text may challenge these very same fore-meanings that were the stepping-stone for entering it in the first place. That is why "the hermeneutically trained mind must be sensitive to the text's quality and newness. But this kind of sensitivity involves neither 'neutrality' in the matter of the object nor the extinction of one's self, but the conscious assimilation of one's own fore-meanings and prejudices. The important thing is to be aware of one's own bias, so that the text may present itself in all its newness and thus be able to assert its own truth against one's own fore-meanings" (p.238).

The above description by Gadamer suggests that there is some sort of iterative process involved in understanding. When we are confronted with a text, the first iteration starts with our fore-meanings and prejudices. For an adequate understanding it is necessary to continually re-evaluate in terms of the meanings that come to the fore in the text. In these iterations, the meaning of the text is continually reappropriated. This iterative process is know as the hermeneutic circle.

The hermeneutic circle

The hermeneutic circle is one of the most important conceptual contributions offered by hermeneutics. The hermeneutic circle expresses the principle that one must understand the parts from the whole and the whole from the parts. Gadamer (1989) explains it as follows: "The anticipation of meaning in which the whole is envisaged becomes explicit understanding in that the parts, that are determined by the whole, themselves also determine this whole" (p.259). The hermeneutic circle is not a vicious or a subjective circle. It is neither formal nor methodological. In the hermeneutic circle, we *project* significance onto the text, based on the form of life within which we interpret; we then allow the text to inform the tradition, which is the living context from which we seek to

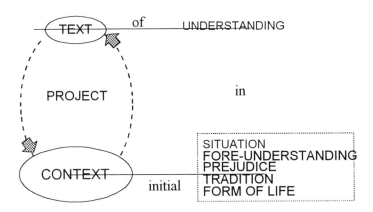

Figure 3.1: The hermeneutic circle

understand. In the hermeneutic circle, we continually adjust our point of view, perspective or horizon, always within our own tradition and situation, in an effort to fuse these points of view, perspectives or horizons. We do this in order to achieve understanding and in order to maintain a living and current form of life. The hermeneutic circle is utilized by such diverse people as Kuhn (1977, p.xii), in his effort to understand the physics of Aristotle, and Feyerabend (1993, p.251), in describing what he called the "anthropological method".

Figure 3.1 depicts the operation of the hermeneutic circle. It starts in a heuristic manner, the interpreter uses her fore-understanding and pre-judices to establish the initial meaning of the text; assuming it to be in some way coherent and understandable. She then relates this meaning to her current situation, tradition or form of life. She now possesses a new understanding of her context; this new understanding is projected back onto the text which opens up new meanings to be projected back to the context. This movement to and fro between text (the part) and context (the whole) creates possibilities for understanding, but only if the interpreter persists and continually opens herself to the text. The hermeneutic circle is, in a sense, the dialectic process of understanding. In the movement to and fro, "(the) harmony of all the details with the whole is the criterion of correct understanding. The failure to achieve this harmony means the understanding has failed" (p. 259).

The notion of the hermeneutic circle enables an understanding of the concept of multiple perspectives. The first perspective is based on current understanding or prejudices. The interpretation process will try and render it coherent with this understanding. If this is not possible the perspective must be adapted for a new understanding to be possible. The new understanding becomes the new perspective that is again projected onto the text from which emerges a new meaning and thus an expanded understanding. This process of repeated and reiterated projection of perspectives onto the text will expand the interpreter's understanding of the text. However, this process, as explained above, requires an *openness* to the text. The more the process is reiterated, the more comprehensible the text becomes and the 'greater' the interpreter's understanding of the text becomes. However, if the process is prematurely terminated (the inter-preter closes to the text) then the interpretation and thus the understanding of the text is incomplete and to a degree subjective. It is clear that subjectivity is not a choice. It is in reality a given. It is not an evil, it is an essential ingredient in the process. It is the interpreter's task to use it creatively and also to struggle beyond it towards the never-ending possibility of further interpretations.

If this notion is applied to dialogue, its power clearly emerges. In the description of the interpretation of a fixed text the responsibility of projecting the new perspective onto the text lies with the interpreter. In a dialogue, each partner in the dialogue injects a new perspective and places both the participants in a hermeneutical circle. Dialogue essentially ensues when two parties from different perspectives engage to understand a text by means of the hermeneutical circle. The dialogue is not the joint interpretation of a given text but the interaction in the production of a continually changing text; the text itself and not just the interpretation mutates. Dialogue has the following characteristics, according to Gadamer (1989, p.347):

- two or more participants committed to the process;
- the acknowledgement by both parties that they individually do not have complete understanding, as this would eliminate the need for dialogue;
- both participants take seriously the truth claims of the other party and do not try to destroy the other party's position;
- the reciprocal illumination of positions by the other party;
- if successful, the conclusion of the dialogue will take the participants beyond their original points of view in the sense that these are transformed or consolidated by the encounter with alternatives.

Interpretation and Erlebnis

Erlebnis (lived experience) is a key concept for Gadamer. Hegel (in Gadamer, 1989, p.318) described lived experience as follows: "The principle of experience contains the infinitely important element that, in order to accept a content as true, the man himself must be present or, more precisely, he must find the content in unity and combined with the certainty of himself."

Erlebnis is not merely an experience such as knowing or remembering that 'something has happened to me sometime and somewhere' – a sort of cluster of facts, ordered in time and space, that can be recalled. Erlebnis has a "condensing, intensifying meaning. If something is called or considered an Erlebnis, that means it is rounded into the unity of a significant whole... Every experience is taken out of the continuity of life and at the same time related to the whole of one's life.... Because it is itself within the whole of life, the whole of life is present in it too" (Gadamer, 1989, pp66-9). Erlebnis can be understood as that whole within which the part is already significant.

Crucial to *Erlebnis* is the openness of the person to all possibilities. To experience, the interpreter must not be dogmatic. Experience has a very definite *not-ness* of character. We can only experience something if it is *not* as we assumed it would be. This not-ness opens us to the possibility of experience. Experience can be painful, since an element of disillusionment is always involved. As Aeschylus, the Greek tragedian wrote, *"through suffering [we] learn"*. Experience puts us face-to-face with the reality of the finiteness of human existence for it is in experience that the limits of expectation are displayed.

Erlebnis is the significant whole – the form of life, the involvement whole – that provides the *horizon*, the possibility and the boundary that describes the space within which interpretation becomes possible. Hence, every interpretation is rooted into an already present and significant whole; my life, my Erlebnis. (Gadamer, 1989)

Understanding and practical wisdom

One question that emerges from this discussion is how does hermeneutic understanding relate to practice and to knowledge? It is easy to mis-conceive hermeneutic understanding as removed uninvolved reflection, but Gadamer argues that hermeneutic understanding is rooted in *phronesis* (practical wisdom).

Aristotle developed the concept of *Episteme*, scientific knowledge. It is, as Bernstein (1983, p.146) explains, "knowledge of what is universal, of what exists invariably, and takes the form of scientific demonstration". *Episteme* exists, that is not the issue at hand. Gadamer, in his hermeneutic theory argues, rather, that it is *phronesis,* practical wisdom, that is required in order to achieve understanding. *Phronesis*:

- is a form of reasoning and knowledge that involves a distinctive mediation between the universal and the particular (Aristotle, 1962, p.1141b; Bernstein, 1983, p.146);
- combines the generality of reflection of principles with the particularity of perception into a given situation (Hoy, 1978, p.58);
- is not, however, merely a rational *phronesis* characteristic or trained ability. An indication (that it is something more) may be seen in the fact that a trained ability of that rational kind can be forgotten, whereas practical wisdom cannot (Aristotle, 1962, p.1140b);
- is a kind of a perception – not sense perception (of colours, sounds, and the like), but rather a question of perceiving what is at stake in a given situation (Hoy, 1978, p.58).

Aristotle notes that practical wisdom is a capability or ability that "*managers* of households and states" should have.

Praxis, for Gadamer, is informed practice and not merely the antithesis of theory. This contrasts with the common view that theory is the 'thinking about' and practice is the 'doing'. As Hoy (1978, p.55) explains, "the reflection never provides completely sufficient reason for action. In fact, ordinary life provides numerous examples of action that does not concur with the antecedent reflective conclusion." *Praxis* is not pure reasoning, it is inseparable from action itself, it is reason in action. It may be likened to the difference between knowing the rules of a game and being able to play the game.

Hermeneutic understanding is not a reflective type of understanding, an understanding removed from the situation. Because of its character within and as part of the situation, it is a misapprehension to try to separate understanding and application in the hermeneutic process. The process is not the traditional epistemology of applying theories or concepts (thus *episteme*) to a practical situation, but is a matter of *praxis*.

For Gadamer, understanding *phronesis* is the result of *phronesis* and vice versa. In a sense, it is within the hermeneutic circle that *phronesis* and *praxis* fuse to create understanding and through this reshape and become part of the interpreter's *phronesis*. Wittgenstein also emphasizes the way understanding is grounded in and constituted by the meaning contexts provided by forms of life. He argues that understanding a rule is at the same time understanding *how to apply it*.

Appropriation

Appropriation is the bridge between the alien and the known, it is the essence of the actualization of understanding. Ricoeur (1979, p.185) explains appropriation as: "...the concept which is suitable for the actualization of meaning as addressed to someone. It takes the place of the answer in the dialogical situation, in the same way that 'revelation' or 'disclosure' takes the place of ostensive [explicit] reference in the dialogical situation."

With the insights gained from the section on hermeneutics, some conditions for appropriation can be examined:

- *The Overlap Principle*: A text can only be understood in terms of a pre-existing whole (fore-meanings, prejudices, assumptions, etc.). If there were no *overlap* with existing then interpretation would be blind. To put it differently: the hermeneutic circle has to have some point of entry.

- *Common lexicon*: A level of shared understanding present for interpretation to make sense. This may imply sharing a particular form of life.

- *Phronesis*: The ability to separate the essential from the non-essential, the ability to translate from the universal to the particular.

- *Erlebnis*: As Gadamer has argued, understanding can only be grounded in Erlebnis. Erlebnis provides the referential whole that allows the interpretation to be significant in the first instance. Without Erlebnis of a form of life the background for significance to display against will be lost.

- *Hermeneutic circle*: Understanding comes alive in the hermeneutic circle. In order to understand, the receiver must engage in the hermeneutic circle. This implies an understanding of Erlebnis, the context or larger whole from which the text emerges.

- *Openness to text*: This openness implies: a commitment to being prepared to be challenged by the text; a continual willingness to 'listen' to the text and not to jump prematurely to conclusions thereby closing oneself to the possibilities of understanding; and being aware of the role of prejudices and fore-understanding (and using them to facilitate understanding but not to be dominated by them). To be closed to the text is to fall into subjectivity.

Some provisional conclusions on hermeneutic understanding

If information is all about meaning and understanding, as was suggested in the previous section, then the following conclusions can be drawn:

- Hermeneutic understanding is understanding that comes into being by active interpretation that is based on Erlebnis and not on distant reflection. It is the result of applying phronesis in praxis. It is always within a context and coloured by that context. It is historical, always fusing past, present and future. It is created in the situation, through hermeneutic dialogue between the interpreter and the text, in the situation. And finally, it is the act of appropriation of meaning.

- For hermeneutic understanding to come into being requires: presence in the situation; the openness to fuse past, present and future into the process; the application of phronesis; an openness to the text; a conscious awareness of fore-understanding and pre-judice; an active, never-ending, hermeneutic dialogue with the text and engagement in the hermeneutic circle.

- Hermeneutic understanding is not the same as representational know-ing. Representational knowing (occurrent knowing) requires only that the knower has access to an adequate representation. We could say we know of "Peter Smith" if we can locate him from an entry in a directory. However, for this sense of knowing to be-in-a-world it needs a hermeneutic understanding that can contextualize this representation back into an involvement whole: to know Peter Smith is to be acquainted with him as a friend or antagonist.

A postmodern critique of hermeneutics

The above the discussion of hermeneutic theory makes the assumption that a text does in some minimal way refer to, or point to, a reality. In other words that it has some final referent that it is ultimately grounded in. This assumption has been *deconstructed* by the postmodern movement. Derrida (1982) argues that humans exist within a linguistic play, a text, in which there are no grounding absolutes, only an endlessly differentiating play of signifiers. All attempts to ground language (and interpretation) are futile, since there is no one term which has any *intrinsic* meaning. All terms acquire meaning only by their *differentiation* from all the other terms in the language.

What Derrida is saying has truth, yet it cannot be absolutely true. In the pragmatic dealings of everyday, we establish some, albeit very limited and mostly implicit, agreements about the relationship between a set of signifiers and that which it may signify. If this does not happen then all communication and interpretation becomes meaningless. In some vague sense we all believe – and it must be that Derrida would include himself in this all – that a newspaper of record does in some way refer to a 'real' world in a way that a Tolkein novel does not. It is not that there is no 'real' and that it is all 'text'; rather it is our inability to escape language. It is the knowing beyond the representation that continually inspires us: this is why we continue to read a daily paper. This is why we continue to be involved in the world.

A possible answer to the dilemma of infinite regress is to break the link between understanding, or knowing and representation.

Heidegger on understanding and interpretation

In the discussion of Gadamer's notion of hermeneutic understanding it was demonstrated that interpretation is to be seen as a process of appropriation of, rather than recovery of, meaning *in* the situation. The appropriation becomes necessary in moments of breakdown when the interpreter is distanced or alienated form the world as text. Interpretation is the mode through which this distance is dissolved and the text is rendered alive in-the-world again and made available. To put it simply: for Gadamer understanding occurs *in* interpretation (1989, p.389).

From Heidegger's perspective the notion of distance has the potential to reinstate the Cartesian dualism, that of the observer removed from-the-world. Understanding is not something we come to – by dissolving the distance. To be in the world means to always already understand the world. Our involvement in the world always already assumes this under-standing. As Kockelmans (1972, p.16) explains: "Man's interpretation does not throw a meaning over some 'naked' thing that is present-at-hand, nor does it place a value on it. The intra-mundane thing that is encountered as such in the original understanding, which is characteristic of man's concernful dealing with things, already possesses a reference that is implicitly contained in man's co-understanding of the world and thus can be articulated by interpretation." If interpretation does not lead to or restore understanding, what, then, is the function of interpretation? Before trying to answer this question it is necessary to articulate more precisely Heidegger's notion of understanding.

Understanding as projection

For Heidegger understanding is a primordial existential of Dasein; "to exist is essentially, even if not only, to understand" (Heidegger, 1988). This primordial understanding does not mean to have some cognitive content, a picture or idea in our heads, about something or some situation, or to grasp it thematically. Rather, it refers to that mode of being which is characteristic of humanity as being-in-the-world. In this original understanding Dasein manifests itself as being-able-to, as having possibilities. To understand a situation is to have a comportment towards the possibilities within the involvement whole. Hence, understanding is rooted in-the-world and has the structure of *projection* (p.184/5). Projection means that understanding makes the possibilities within the referential whole stand out, become visible. In coping in the world Dasein continually presses forth into these possibilities and in so doing creates leeway for movement (or room for manoeuvring as Dreyfus (1991) puts it). This leeway for movement is the space of possibilities, the clearing that opens up and, simultaneously, limits the range of that which it makes sense to do. Being thrown into-the-world means that Dasein is always limited to a space of sensible possibilities which it already understands or is projected onto; the space that is necessarily tied into the involvement whole which Dasein is already in. Dasein knows, without reflection, this space of possibilities, this room for manoeuvre, for it is the always already understood background of concernful circumspection implied in being involved in the world.

Understanding and interpretation

In interpretation, understanding "does not become something different. It becomes itself" (Heidegger, 1962, p.188). We can only interpret that which we already understand. In interpretation we do not acquire additional information about what is already understood; rather interpretation is the "working-out of possibilities projected in understanding" (p. 189).

In understanding we already have a primordial sense or reference in the form of an already there network of for-the-sake-of-whichs or of in-order-tos about ourselves and our tools within the referential whole. However, this primordial understanding can be further interpreted in such a way that the ready-to-hand comes explicitly into that sight which understands it. This is accomplished by the taking apart, as it were, of the in-order-tos that are already circumspectively understood, and concerning ourselves with what becomes visible through this process. This in-order-to that is now explicitly understood has the structure of something *as* something – as a thing for doing this or for doing that. It follows that interpretation is the laying out, the making explicit, as this or as that, of something already understood in its in-order-to as this or as that. The 'as' constitutes the interpretation; it makes up the structure of the explicitness of something that is understood (Heidegger, 1962, p. 189). If asked "what is this?", we can answer (explain or interpret), that it is something which functions as this or as that – we take it to be a chair or a table or a pointer. This is why Heidegger argues that, in interpretation, understanding does not become something else; it becomes itself; it makes explicit its own possibilities to be as this or as that.

A simple example of a computer mouse may help to illustrate these notions. We understand a mouse in using it to point to various places on the screen in-order-to open files, open applications, select menu options, print, select text, ...; in-order-to write letters, maintain disk space, or do Internet searches, ...; for-the-sake-of getting our work done; for-the-sake-of being a good worker. In understanding the mouse we already know the space of possibilities for which it *makes sense* to use – since we are involved in doing things on the computer, which is the referential whole of which it is an in-order-to. We know that we are able-to-use-it to point and execute. Yet we may not have made this explicit, although it is always possible in principle. If someone would point at the mouse on the table and say, "what is this?", we may explain, that is interpret, by responding, "it is a something normally used *as a pointing thing*; to point at menus, icons, etc. to activate them in order to get things done, like opening files, or selecting text." In this explanation we have made explicit what we already knew, not as an idea in the head, but as an in-order-to that is always already embedded in an involvement whole that makes it significant, and which we may call "working on the computer."

Meaning and meaningful

According to the functionalist model of communication words, symbols, signs and texts possess meaning. In the communication process this meaning may get lost. The purpose of the interpretation process is to recover this meaning. When this recovery has happened, a person may now claim understanding. Thus, in this way of thinking understanding is merely a matter of linking the signifiers (words or pointers) to the signified (things or ideas of things) in a way commensurate to that of the speaker or sender. Interpretation in this context would be the process of correcting any muddled signifier to signified relationships. This notion of understanding is also implied in the statement, "the computer understands my input" – a way of saying that the computer performed the action intended by the command. The computer established the same relationship between the signifier (the command) and the signified (the action to be performed) that the sender had in mind when 'talking' to it through the medium of the keyboard.

Wittgenstein (1956) argues that this view of understanding may be in some sense right. For him, however, it is an example of a very primitive *language-game*; one that is not very useful for thinking about the complexities of everyday language. The idea that words or signs have stable and persistent associations linked to them is too static a view for understanding everyday language. The meaning of a sign is not a "meaning-body, an entity which determines its use. A sign becomes meaningful not through being associated with an object, but through having a rule-governed use" (p. 432). The sign does not have an intrinsic meaning, the sign by itself is dead: "What gives it life? In use it is alive" (pp. 431-2). His argument is that we do not use language to convey meaning as such. We do not have an idea and then convey it by carefully selecting the words that best represent it, rather we use language as part of doing. Using language in doing things is like using a tool in doing things. It does not make much sense to talk about using a tool without thinking about doing something. What we *mean* by an utterance is linked to a language-game (a set of signs and rules for applying them), which is linked to a form of life (a practical everyday doing of something). Therefore, "(whether) a sign is meaningful depends on whether there is an established use [in a language-game], whether it can be employed to perform meaningful linguistic acts [in a form of life]; what meaning it has depends on how it can be used. The meaning of a word is its use in the language" (p. 43). We understand the meaning of a word, a sign, or a text if we use it appropriately as part of some doing.

Heidegger would agree with Wittgenstein's analysis but he would go one step further. He argues that the primordial origin of our apprehending anything as meaningful is our presence in the world. Meaningfulness is "first of all a mode of presence in virtue of which every entity of the world is discovered." (Heidegger, 1992, p. 213) Meaning is not something we inject into a meaningless world. Since our existential structure is that of *being-in*, the referential whole is always already meaningful. We discover this meaning in our concerned understanding. Thus words as signs do not contain meaning. They are only meaningful as part of the referential whole that is our world.

This notion of meaning may best be made explicit through the computer mouse example. The words "mouse" and "point" do not contain meanings. To say "point the mouse to the 'open file' icon" will only mean something as part of 'working on my computer' in-order-to get something done. The meaning is not that an object can be assigned to the word "mouse" and an action to the word "point". The meaning arises from there already being significance in the request to "point" the "mouse" in this form of life called working together to get something done. In this involvement whole the meaning of the request is already present. It is already understood.

Understanding and the information concept

This section will endeavour to bring the discussion back to the concept and nature of information by examining the notions of information, data, knowledge, and wisdom. Firstly, the relationship between knowledge and data will be discussed; secondly the relationship between information and wisdom will be elaborated. And, finally, the notions of data and information will be discussed and contrasted.

Before embarking on the discussion it must be noted that the purpose of this discussion is to *contrast* two views of the same reality. The removed observer view and the involved Dasein view. In order to make this contrast as sharp as possible the discussion must present them as discretely as possible. This will necessitate leaving many potentially ambiguous notions unchallenged, obviously such neat demarcation is not feasible in reality and should not go unremarked. Nonetheless, a simultaneous decon-struction might also dilute the distinction to the point that the contrast itself fades. Consequently, the emphasis in the discussion will be on facilitating a flow such that the general theme emerges.

Data and knowledge: the epistemological domain

Within what may be called the *epistemological domain*, data are basic facts; facts that can be shown or demonstrated to be true because they correspond to reality (the correspondence theory of truth). Data are particular instances of reality. Knowledge (*Episteme*) consists of truths deduced (or created) from facts by reasoning, using the tools of logic. Knowledge strives to discover universal truths. With these truths, know-ledge can attempt to explain certain aspects of reality, by explaining why.

The process of knowledge creation starts with basic facts and moves, via logical reasoning, to more universal truths. This process of knowledge creation is conceived to be objective in that the subject (the investigator) explicitly excludes herself (her pre-convictions, fore-understandings and pre-judices) from the reasoning process.

This reasoning process is a-contextual (not embedded within an involvement whole), a-historical (not based on and facilitated by a *tradition*) and a-perspectual (not based on a particular point of view). The investigator only accepts facts that are shown to be true (meet the conditions for truth), irrespective of context and time. The investigator does not adopt any particular point of view when evaluating the facts and reasoning about the facts. In the reasoning process the investigator's own prejudices are removed from the situation and there is objective reflection on the facts and the reasoning about the facts.. Thus, within the epistemological domain, the domain of the removed observer, the *scientist* explores and discovers the nature of things. In this epistemological world, observation and reason rules and the discovery of universal truths is the ultimate and final aim.

Information and wisdom: the hermeneutic domain

Within the hermeneutic domain, information is the referential network of significant relationships which we always already understand as part of being in the world. We do not become informed. To be-in-the-world is to be always already informed. Interpretation is the working out of the possibilities already given in our understanding of the world we are *in*, which leads to *in*-sight. Wisdom comprises the critical working out of these *in*-sights. We say someone is wise when that person acted sensibly;

acted within the possibilities made explicit by the process of interpretation. Insight is therefore, knowing what makes sense *to do* within the room for manoeuvre. Based on this insight, sensible judgements in, of, and about the specific situation at hand can be made. Continued interpretation, working out of the possibilities available in a person's coping, will lead to insight and, if persistent, to wisdom.

The interpretation process starts with *Erlebnis*, existing historical insight and historically rooted understanding, and projects it on to the situation at hand. The interpretation process is not subjective, it merely acknowledges the fact that we cannot escape our own historicity and contextuality (thrownness). The interpretation process draws upon its historicity and contextuality as a baseline from which to project new attempts at working out of possibilities in the situation. It is from this base and by means of the hermeneutic circle that we develop the space of sensible possibilities for the situation at hand. Thus interpretation is historical, contextual, and perspectual.

Information and wisdom exist in the *hermeneutic* domain. In this domain insight and wisdom are the ideals. This is the domain of the everyday *involved* person, the domain in which the involved person is thrown but within which there is always a pressing forward into possibilities – a rendering sensible of that which is already understood.

Data and information

The technical-functional notion of the relationship between data and information is that information is data that has been processed (or interpreted) in order to make it useful, sensible, or meaningful. The idea of data as independent (present-at-hand) facts about the state of affairs in the world assumes a more primitive notion of a background understanding (information) that, the previous discussion has argued, is to be seen as always already present (ready-to-hand). The manager's interpretation does not throw a meaning over some raw data that are present-at-hand, nor does it place a value on the data. The data encountered in original understanding, which is characteristic of the manager's concernful dealing with things in the world, *always already possesses a reference* that is implicitly contained in the manager's involved understanding of the world. The manager can only act as if she can isolate facts as data because the manager always already understands, is in-formed, about the world that she is involved in. Therefore, the hermeneutic domain is primary (primordial) and the epistemological domain is secondary (derived).

This has been the mistake made by the pioneers of management information systems. The management information systems 'failed' on two accounts:

- either the manager already understood the issues because she is concernfully involved and finds the information represented through the system to be a crude approximation of what she already knows;
- or, the manager is not involved and therefore finds it impossible to make sense of the information presented by the system and has to rely on personal dialogue to interpret it.

In either case the system is seen to be of relatively little use and is ignored. The involved manager would argue that the system merely informs her of what she already knows and thus merely drowns her in useless data. Conversely, the removed manager would argue that the data do not make sense and might therefore continually request more or different data while preferring to rely on personal contact to resolve the distance. The role of traditional technical-functional information systems, and the reason for their continuing introduction, are therefore brought into question. Before addressing this question it may be sensible to summarise some conclusions about information from the hermeneutic perspective.

Hermeneutic conclusions about information

There are many conclusions that could be made and the perceptive reader may, by now, sense the important contributions that Gadamer, Heidegger and Wittgenstein have made to our exploration of information.

Hermeneutics not epistemology: The technical-functional paradigm of information draws on the natural science model of epistemology deriving from the Enlightenment. It is based on the idea of a detached objective observer (the manager) who indirectly observes the current state of affairs by receiving facts about the world from the computer. The computer is merely a sophisticated measuring tool that is accurate and efficient: it can be present at many places at the same time (through various input devices); it can accurately organise and retain many facts; and it is very efficient in computation. The manager can use this computer 'magnifying lens' to know the world and act accordingly. This view of the information system is of course in some limited sense correct. It is similar to the language-game "words are signifiers that point to objects". This view presupposes another, the hermeneutic. This is the world of the involved manager. A manager who always already understands. A manager who is continually pushing forward to insight, working out the possibilities of that which is already understood.

Hermeneutic understanding: Information is hermeneutic understanding. It is always already projected, yet, the possibilities of this projection need to be worked out. The manager, through interpretation, becomes aware of what is already known. This working out happens through appropriation; it is the appropriation of an understanding, an understanding that is always already understood. Information, therefore, cannot become meaningful through being processed. If the manager is involved in-the-world then it will already be meaningful; if not, it will always stay present-at-hand.

Certainly some managers do find some computer-generated reports useful or meaningful. In this context 'useful' or 'meaningful' denote that these reports make certain possibilities apparent as being sensible to do in the situation. These possibilities, the being-able-tos, however, do not flow from an interpretation of a confused text which becomes endowed with meaning through a process of interpretation. These possibilities are already present because the manager already understands. If the manager then declares (after reading the report), "now I know what it makes sense to do", he is not implying that the sense emerged from the report. The manager is implying that the possibilities, already pre-constituted by being involved in-the-world, are now more lucid, more explicit.

From informing to sense-making: In the hermeneutic domain the shift is from informing to sense-making. The technical-functional notion of information is based on the idea that someone does not know what to do and then receives the information and consequently knows what to do. If we were computers that applied facts to rules to make decisions then this notion of information might be appropriate. From a hermeneutic point of view, however, we are always already in-the-world. This means we already have a landscape, a horizon of possibilities that we understand. When the manager receives the information, the in-order-tos of the referential whole may become more explicit and what it makes sense to do will become clear. Hence, information does not add to our understanding, it merely makes explicit that which we always already understand as part of what it means to be in-the-world.

References

Ahituv, N. and Neumann, S. (1990), *Principles of Information Systems for Management*, Dubuque, Wm. C. Brown Publ.

Aristotle (1962), *Nicomachean Ethics*, Indianapolis, Bobbs-Merrill Publ.

Bateson, G. (1972), *Steps to the Ecology of Mind*, Northvale, Jason Aronson Inc.

Bernstein, R.J. (1983), *Beyond Objectivism and Relativism: Science, Hermeneutics and Praxis*, London, Basil Blackwell.

Boland, R.J. (1983), 'The In-Formation of Information Systems', in Boland, R.J. and Hirschheim, R.A. (eds), *Critical Issues in Information Systems Research*, New York, John Wiley & Sons.

Boland, R.J. (1993), 'Accounting and the Interpretive Act', *Accounting, Organizations and Society*, 18, 2/3, 125-146.

Boland, R.J. and Tenkasi, R.V. (1993), 'Locating Meaning Making in Organizational Learning: The narrative basis of cognition', *Research in Organizational Change and Development*, 7, 77-103.

Burch, G.C. and Grudnitski, G. (1989), *Information Systems: Theory and Practice* (5th Edition), New York, John Wiley & Sons.

Davis, G.B. and Olsen, M.H. (1985), *Management Information Systems: Conceptual Foundations, Structure and Development* (2nd Edition), London, McGraw-Hill.

Derrida, J. (1982), *"Differance", Margins of Philosophy*, Chicago, University of Chicago Press.

Dreyfus, H.L. (1991), *Being-in-the-world: a Commentary on Heidegger's Being and time, Division I*, Cambridge, Mass, MIT Press.

Feyerabend, P. (1993), *Against method* (3rd Edition), London, Verso.

Gadamer, H.-G. (1989), *Truth and method* (2nd revised Edition), London, Sheed and Ward.

Heidegger, M. (1962), *Being and time*, Oxford, Basil Blackwell.

Heidegger, M. (1988), *The Basic Problems of Phenomenology*, Bloomington, Indiana University Press.

Heidegger, M. (1992), *History of the Concept of Time*, Bloomington, Indiana University Press.

Hoy, D.C. (1978), *The Critical Circle: Literature, History and Philosophical Hermeneutics*, Berkeley, University of California Press.

Kockelmans, J.J. (1972), 'Language, Meaning, and Ek-sistence', in Kockelmans, J.J. (ed.), *On Heidegger and Language*, Evanston, Northwestern University Press.

Kuhn, T.S. (1977), *The Essential Tension: Selected Studies in Scientific Tradition and Change.*, Chicago, Ill., The University of Chicago Press.

Laudon, K.C. and Laudon, J.P. (1996), *Management Information Systems* (4th Edition), New York, Prentice Hall.

Palmer, R.E. (1969), *Hermeneutics*, Evanston, Northwestern University Press.

Pratt, A.D. (1982), *The Information of Image*, New Jersey, Ablex Publ. Corp.

Ricoeur, P. (1979), *Hermeneutics & the Human Sciences*, Paris, Cambridge University Press.

Roszak, T. (1986), *The Cult of Information*, New York, Pantheon Books.

Senn, J.A. (1990), *Information Systems in Management*, Belmount, California, Wadsworth Publ.

Shannon, C.E. and Weaver, W. (1949), *The Mathematical Theory of Communication*, Urbana, University of Illinois Press.

Singh, J. (1966), *Great Ideas in Information Theory, Language and Cybernetics*, New York, Dover Publications Inc.

Stamper, R.K. (1985), 'Information: Mystical Fluid or a Subject for Scientific Enquiry?', *The Computer Journal*, 28, 3, 195-199.

Wildavsky, A. (1983), 'Information as an Organizational Problem', *Journal of Management Studies*, 20, 1, 29-40.

Wilden, A. (1980), *System and Structure: Essays in Communication and Exchange*, Bungay, Tavistock Publications.

Wittgenstein, L. (1956), *Philosophical investigations*, Oxford, Basil Blackwell.

Wurman, R.S. (1989), *Information Anxiety: what to do when information doesn't tell you what you want to know*, New York, Bantam Books.

4 Management: and *manus*

- *Introduction*
- *The evolution of management*
- *The first-order cybernetics perspective*
- *The first-order cybernetic management concept*
- *The second-order cybernetic paradigm*
- *The principles of management as manus*
- *Addendum: systems and cybernetic concepts*

Introduction

> *Everything must be made as simple as possible, but not simpler.*
> **Albert Einstein**

Chapter 4 will explore the concept of management. The first section contains a brief overview of the development of the management concept and of some of the current archetypes of management. Although these concepts are helpful, they do not provide a framework to explore the issues of the management concept. For this purpose the concepts of systems and cybernetics will be explored as a, hopefully, more appropriate perspective or point of reference. Firstly, classical, first-order cybernetics will be discussed. This cybernetics perspective has the advantage that the concepts of management can be explained in very general and conceptual terms in order to reveal more of the actual issues of management. This analysis will show that management faces a fundamental problem that cannot be solved within the first-order perspective. Secondly, the more recently developed second-order cybernetic and systemic concepts of autopoiesis and self-organization will be examined. These theories will lead us to the core of the issues faced by management today. In the final section, these principles of second-order cybernetics and systems will be applied to the management situation to define some general principles of self-organising management. The logical structure of this chapter is depicted in Figure 4.1.

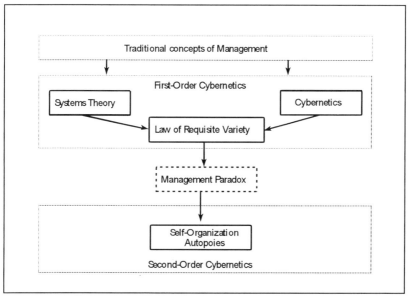

Figure 4.1: The logical structure of Chapter 4

The evolution of management

What is management? How did it come about? To open the discussion it may be useful to start with some current definitions of management.

> *Management may be defined as getting things done through others (Holt, 1987).*

> *Management is the art of getting things done through other people (Hellriegel & Slocum, 1989, p.6).*

> *The term management refers to the process of getting activities completed efficiently with and through other people (Robbins, 1988, p.6).*

> *Management is the process of working with and through others to achieve organizational objectives in a changing environment. Central to this process is the effective and efficient use of limited resources (Kreitner, 1989, p.6).*

> *Management is the process undertaken by one or more individuals to co-ordinate the activities of others to achieve results not achievable by one individual alone (Donnelly & Gibson, 1990, p.7).*

These definitions suggest a summarizing of the concept of management in terms of:

- *The aim*: getting desired things done;
- *The process*: through others (the doers);
- *The rules*: effectiveness and efficiency;
- *The reason*: limited resources.

But this list does not progress beyond the obvious. The management theorist Peter Drucker (1974, p.40) states that management can only be understood in terms of its tasks or its contribution to the organization. He lists the following management tasks:

- achieving the *purpose or mission* of the enterprise, i.e. achieving economic performance;
- making work productive and getting the worker to achieve;
- managing the social impact and responsibility of the enterprise.

The problem with such types of list, and for that matter the definitions above, is that they seem to get produced and reproduced without any significant reflection on what management *is* and *why* management is. They only function well as lists of what management *ought* to do. They start with the *what* without first penetrating the 'is' and the 'why'. This results in an *ad hoc*, cut and paste, approach to the issues of management. It is not surprising then that management seems to get dragged along with every new fad that comes along (whether MBO in the seventies, TQM in the eighties, BPR in the nineties, or their sons and daughters in the new millennium). It would not be outrageous to say that much of what we know about management today could be viewed as a patchwork of fads. Notwithstanding this many organizations succeed in this manner anyway, so it is not necessarily a disaster. However, this process may be better understood with access to a more fundamental understanding of management as such. Such an understanding may even suggest that the patchwork approach is the right one. Then at least we would know why it is the more appropriate way to manage. The aim of this chapter is to develop that more fundamental understanding.

Management and manus

The modern word management derives from the Latin word *manus* which simply means hand. *Manus* comes from the root *man* which means measure. This in itself does not tell us much; however, if we look at the contexts in which *manus* was used a more interesting picture emerges. In Lewis and Short's Latin dictionary (1879, p.1111) the following contexts of the use of *manus* are highlighted: to be in everybody's hands, to be well known; to be near; to have in hand, to be engaged on a thing; to know for certain; to come to hand; to fight at close quarters; at hand, in readiness, in hand; a secretary; to give with one's own hand; to deliver from hand to hand, with great care; and so forth. These contexts seem to suggest the idea of involvement, of being close and ready and also the idea of a hand-to-hand battle in which the participants are intensely absorbed. It also seems to have the sense of here and now. Other English words that have the same root are *manual* – both in its sense of a book that is kept close to hand and in its sense of labouring by hand; and *manifest* – as in clear and obvious. From this brief analysis the manager as *manus* can be described as the hand that is present, ready, actively involved; the master hand that makes clear or obvious the hand that is close at hand, dirty and even bloody as against the hand that is distant, cold and clean. In short: the hand that is at hand to give a hand. When, why and how did management evolve from *manus*?

Management is not an idea that solely emerged out of the industrial revolution, as is often suggested. It is true that the industrial revolution was a period of particular intensity in terms of the upsurge in management thought. Nevertheless, management existed in many periods of history before then. The temple corporations in Mesopotamia (*c.* 3000 B.C.) developed systems of management which included a management hierarchy, planning, division of labour, supervision and reporting (Sterba, 1976). Interestingly enough, these systems of management were also supported by their own information system, in that case detailed records on clay tablets. A similar system of management is described in the sixth century B.C. writings of the Chinese general Sun Tzu (Giles, 1910). He wrote of organizing an army into divisions, the importance of extensive planning before entering a battle, and the use of a system of gongs, flags and signal fires for communication.

In contrast to these very early descriptions of the explicit use of the idea of management in the middle east and Asia, in the European, pre-industrial era of cottage industry a system of *manus* existed. Here artisans with craft skills made products for merchants who provided the raw materials. In this environment the ideal was that the *manus* would work with the apprentice in close proximity (at hand). The *manus* would guide the gifted apprentice to craftsmanship through the socialization of craft knowledge. Within contemporary society there is a parallel in the relationship between medical consultant and junior doctor, where, at least in medical mythology, the master raises the ingénu to his level.

The emphasis is not merely on output but also on learning – the transfer of the craft skills. In this system we find only limited division of labour – mostly to do with the level of the apprenticeship rather that the production of the product itself. The emphasis is on the ability to produce a whole product independently, to synthesize skill, material, design, and process into a coherent whole. To be a craftsman is to be a master of every aspect of the craft. In this context the work of the apprentice is closely supervised by the *manus*, not for purposes of control, but for identifying opportunities to impart knowledge – not through explanations but through example, through doing. Thinking about the work and doing the work is fused together in one coherent whole. The tools, the material, the skill, are all brought together in a coherent whole, in the product – a hand-crafted object of utility. It may be a violin, or a dinner set, or a piece of furniture. The relationship between the *manus* (master hand) and the apprentice is profoundly different from the relationship between the manager and the labourer; it is a teacher–pupil, not a thinker–doer relationship.

The dominance of *manus* in the cottage, the pre-industrial commerce, was broken by the rapid development of technology. Craft knowledge was recorded and was being disseminated through books, such as the *Encyclopédie*, and the technical schools of the eighteenth century (Drucker, 1978). They "converted experience into knowledge, apprenticeship into textbook, secrecy into methodology, doing into applied knowledge" (Ibid., p. 26). Slowly the craftsmen's shops were being replaced by the factory, skill by machines, and *manus* by management. However, it was the work of Frederick Winslow Taylor (1856-1915) that seems to most lucidly represent the notion of management. Not only Taylor's ideas but his very person typified the spirit of management. As a young man Taylor had "a passion for improving and reforming things on the basis of fact, and early was filled with a divine discontent with anything short of *the one best way*" (Wren, 1979, p. 120). Taylor's scientific management was based on four principles (Taylor, 1990):

- *Separate* thinking and doing. The task of the manager was to extract traditional knowledge through time and motion studies using the action of "first class men" as the basis for the analysis. These observations must then be used to develop general laws (and standards) of conduct. Every type of work, from pig iron handling to shovelling, to machining, must be subjected to scientific analysis.
- *Select* men according to their abilities. Select the right man for the job. Let every man find the type of work that best suits his physical and intellectual capabilities.
- *Integrate* man and task. Integrate the optimized and standardized task (according to the laws of science) with the specially selected

(developed) man. This will be done by the manager who will see to it "that we do our work in accordance with the principles of science".

- *Co-ordinate* management work and the optimized task. The thinking and inspection by management must now be "dove-tailed" with the performance of the task by the workmen so that "there is hardly a single act or piece of work done by any workmen in the shop which is not preceded and followed by some act on the part of one of the men in management".

With these principles every act of work in the factory becomes part of a large game of chess that is carefully thought out and precisely controlled. Taylor's explanation of work at the steelworks makes this clear: "Thus planning the work one day ahead involved ...the equipping of that office with large maps showing the movements of the men from one part of the yard to another which could be laid out in advance so that we could assign to this little spot in the yard a certain number of men... each to do a certain kind of work. It was practically like playing a game of chess in which four to six hundred men we moved about so as to be at the right place at the right time" (p. 213). From this discussion of *manus* in the craft based industry and Taylor's scientific management a sense of the difference can be gleaned between *manus* and management. This is shown in Table 4.1.

Table 4.1: *Manus* and management

Manus	Management
Tools and skills	Machine and labour
Synthesization	Specialization
Decentralization	Centralization
Local	Global
Heuristic 'rules'	Command and Control
Doing and thinking fused together	Thinking and doing separated
Apprentice	Subordinate
Learning	Information
Network	Hierarchy
Socialization	Training
Bricolage	Planning
Involved	Removed
Inside	Outside
Coherence	Product output

Did management evolve from *manus* or the other way around? Each seems to have occurred in its own right, with its own logic, at different periods of history and in very particular situations. For example, we saw that management already existed in Mesopotamia in 3000 B.C. It may be that particular circumstances gave rise to management and others to *manus*. In some situations they may even have existed side by side, as one would expect in the transitionary period from the pre-industrial age to the industrial age. Some management theorists argue that we are again in a period of transition. After 200 years of the industrial revolution and 75 years of management they suggest we are now shifting back in the direction of *manus* – the post-capitalist society, or the knowledge society (Drucker, 1978).

Drucker now calls the manager a "conductor". The manager's job is no longer to "command...it is to direct" – to become a *manus*? Peters talks about "managing by walking about" (Peters & Austin, 1985), perhaps this is being in-the-world? Later chapters of this book will question whether management information systems are a help or a hindrance in achieving this ideal.

The relationship between management and manus

There seems to be a direct parallel between the development of the idea of management and the emergence of the Cartesian subject–object dualism. In some sense Taylor is the Descartes of management thought. For Descartes the only firm basis of any knowing, the only thing that cannot be doubted, is the existence of the thinking subject. There is nothing certain except myself. And "I" am nothing more than a thing that thinks – for Descartes this was self-evident. Hence, his famous '*cogito ergo sum*'. By granting this irrefutable basis of the thinking subject (*res cogitans*), the objective world (*res extensa*) can now be investigated. Every fact must be brought before the seat of reason and be judged. By making the subject the foundation of all knowledge Descartes separated the inquirer from the phenomena of enquiry. The 'real' world now becomes that which can be brought before, can be set before, the subject (reason). This separation generates a third dimension, namely that of representation (maps). Science becomes a matter of creating maps (theories, laws, descriptions), reading them, interpreting them, and evaluating them against that which has, in this perspective, the status of facts from the world. The key issue in science becomes the creation of true, valid, correct, etc. maps – mirrors of nature.

In Taylor's world of scientific management the same logic can exist. The manager, through science, sets up a secure basis for control; the certainty of his own thinking. A dualism is established between, on the one hand, the thinking manager (*res cogitans*) and the task (*res extensa*), and, on the other, the men that perform them. The only true knowledge is that which the manager can extract, using the methods of science (time and motion studies) from the world. Management becomes a matter of creating maps (such as plans, policy and standards), reading them, interpreting them, and evaluating them against what the information system supplies as the facts from the world. The key issue in management becomes the creation of valid and correct maps: plans, policies, procedures, and so forth. This resemblance between the ideas of these two perspective figures can be depicted as in Table 4.2.

This analysis suggests that the separation of *thinking* and *doing*, the setting up of the world as a thing to be managed, made management emerge from its primitive and primordial basis, namely *manus*. This separation made explicit, and problematised, things such as planning, controlling, decision-making and information. These management activities were created by this separation, this dualism. They become explicit as the interaction between the subject and the world, the manager and the organization, becomes mediated via explicit representations. It is, therefore, being postulated that *manus* is the primordial notion of management and that modern management is a derivative created by the dualism.

Table 4.2: The dualisms of Descartes and Taylor

	Descartes	**Taylor**
Res cogitans	The rational subject	The rational manager
Res extensa	The world	The task (workmen)
Representations	Laws, theories, models	Plans, policies, procedures

It was Kant in his *Critique of Pure Reason* who tried to resolve the Cartesian dualism. In sociology, Giddens tried to resolve the dualism with his structuration theory (Giddens, 1984). In management thought there have been various authors such as the later work of Mintzberg on strategy as 'crafting' (Mintzberg, 1994). In organizational learning theory the key issue is to *return* thinking to the task. Organization learning theory is a bold step to resolve the Taylorist dualism (Argyris, 1993; Nonaka, 1994; Pentland & Reuter, 1994). Certainly, these new theoretical developments are important in defining ways in which to think about dealing with the Taylorist dualism. The current argument, however, is that the logic of the Taylorist dualism must be understood first.

The next section will argue that the Taylorist dualism cannot be sustained for an indefinite period of time, by using the concepts of systems theory and first-order cybernetics; or, at least that it can only exist in a very limited category of environment. It will show that this limit is due to the *paradox of control* which emerges as a consequence of the separation. The next stage in the argument developed in the following section, is that manus, authentic management, can only happen when dualism, the inauthentic separation, is surpassed. This surpassing of the Taylorist dualism will be the basis of the final section which will attempt to develop a perspective of *manus* by using the theory of self-organization and, specifically, the work of Varela and Maturana (1987)

The first-order cybernetics perspective

In this section, management as a concept will be explored by means of a general systemic view using, as a basis, the theory of first-order cybernetics. The main concept employed for the exploration will be the *law of requisite variety* (LRV) as defined by Ashby (1957). The use of first-order cybernetics will create an understanding of the limits of the Taylorist dualism.

Systems and cybernetic theory

A full exposition of the theory is beyond the scope of this work, but may be found in the following works (Ashby, 1957; Capra, 1982; Churchman, 1968; 1971; 1988; Flood & Jackson, 1988). A definition of the concepts used can be found in the excellent exposition by Russell Ackoff (1971). A short definition of the key concepts used here, based on Ackoff's work is given in the *addendum* to this chapter. Readers not familiar with these concepts are advised to read the addendum first. These systems concepts will be utilized to describe and interpret the concepts of cybernetics that will form the basis of the first order cybernetic management perspective. The central theme in cybernetics is the notion of control. The word itself derives from the Greek word for steering.

While systems theory provides powerful metaphors for describing and analyzing phenomena from the world, it does tend to require an anthropomorphic vocabulary. This appears to ascribe human attributes to inanimate objects and to imply that organizations have beliefs separate from the human beings who comprise them and to have intentionality. This will not affect the main tenets of the argument but may produce erroneous interpretations which need to be guarded against.

The law of requisite variety

One of the most fundamental laws of control was defined by Ross Ashby in his work *An Introduction to Cybernetics* (Ashby, 1957).. The Law of Requisite Variety (LRV) can be stated as follows: a controlling system can only control a system if it can generate the *requisite* variety to equal the variety generated by the system it wishes to control.

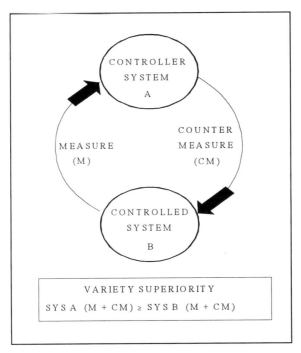

Figure 4.2: The law of requisite variety

The application of this seemingly simple and obvious law can lead to an amazing depth of understanding. Thus, in order to control a system, a controller must be capable of taking at least as many distinct measures and countermeasures as the system which it seeks to control may require (see Figure 4.2).

A simple example may help to illustrate the law. If a tennis player consistently generates shots for which the opponent does not have countershots then that player will tend to control the game; assuming, of course, that the first player can return the shots generated by the second player. Beer (1985, p.30) restated the law as follows: *"Only variety can absorb variety."*

Another way to describe the law of requisite variety is the seeing of *control* as *variety superiority*. If two teams play a football game, they each try to win (control) the game by achieving variety superiority. This can be achieved in many different ways:

- They could *increase* their own variety by using a different or unusual pass or any other trick or move that they know their opponents do not expect.
- They can *limit* their opponents' variety by not allowing them to perform any move for which they do not have a counter-move.

Both teams are controlled by the rules of the game that define what states and what variety are acceptable and what are not. The teams are, as a result, both limited in their ability to generate variety. As the two teams play against each other, their desire to achieve variety superiority will assist them to realize their potential to generate variety (within the rules of the game). They will thus become more and more variety abundant and complex. Competition, in all walks of life, forces all systems to continually increase their variety. All surviving systems are driven to an ever-increasing level of complexity. It is an evolutionary process, driven by a desire for survival through variety superiority.

It is important to note that the LRV is a *relative*, and not an absolute concept. The case of the AIDS virus demonstrates this. In absolute terms the human system has an infinitely higher level of variety, yet the AIDS virus is in control. One of the states that the virus can produce is the rate at which it mutates. Human ability to produce antibodies cannot match this rate of mutation, hence, the AIDS virus has the variety superiority. It is irrelevant that human beings can do many other things very well. At the level of requisite variety the AIDS virus is winning.

Communication of variety

To have an effect variety must not only be locally generated, it must also be communicated; for this two concepts are important:

- *Channel capacity or variety*: Variety is communicated via a communication channel. The communication channel must be able to absorb the variety it wishes to communicate.
- *Transducer variety*: The transducer is the system that encodes and decodes the variety that enters or leaves, that crosses the boundary of the system. The transducing system must be able to absorb the variety it wishes to translate.

The communication of variety is fundamental to the concept of variety itself. Variety that is not located and communicated will have no effect and will be transitory. In this regard the following issues seem to emerge. Since a computerized information system, as a symbolic processor, clearly does not have the channel capacity to absorb the variety of actual social events in-the-world, then what can a computerized information system communicate except for severely decontextualized chunks of reality. A computerized report emanating from the world of the supervisor cannot be in-the-world of the manager for the manager is not in-the-world of the supervisor. The manager can only decode the report mechanistically. There is insufficient transducer variety to communicate the variety that is present in-the-world of the supervisor into the *Erlebnis* of the manager.

The first-order cybernetic management concept

In this section the concepts of the system and cybernetic theory will be applied to the management situation in order to develop a first-order concept of management. Firstly, the management situation, based on the Taylorist concept of separation, will be discussed; then the law of requisite variety will be applied to the management situation; finally, a strategy to deal with management control using first-order cybernetics will be explored.

The management control system

In Figure 4.3 the following elements can be defined for any management control scenario from the perspective of control or the law of requisite variety:

- the control system;
- the controlled system;
- the controlled system's environment.

Each of these three elements is present whenever a manager seeks to control or manage a particular system or situation. Consequently, the elements need to be clearly defined and understood.

In the management, the control system is the manager. The control system is the system that defines and/or decides on the appropriate action required to steer the controlled system towards its final state. The decision(s) will be based on the variety generated by the controlled system and its environment and on the expected or anticipated behaviour inscribed in the control model.

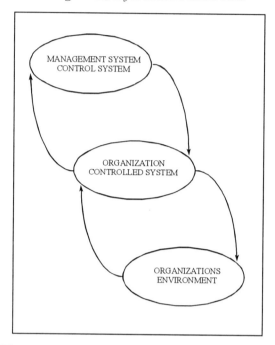

Figure 4.3: The management control scenario

The controlled system

The controlled system is the system that the control system wishes to steer. In the management situation, the controlled system can be an organization, an organizational unit or an individual. In the organizational context both the control and the controlled systems are *purposeful* systems. This is what makes it easy to drive a car but difficult to manage an organization or an individual. As purposeful systems both systems can autonomously select goals (or rather comportments).

The controlled system's environment

The controlled system's environment refers to those entities or elements that can have an impact on the system, but that the system can only influence. The survival of a system is, in *all* cases, predominantly determined by the ability of the system to *influence* (generate the requisite variety of) its environment. In influencing its environment, the system must not make its environment uninhabitable, for to do so will cause the destruction of the system itself.

Levels of control

In the model in Figure 4.3 it is possible to identify two levels of control:

- Between the control system and the controlled system
- Between the controlled system and its environment

Both of these levels are crucial to the discussion that follows.

The management paradox

In the light of the previous section the following formulation of the law of requisite variety can be derived:

There will only be successful management control of the system if, and only if, there is a homeostatic balance of variety on all three levels within the management situation, with the centre of gravity of variety abundance within the control system (as shown in Figure 4.4 block A).

The manager must continually find ways to achieve variety superiority. If the organization's variety increases, this would necessitate more variety abundant (and more complex) control systems so as to maintain management control. The manager is, in a sense, caught between the desire to limit the variety of the organization (so as to control it) and the risk of so limiting the variety of the organization that it cannot control its environment. This can be termed the *management control paradox.*

The organization must seek to influence its environment in order to survive. This is, in fact, more complex than the management control of the organization, as the organization can only influence its environment and not guide or steer it in any direct manner.

Many of the current management models are attempts to deal with the management control paradox. One option is democratic management (block B in Figure 4.4). Here the manager becomes an administrator. The manager merely coordinates, documents and reports the events that the manager is responsible for.

This model is often favoured in turbulent markets where the employees are mature professional experts. The problem with this model is the ambiguity that it creates. In the bureaucratic management model (block C in Figure 4.4) the paradox is resolved by ignoring the relationship of the organization to its environment. In a competitive environment this will lead to the 'death' of the system. Hence, bureaucratic organizations can only exist in non-competitive environments. This may be why it is often used in governmental institutions. Chaotic control (block D in Figure 4.4) is less usual. However it can be found in organizations based upon self-directing, usually professional, staff and where the organization does not seek to influence key elements of its environment. A possible example is a traditional university department.

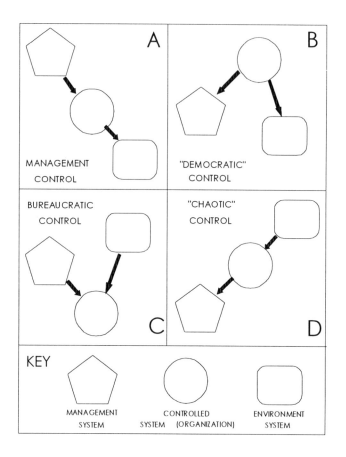

Figure 4.4: Management control possibilities

It is clear, from this brief analysis, that the problem in this second-order model is how to balance the two levels of variety absorption. This is an ongoing, though implicit, debate in much of the more traditional management literature. It is argued then that the real art and science of management is to be able to balance the requirement for management control with the need for the organization to control its environment.

It is vital to realize the importance of the word 'requisite' in the LRV. Too much variety can be as detrimental as too little variety. Thus increasing the variety to a level beyond that required will increase the complexity without any gain in ability to control the environment. This non-required complexity will only decrease the efficiency of the system. Thus it may be that some systems need to decrease their variety in a given situation and increase it in another. It is therefore important to know or to be able to determine the appropriate level of variety required.

Achieving first-order management

How can management control be achieved, *given* the inevitability of the management paradox? It may be useful to reflect on this question to gain a better understanding of why certain concepts have particular prominence in management literature today. In order to achieve management control and ensure the long term survival of the system, the following prerequisites must be met:

- The organizational system must achieve variety superiority over its environmental system;
- The management system must achieve variety superiority over the organizational system.

The key question that flows from these requirements is: how can the required variety superiority be achieved? There are three core processes in the achievement of variety superiority (see Figure 4.5):

- Variety matching;
- Variety innovation;
- Adaptation.

These processes will be discussed for each prerequisite in turn.

Variety Matching (evolution)

Variety matching is an essential process in the achievement of variety superiority, since the system must be able to absorb, as required, the variety generated by the environment. Without variety matching, the environment will gain control and the system will cease to exist. In order to match the environment variety effectively the system must be able to anticipate the next relevant environmental state and to adapt accordingly. In order to anticipate the next state, the system must have both adequate environmental information and the necessary transducer variety to make sense of it. The organization must, therefore, be involved in the environment. This involvement does not mean that the organization must from time to time contract a market research company to do a market research. This is an occurrent mode of being that would add very little to any real understanding of the environment. The involvement must be based on involvement as part of an involvement whole. This may mean membership of trade, consumer and other organizations; it may mean sponsoring and participating in community events; it may mean continuing contacts with clients and suppliers. It is only as part of a larger involvement whole that the know-how will be created for significant action.

The information must provide the system with a sufficient understanding of what to expect from the environment in the next time period. The system must decide what to do, in the current time period, to match the expected future state or states of the environment. This process will result in the identification of the desired state for the system in the next time period.

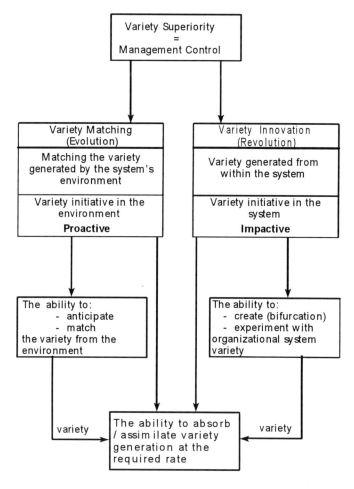

Figure 4.5: First-order management processes

Variety innovation (revolution)

In variety innovation, the system seeks control by taking the initiative and generating variety that it believes the environment cannot match. The processes involved in variety innovation are creative by nature. The system must experiment and generate points of disequilibrium where new ideas, structures, relationships and so forth can emerge. Using processes such as these a new or desired state can be established that will give the system the initiative. These processes are not evolutionary in a sense that they build on any previous rules, models or states as such. Instead they are new orders generated through creative leaps.

Adaptation (diffusion)

Given a desired state (generated by variety innovation or variety matching) the system must successfully change or adapt from the current state to the desired state. Ideally, the change must be instantaneous *and* the benefit must outweigh the cost of making the change. The rate of change of adaptation is a key parameter in successful change. Some systems need to adapt in a matter of seconds to match or innovate variety; in other cases the environment permits the system a period of years to adapt.

Management is thus a synthesis between evolutionary and revolutionary change. Evolutionary change will ensure integration into the environment. Revolutionary change will ensure competitiveness in future environments. Irrespective of the nature of the change the system must be able to absorb it.

Some conclusions about first-order cybernetic management

A number of conclusions can drawn from this discussion. Within the limits of the first-order perspective, itself based upon the Taylorist dualism:

- Management is the continual improvement of the system (organization) to ensure its long-term survival. The system will only survive if, and only if: (i) there is a homeostatic balance of variety between the system and its environment, and between the management system and the rest of the organization; (ii) there is a homeostatic variety balance between the different systems in the organization; (iii) the organization continually scans its environment. Homeostatic variety balance can only be achieved if the systems can generate, limit and communicate variety.

- Management cannot escape the management paradox. There is no simple heuristic or rule of thumb that will determine the appropriate level of variety for any given system. The variety struggle is a continual battle for management to cope with.
- Management is achieved through purposeful systems (people) as the generators and communicators of variety. However, purposeful systems make variety proliferate in all aspects of organizational action.
- Management success is a dialectical relationship between evolutionary and revolutionary change. They are both essential.

Management is based upon the transmission and negotiation of representations. Representations are, of their nature, less variety rich than the reality that they purport to represent. Although variety comes into being by being communicated, an involved manager communicates not only through representations, but also by example, by presence and by what is commonly described as moral stature.

Having established some concepts of management from a first-order cybernetics point of view, it may be worth while to stop and reflect on these new understandings. What are the limitations of this first-order management model?

A critique of the first-order view of management

The first-order view provides some very useful concepts about the dynamics of control in the organization. However, the major problem with the first-order application of cybernetics is the Taylorist dualism in the form of the *management paradox* which cannot be escaped. To limit the organization's variety, so as to control it, is also to limit the organization's ability to respond to the environment. Increasing organizational variety – so that it can respond appropriately to the environment – means that management variety is absorbed and, in so doing, management loses control or management must become increasingly complex.

This paradox was the inspiration for the development of second-order cybernetics. The key conclusion is that the control dilemma can never be solved if the control is located in a separate control system; if the control system and the system being controlled are *separated* the variety paradox always recurs. The first-order view is useful in addressing the relationship between the organization and its environment, but not in the relationship between the manager and the organization. To resolve the variety problem the control must be located within the system: the system must *control itself*. In second-order cybernetics control becomes autopoietic (self-generative) and self-organizing. The key notion operating in the second-order paradigm is that of putting control within the system and hence defusing the variety dilemma and resolving the paradox.

The second-order cybernetic paradigm
The theory of self-organization

The theory of self-organization has its roots in the natural sciences initially through the work of Prigogine (1985) in thermodynamics; Varela and Maturana (1987) in biology; Ashby and Von Foerster (1984) in second-order cybernetics; and also synthesized by Jantsch (1980) in his acclaimed work *The Self-Organizing Universe*. Although natural science theory does not necessarily apply to the social domain, the theory of self-organization has also been extensively applied by Luhmann (1990) to the analysis of social systems in general and by others such as Teubner (1993; 1992) in analysing legal systems. Consequently, there seems to be sufficient demonstration that it can be useful to apply the theory of self-organization to social systems.

In the theory of self-organization there are two major schools of thought. The first, based on the work of Prigogine, deals with the notion of systems *far from equilibrium* using the concept of a *dissipative structure*. The other school, based on the work of Varela and Maturana, focuses on the notion of *self-reference* using the concept of *operational closure*.[1] The second school of thought is the least explored and will be the focus of this section.

Self-reference and operational closure
The concept of operational closure

Systems can be self-organizing if, and only if, they are operationally closed (Varela, 1984). This implies that the systems must have access to their own descriptions (definitions or structures). Or as Varela and Maturana (1987) state elsewhere: "their identity is specified by a network of dynamic processes whose effects do not leave that network" (p.89).

---

1. For papers dealing with the application of dissipative structures in social systems refer to: Zimmerman, B.J. (1993), 'Chaos & Nonequilibrium: The Flip Side of Strategic Processes', *Organization Development Journal*, 11, 1, 31-38., Smith, C. and Gemmill, G. (1991), 'Change in the small group: A dissipative structure perspective', *Human Relations*, 44, 7, 697-716. and Gemmill, G. and Smith, C. (1985), 'A Dissipative Structure Model of Organization Transformation', *Human Relations*, 38, 8, 751-766..

Varela argues that to understand operational closure it is necessary to move away from *input-type* description to a *closure-type* of description. In the input-type description the system is seen as taking inputs from the environment and transforming them into outputs via the transfer or transformation function. This is the description of classical systems theory and the one most commonly used and was also the basis of the previous discussion. It is the type of description used in such mathematical functions as:

$$f(x) = 2x$$

Which implies:

if $x = 1$ then $f(x) = 2$
if $x = 5$ then $f(x) = 10$
if $x = 0$ then $f(x) = 0$

Note that the value of $f(x)$ is *determined* by the input (the value of x) applied to the transformation function ($2x$).

However, in the closure-type description, a system is characterized not by its inputs and transformations but by its *internal coherence* which arises out of its interconnectedness. In this description systems are not seen as isolated from their environments, "specific environmental inputs are bracketed as unspecific perturbations or simply noise. An input becomes a perturbation when it is *no longer necessary to specify the system's organization*, i.e. it has become noise." (p.26, emphasis added) Thus, the environment can cause changes in the system but can never determine these changes.

A relatively simple example of such operational closure is a normal, everyday conversation. Every participant tries to make a point, but only in regard to what has already been said (by each participant). Every statement is added in order to keep the dialogue coherent (and alive), not to transform input into outputs. Every statement is reflected upon and changes the selection of the next statement in such a way that it is impossible to know what the next statement in the conversation will be (or what will be said at any point in the conversation). If another participant enters from the environment then these statements are treated as perturbations that will not be incorporated at the expense of the internal coherence of the existing dialogue. The conversation is both medium and outcome; other examples are nervous systems, ecologies and consciousness.

The key element of all these systems is the level of self-involvement, circularity, of the system in its own structure and coherence. An operationally closed system could be depicted as a collection of interconnected systems with negative and positive feedback loops that create self-referring circular behavioural patterns. Varela (1987) concludes: "Autopoietic systems are distinctive in that their organization is such that their only product is themselves, with no separation between producer and product. The being and doing of an autopoietic unity are inseparable" (p. 49).

Varela and Maturana clarify the difference between the input definition (behaviour) and the closure definition (coherence) by way of a thought experiment of a submarine pilot. Let us assume a person who always lived in a submarine. The person has never left the submarine but is trained how to handle it. An observer sees the submarine float gracefully through very dangerous reefs and obstacles and surface in the still waters of the bay. Let us assume the observer has radio contact with the submarine. On surfacing the observer contacts the submarine pilot and announces: "Congratulations! You avoided the reefs and surfaced beautifully. You really know how to handle a submarine in dangerous circumstances." The pilot in the submarine is, however, perplexed: "What is this about reefs and surfacing? All I did was push some levers and knobs and make certain relationships between indicators as I operated the levers and knobs. It was done in a prescribed sequence which I am used to do. I did not do any special manoeuvre, and on top of that, you talk to me about a submarine. What is that? You must be joking!" All that exists for the pilot of the submarine are the readings of different indicators, their transitions and sequences of actions for obtaining specific relations between the readings. It is only for the observer that the dynamic relations between the submarine and its environment exist. These are representations which the submarine pilot does not have or need.

In the example, an input-model of reality existed for the observer; the model described what actions by the pilot created what relationships between the submarine and its environment. For the pilot, a closure-type description existed; the inputs from the environment were mere disturbances that had to be dealt with by restoring a particular relationship between certain indicators by applying certain levers or knobs. For the pilot there is an internal coherence that must be maintained. If this coherence is maintained his world will stay intact, if not it will disappear. In the business world this striving towards continual internal coherence (piloting) is often characterized by the notion of *getting the job done*. The most primordial understanding that people have of their work is what is required to get the job done; be it answering phone calls, writing letters or having a chat in the corridor.

Closure and behaviour

But what about seemingly intentional behaviour that observers believe they see in systems? Are they not *determined* by transformation functions such as theories, attitudes and norms? Varela argues: "as a rule, all behaviour is an outside view of the dance of internal relations of the organism." It was clear from the submarine thought experiment that observers impose behaviour onto the system; it is a view from outside the system. From a viewpoint inside the system, it is merely maintaining its internal coherence. If the system cannot maintain its internal coherence it will lose its autonomy and dissolve into the environment. Autopoietic systems have only one goal and that is to maintain themselves. All environmental inputs are merely noise that will be dealt with in terms of maintaining the integrity of the system's organization. Without the closure-type description self-reflection and self-reference cannot be understood: all descriptions will merely become deterministic. They will reduce all systems to trivial machines as Von Foerster (1984) describes them.

The principle of self-reference, or self-organization, is exactly what Giddens (1984) describes in his structuration theory when he says that societies, the structures of his theory, are both the medium and the outcome of reflexive agents. Societies emerge over time as the continual mediation between individual action and the structural properties that both influence this behaviour and were, themselves, created by the behaviour. Social systems do not behave in a teleological way. Their behaviour is not intentional, in as much as they make plans and then systematically implement them. This is exactly the problem of first-order thinking. It insists on behaviour based on representations. It is clear that represent-ational thinking is rooted in input-type thinking. It is also clear that representation does not play a role in closure-type thinking. The des-cription of internal coherence has parallels with Heidegger's description of being-in-the-world. Closure (or getting the job done) can be seen as a ready-to-hand mode of being and the observer point of view as the present-at-hand mode of being. Heidegger argues that the former mode of being is more primordial than the latter; this will be further explored in the final chapter.

Closure and environment

In the input-output definition the environment is viewed as some fixed whole that *determines* the behaviour of the system. In the closure description the environment is not some abstract whole; it too consists of a set of self-organising systems, each trying to maintain internal coherence. This leads to the notion that there is a *co-evolution* between structure and agent, in this case system and environment: not, as classical Darwinism and systems theory would hold, that the environment determines the system. This co-evolution emerges through *interaction* and nothing else. Varela (1987) speaks of this co-evolution as structural coupling: "We speak of structural coupling whenever there is a history of recurrent interactions leading to the structural congruence between two (or more) systems" (p. 75). It is this congruent structure that makes the recurrent interactions persist and not the adaptation of the system to a fixed environment. The environment is both medium and outcome for and of the interaction.

Structural coupling is always mutual; both organism and environment undergo transformations in and through their interactions (p. 102). This congruence based on structural coupling is also referred to as structural drift. To summarize, systems must succeed in two dimensions in order to survive:

- They must ensure their own autonomy by maintaining internal coherence or organization[2]. This implies the location of environmental input as perturbations and appropriating this input in such a way that their internal coherence, sense of self, mission or vision is not lost.
- They must maintain their structural coupling with the environment through continual interaction that will ensure co-evolution or the "ongoing structural drift that follows the course in which, at each instant, the structural coupling (adaptation) of the organism to its medium of interaction is conserved." (Maturana & Varela, 1987)

Implications of operational closure

In adopting the closure-type description there are certain implications that need to be made explicit.

---

2. Varela explains the difference between organization and structure as follows: "Organization denotes those relations that must exist among the components of a system for it to be a member of a specific class. Structure denotes the components and relationships that actually constitute a particular unity and makes its organization real" Maturana, H. and Varela, F. (1987), *The Tree of Knowledge: The Biological Roots of Human Understanding*, Boston, Shambhala.

Historicity

Operationally closed systems are historical. Varela (1987) defines historical phenomena as follows: "Each time in a system that a state arises as a modification of a previous state, we have a historical phenomenon" (p.57). The state of the system, from a coherence point of view, at any point in time is the cumulative result of self-reference upon self-reference upon self-reference. Such systems cannot be understood simply through the application of ahistorical models. Conversely, in the input-output mathematical model any specific input determines the output of the system, irrespective of any previous input, transition or output; any given value x always produces the same $f(x)$ irrespective of any previous operation.

This result ties in with Heidegger view that systems are only significant within an involvement whole. Historical systems cannot be abstracted from their embeddedness. It may be this mismatch between the ahistorical methods of software engineering and the historicity of the organization that creates a barrier that engineering, *ipso facto*, cannot solve.

Non-linearity

Operationally closed systems are *non-linear*. This implies that the behaviour in the past is no indication of what the behaviour in the future will be. We cannot understand the future by analysing the past. We can only know one thing for certain: the system will act in a manner that will maintain its internal coherence and, since this internal coherence is recursively defined, we can never predict it. Prediction is a mode of input-output thinking. It has, as its base, the notion of behaviour in an environment. Since both the system and its environment have co-evolution, through structural coupling, as their base, they cannot be predicted. The only way to understand systems is be-in-the-world of the system. This type of understanding is however not very useful for generalization and the building of grand models; such models may be useful as a starting point but can never replace situated understanding.

Locality

Knowledge of operationally closed systems is tacit and local. Knowledge of the system logic becomes *localized* and sedimented within the system itself. In most cases, due to the historicity of the system, the system itself would find it difficult, if not impossible, to express this knowledge (see the discussion in Chapter 3). The most primordial basis of knowing is interaction; only through interaction will structural coupling be conserved. Again, this accords with Heidegger, "we know by using".

These are but some of the conclusions that can be drawn from the concept of operationally closed systems or self-reference: from the above it is safe to conclude that a theory of the self-organization of management should at least be able to address the notions of historicity, non-linear behaviour and localized knowledge.

Autopoiesis and social systems

The important question now is how do social systems maintain internal coherence? What is the mechanism involved? The answer is quite simple: communication by language. That is why the essence of maintaining internal coherence and structural coupling in organizations is bound to what Varela calls languaging.

Languaging

Communication is the basis of social behaviour. Communication can be defined as the *co-ordinated behaviours* mutually triggered among the members of a social unity. Clearly this view is totally inconsistent with the traditional idea of communication as the transfer of information. Varela (1987) argues that: "...biologically, there is no 'transmitted information' in communication. Communication takes place each time there is behavioural co-ordination in the realm of structural coupling. ... each person says what he says or hears what he hears *according to his own structural determination...* The phenomenon of communication depends on not what is transmitted, but on what happens to the person that receives it" (p.196, emphasis added). Thus, when two ants exchange chemicals they communicate; they are being social. Social systems are structurally coupled through communication; in the linguistic domain, each participant in the social network maintains itself through a history of linguistic structural couplings within the group.

What is peculiar to humans is that humans do not only communicate as part of their structural drift in the group, they also communicate about communication. As Varela (1987) explains: "Human beings are not the only animals that generate linguistic domains in their social existence. What is peculiar to them is that ... they give rise to ... the domain of language. This comes about through the co-ontogenic co-ordination of their actions. ...[L]anguage appears when the operations in the linguistic domain result in co-ordinations of actions about actions that pertain to the linguistic domain *itself.* As language arises, objects also arise as linguistic distinctions of linguistic distinctions that obscure the actions that they co-ordinate... In other words, we are in language or, better, we "language" only when through a reflexive action we make a linguistic distinction of a linguistic distinction" (p.210).

Varela is arguing that it is in such reflexive actions as the following statement," What I mean with this distinction (word)... is this distinction (word)" that language emerges. Language, itself an autopoietic system, does not merely function as an abstract system of representation. It is in the co-ordination while doing, or rather co-ordination *of* doing, that distinctions are made and remade. Language becomes a network of distinctions of distinctions, of and for action. Language brings forth a world and a world brings forth a language. Hence, Varela argues that we only *are* in language (p.212) or, in Heidegger's terminology, we *dwell* in language. Therefore, words are distinctions for linguistic co-ordination of actions and not things that we move from one place to another. They exist and make sense only through our history of recurrent interactions that make possible ontogenic drift in our structural coupling; this takes place in a world we share *because we have specified it together through our actions* (p.232-3). This link between action and language allows Varela to make his claim that we exist *in* language. Moreover, it is in language that we become part of our domain of existence and constitute it as part of the environment within which we have to conserve our identity (p.234).

Language is not a tool for representing or for revealing the world: language is an act of knowing. It is an autopoietic system of distinctions of distinctions that is sedimented in the structural coupling of everyday interaction. Language gets continually reinvented in the discourse of everyday life. It is in this discourse that we bring forth a world. As an autopoietic systems language is also operationally closed; therefore also historical, local and non-linear.

The principles of management as manus

From our discussion of second-order cybernetics, of self-organising theory, it is clear why the first-order thinking did not provide the answers that are needed. First-order thinking is based on the input-output description of behaviour (the observer perspective) and is not based on situated understanding. It was a legacy of the Taylorist dualism. This perspective can enable an explanation of why many businesses without elaborate business plans and resounding mission statements survive for many years by just doing well what organizations do everyday (piloting submarines, getting the job done). These insights can be summarized as *principles for self-organising management*.

Operational closure

From the operational closure perspective the following insights may be deduced:

• *Variety can only be absorbed by locating control in the system by manus.* Variety from the observer perspective (the Taylorist dualism) explodes and produces the management paradox. Variety must be absorbed *in* the system itself. This requires treating social systems as the autopoietic systems that they are. Autopoietic systems behaviour is not determined by inputs and does not transform inputs (or instructions) into actions in any predetermined way. Therefore any environment can only influence it, not determine it. The degree of the influence will depend on the sense of identity, the internal coherence, of the system and the intensity of the interactions with the environment. There are, of course, those inputs that are so intense that they may destroy the system's internal coherence – such as the hunter killing the animal; or radically change its internal coherence – as in the use of hallucinogenic drugs.

• *Planning and controlling is an observer perspective, a legacy of Taylor.* Planning assumes behaviour and representations that are not commensurate with the autopoietic organization. Management must, therefore, be at the level of local logic. Co-ordination of activities must be the result of structural drift in a history of *interactions*. The best way to exercise control of an autopoietic system is as part of the doing. Employees do not act in accordance with plans, they just focus on the everyday of getting the job done. If communication about the future cannot be embedded in the local logic it will have no significance to the system.

• *Organization is maintained through identity.* The most important management task is to develop the identity of the organization and the individuals in it. Identity is more important that planning (who, what, when). Identity is created in organizational languaging. Many organizations with strong traditions and values, shaped through interaction, have survived without modern strategic management concepts. Maybe management interventions such as Business Process Reorganization are destroying the very identity that has provided the internal coherence for so long. Maintaining the systems identity is not a matter of labelling it is a matter of infusing it as part of the local logic, of embedding it in the work practice of the everyday.

Structural coupling

The earlier discussion showed that the systems need to succeed in two complementary ways: first, to maintain internal coherence; second, to maintain structural coupling with the environment. The essence of structural coupling is *interaction*. Every minute variation in the environment must be appropriated by the system. Hence the structure of the system will have to change (without changing the identity of the organization). The structural drift of the system cannot be predicted since there is a co-evolution taking place between the organization and the environment. Any observer attempt to 'radically shift' the system relative to its environment would place the system at hazard of the organization's identity being lost. In situations of turbulence within the organization, the individual sub-systems will focus on maintaining their own identities at the expense of the identity of the organization. Clearly the idea that seems to be so popular, that of radical change, has its limitations. Radical change always has the risk of extinguishing identity, internal coherence. If structural coupling is maintained then radical change need not happen. It should only be necessary in situations of structural dislocation, violent intervention. A strategy of pre-empting structural drift may be very dangerous, yet sometimes the only option for survival, for structural drift takes time.

Languaging

• *Language in-the-world is the essence of management.* Languaging creates the distinctions that make social action possible; social action creates the distinctions that make language possible. In human systems, there can be no language without social action and there can be no social action without language. It is through and in organizational dialogue and discourse that our world of work, and of play, becomes real. It seems then that the most important management task is to engender organizational dialogue and discourse in every sub-system and between sub-systems.

• *Organizational dialogue is historical,* therefore, through ongoing interaction, every new distinction that is introduced must be made coherent with the existing network of relations.

• *Distinctions themselves are part of a structural drift.* This again implies that the system cannot merely be directed by introducing a few key phrases. Each sub-system will localize, within the context of its existing world, the particular meaning of the distinction introduced into the discourse. The distinction "empowerment" may become the distinction "opportunity to negotiate better benefits" for the employees and it may become the distinction "opportunity to make liable" for the managers; each embedding it in their own repertoire of social action. For such a notion to influence the organization as a whole there needs to be organizational discourse to achieve structural congruence. Only then will it become part of organizational identity and hence part of that which the autopoietic system will maintain.

Addendum: systems and cybernetic concepts

This addendum provides a brief discussion of system and cybernetic concepts that are used in this chapter. They are mostly based on the work of Russell Ackoff (1971) and Ross Ashby (1957).

System concepts

A system

A system is a set of interrelated entities or elements designed or structured to achieve an explicit or implicit objective. Alternatively, a system is an assembly of elements, parts or components which has been identified to be of interest or which may do something, the elements of which are connected in an organized way and are affected by being in the system, and are changed if they leave the system.

Having said this it must always be remembered that the idea of viewing a situation as a system is a human construction. It is a representation, a metaphor, and not the reality. Furthermore, a system is designed or structured to achieve an objective (defined by the designer). Finally, the definition of the situation as a system is dependent on the observer of the situation's frame of reference and knowledge of the system, its structure and its behaviour.

Environment

The environment of a system is a set of elements, and their relevant characteristics, which are not part of the system, but a change in any of them can produce a change in the state of the system. Thus a system's environment consists of all those variables that can affect it. Consequently the environment of a system can have an impact on the system, but the system can only influence and not directly control the environment. If an element in the environment is directly controllable then it is no longer part of the environment, but is part of the system. A system will only survive, in the long run, if it correctly and consistently influences its environment. The system is embedded in the environment and will destroy itself if it makes its environment uninhabitable.

State

The state of a system at a given moment in time is the set of relevant characteristics which the system has at that time. The relevant properties of the system consist of :

- *Entities*: the elements or sub-systems of the system.
- *Attributes*: the dimensions which uniquely identify an entity.
- *Relations*: the way in which two or more entities are dependent on each other, that is a change in the one leads to a change in the other.
- *Structures*: the given set of relations at any given point in time.

Relatively simple systems may be able to generate enormously large numbers of states. Take, for example, an array of 20×20 light bulbs. The different states of the system are the different patterns which this system can display. If every bulb can be either on or off then the systems can display 2^{400} different states (patterns) or roughly 10^{120} – this assumes that you ignore symmetries. If something as simple as a light bulb system can display so many states, imagine the state possibilities of the human brain. It has been suggested that the minimum number of states of the brain must be at least $10^{3\ 000\ 000\ 000}$, more than the number of atoms in the known universe.

Objective and goal

An objective is the eventual state that the system is designed to achieve. This objective may or may not be quantifiable. Goals are the interim states that the system must achieve in order to reach its ultimate objective. In many systems the objectives and goals are implicit and not explicit. In most cases they are not selected by any identifiable individual or group of individuals; they become adopted as default values of the system's behaviour in a larger whole.

Purposeful system

A purposeful system is one which can change its goals under constant conditions; it selects ends as well as means and thus displays will/choice. Organizations and the humans, or groups of humans, that comprise them are purposeful systems. Purposeful systems *will* select the goals that can lead to their achieving their implicit and explicit objective(s). Purposeful systems are very important systems from a control point of view, as they are usually infinitely complex (this will be discussed again later).

Adaptation

A system is capable of adaptation if it reacts or responds by changing its own state and/or that of the environment so as to increase its efficiency with respect to one or more of its goals, when there is a change in its environmental and/or internal state which reduces its efficiency in pursuing that goal or goals.

Learning

To learn is to increase efficiency in the pursuit of a goal under unchanged conditions. In order for organizational systems to learn, the systems must be able to:

- appropriate or assimilate the data fed back by the system so that they become information;
- interpret the information so as to create insight;
- make judgements about the correct course of action based on these insights;
- initiate the actions required to implement the decisions taken (and execute them effectively);
- get data feedback from the system and its environment to see the effect of the actions;
- adjust the understanding of system behaviour based on the feedback.

The ability to assimilate or appropriate and interpret data is an essential requirement for learning to take place. Adaptive behaviour is a prerequisite for learning. If the system cannot adapt, there can be no change. Without change, there is no possibility of learning. If a system is repeatedly subjected to the same type of environmental and internal change and increases its ability to maintain efficiency in the face of this type of change, then it *learns how to adapt.* If a system exists in a turbulent environment, then learning to adapt will be a key to its long term survival.

Homeostasis

Homeostasis is the *stability* of a system's internal environment, in spite of the system having to cope with an unpredictable external environment. Unless a system can maintain its internal organization over time, within a changing environment, it will cease to exist as an autonomous system. An example of homeostasis is the human body's ability to maintain a constant temperature in all weathers.

Cybernetic concepts

System theory creates the vocabulary for cybernetic theory. Whereas systems theory looks at systems in general terms, cybernetics is concerned with the control of systems as such; hence its importance for management theory. The following are some concepts of cybernetics that are important for further discussion.

Control

Intuitively, control can be defined as a systematic steering towards a defined final state or goal. Control implies:
- insight into the current point or state;
- a defined ultimate point, state or objective;
- the ability to steer the system through the transition, from the current to the final state.

The black box principle

The black box principle states that a system can be effectively controlled without detailed understanding of the processes within the system. The controller of the system must, however, have a clear understanding of the behaviour of the system, i.e. what output will result from a given input? Thus, detailed understanding of system processes is not a prerequisite for effective management or control. With complex adaptive systems, it is difficult to understand system behaviour; the link between inputs and outputs is uncertain and elusive.

Variety

Variety can be defined as the set of all the possible *unique* states that a system can assume or generate. This set may consist of one element for a static system, or of an incalculably large number of elements for a very dynamic and complex system such as a human being or an organization.

Complexity

Stafford Beer (1985, p.26) defines variety as the *measure* of complexity; the complexity of a system increases as its variety increases; or, the greater the variety the greater the complexity. Flood (1988) identifies the following attributes of complexity:
- Significant interaction.
- Numerous of parts, degrees of freedom or interactions.

- Non-linearity: Non-linear systems tend to be unpredictable; a given initial state does not necessarily lead to a known final state as is the case with linear systems. Chaos theory shows that even very simple non-linear systems are potentially chaotic and thus totally unpredictable (Gleik, 1987).
- Broken symmetry or asymmetry exists; usually symmetry leads to predictability.
- Non-holonomic constraints are present. This refers to the tendency of a system to behave in an uncoordinated, non-holistic manner.

Generally speaking, it can be said that management or control complexity increases as: the variety increases; the predictability of the next state decreases; the speed of state transition increases; the set of inter-relationships enlarges.

References

Ackoff, R.L. (1971), 'Towards a System of Systems Concepts', *Management Science*, 17, 11, 83-90.

Argyris, C. (1993), *Knowledge for Action*, San Francisco, Jossey-Bass.

Ashby, W.R. (1957), *An Introduction to Cybernetics*, New York, John Wiley & Sons.

Beer, S. (1985), *Diagnosing the System for Organizations*, New York, John Wiley & Sons.

Capra, F. (1982), *The Turning Point: Science, Society and the Rising Culture*, London, Fontana Paperbacks.

Churchman, C.W. (1968), *The Systems Approach*, New York, Delacorte Press.

Churchman, C.W. (1971), *The Design of Inquiring Systems: Basic Concepts of Systems and Organization*, New York, Basic Books Inc.

Donnelly, J.H. and Gibson, J.L. (1990), *Fundamentals of Management*, Homewood, Boston, BPI Irwin.

Drucker, P.F. (1974), *Management: Tasks, Responsibilities and Practices*, London, Heinemann.

Drucker, P.F. (1978), *Post-capitalist Society*, Oxford, Butterworth-Heinemann Ltd.

Flood, R.L. and Carson, E.R. (1988), *Dealing with Complexity*, New York, Plenum Press.

Flood, R.L. and Jackson, M.C. (1988), 'Cybernetics and Organization Theory: A Critical Review', *Cybernetics and Systems: An International Journal*, 19, 13-33.

Gemmill, G. and Smith, C. (1985), 'A Dissipative Structure Model of Organization Transformation', *Human Relations*, 38, 8, 751-766.

Giddens, A. (1984), *The Constitution of Society*, Berkeley, University of California Press.

Giles, L. (1910), *Sun Tzu on the Art of War*, London, Luzac and Co.

Gleik, J. (1987), *Chaos: Making a New Science*, London, Cardinal.

Hellriegel, D. and Slocum, J.W. (1989), *Management* (5th Edition), Reading Mass., Addison-Wesley.

Holt, D.H. (1987), *Management: Principles and Practices*, Englewood Cliffs, New Jersey, Prentice-Hall International.

Jantsch, E. (1980), *The Self-Organizing Universe: Scientific and Human Implications of the Emerging Paradigm of Evolution*, Oxford, Pergamon Press.

Kreitner, R. (1989), *Management* (4th Edition), Boston, Mass., Houghton Mifflin Co.

Lewis, C.T. and Short, C. (1879), *A Latin Dictionary: Founded on the Andrews' Edition of Freund's Latin Dictionary*, Oxford, Oxford at the Clarendon Press.

Leydesdorff, L. (1993), 'Is Society a Self-Organizing System', *Journal of Social and Evolutionary Systems*, 16, 3, 331-349.

Luhmann, N. (1990), *Essays on self reference*, New York, Columbia University Press.

Maturana, H. and Varela, F. (1987), *The Tree of Knowledge: The Biological Roots of Human Understanding*, Boston, Shambhala.

Mintzberg, H. (1994), 'The Fall and Rise of Strategic Planning', *Harvard Business Review*, Jan-Feb, 107-114.

Nonaka, I. (1994), 'A Dynamic Theory of Organizational Knowledge Creation', *Organization Science*, 5, 1, 14-37.

Pentland, B.T. and Reuter, H. (1994), 'Organizational Routines as Grammars of Action', *Administrative Science Quarterly*, 39, 484-510.

Peters, T. and Austin, N. (1985), *A Passion for Excellence: The Leadership Difference*, Glasgow, Fontana/Collins.

Prigogine, I. and Stengers, I. (1985), *Order out of Chaos*, New York, Bantam.

Robbins, S.P. (1988), *Management: Concepts and Applications* (2nd Edition), Englewood Cliffs, New Jersey, Prentice-Hall International.

Smith, C. and Gemmill, G. (1991), 'Change in the small group: A dissipative structure perspective', *Human Relations*, 44, 7, 697-716.

Sterba, R.L. (1976), 'The Organization and Management of the Temple Corporations in Ancient Mesopotamia', *The Academy of Management Review*, 1, 3, 16-26.

Taylor, F.W. (1990), 'Scientific Management', in Pugh, D.S. (ed.), *Organization Theory: Selected Readings*, London, Penguin Books.

Teubner, G. (1993), *Law as an Autopoietic System*, Oxford, Blackwell Publishers.

Teubner, G. and Febbrajo, A. (1992), *State, Law, and Economy as Autopoietic Systems: Regulation and Autonomy in a New Perspective*, Milan, Dott. A. Giuffrh Editore.

Varela, F. (1984), 'Two Principles for Self-Organization', in Ulrich, H. and Probst, G.J. (eds.), *Self-organization and management of social systems*, Berlin, Springer-Verlag.

Von Foerster, H. (1984), 'Principles of Self-Organization - In a Socio-Managerial Context', in Ulrich, H. and Probst, G.J. (eds), *Self-organization and management of social systems*, Berlin, Springer-Verlag.

Wren, D.A. (1979), *The Evolution of Management Thought* (2nd Edition), New York, John Wiley & Sons.

Zimmerman, B.J. (1993), 'Chaos & Nonequilibrium: The Flip Side of Strategic Processes', *Organization Development Journal*, 11, 1, 31-38.

5 Power: the network of force relations

- *Introduction*
- *Sovereign power v strategic power (Hobbes v Machiavelli)*
- *Foucault and power as force relations*
- *Clegg and circuits of power*
- *The London Ambulance Service CAD system*
- *Conclusions and implications*

Introduction[1]

> *This world is the will to power – and nothing besides! And you*
> *yourselves are also this will to power – and nothing besides!*
> **Friedrich Nietzsche** (1967)

All the thinking in the previous chapters assumes what Burrell and Morgan call the "sociology of regulation" (Burrell & Morgan, 1979). This view of society assumes that there is a consensus based, stable, integrated, co-operative, well regulated social order; a regulated and well functioning co-operative whole that strives to maintain itself over time. This sociology of regulation neglects conflict and power. Power, nevertheless, seems to be very pervasive in organizations, as in society as a whole. Many practising managers will agree that organizational politics pervade everything they do. It seems to be always already present in every organizational event. Consideration of the narrative of the *involved manager*, management, and information in the organization would not be complete, or even adequate, without a reflection on power. This chapter is intended to provide such a reflection.

The chapter will start of by discussing the two streams of thought on power. The conventional view of Hobbes, of power as *located* in the sovereign, and the view of Machiavelli, of power as a play of *strategic*

---

1. This chapter is the product of collaboration with Leiser Silva, a friend and colleague. His contribution to this chapter improved it significantly in content and analysis. In particular I want to acknowledge his insightful contribution to the analysis of the London Ambulance Service case study.

forces. It will be argued that the notion of power as located (which is the dominant view in management theory) is not of much assistance in understanding power in its material form as power in the world of everyday organizational existence. The next section will discuss power as the play of strategic force relations. The work of Foucault and Clegg will be suggested as providing frames for thinking through power in-the-world. Foucault's analysis of power as a grid of force relations provides a general frame for understanding the dynamic nature power in the everyday practices of the organization. Clegg, in contrast, provides a detailed template, the circuits of power framework, for analysing the dynamics of power. Using Foucault's notion of power and Clegg's circuits of power, the chapter will conclude with an analysis of the system failure at the London Ambulance Service. This analysis will demonstrate the way in which power, as strategic force relations, can help to understand the everyday, in-the-world, nature of power – power as a network of force relations which *is always already there*. From this it should be inferred that the involved manager is always already involved in power.

Sovereign power v strategic power (Hobbes v Machiavelli)

Hobbes, in his work *Leviathan* (1962), argues for a concept of power as *located* in the sovereign. The individual members of society acknowledge and accept the power of the sovereign in exchange for social and moral order. With power located in the sovereign the society can be structured to the benefit of all. This notion of sovereign power implies that power is something owned or possessed by a unitary entity, frequently equated with individuals. In order to understand the rationale of this concept of power, it is necessary to take note of Hobbes' political context. Hobbes was rationalising and justifying the position of the English monarch after the bloody English Civil War and the Commonwealth.

In opposition to the Hobbesian notion of power as a means to ensure social and moral stability, the ideas of Machiavelli (1958) conceive of power as a strategy and not as an instrument. Unlike Hobbes, Machiavelli did not look for ultimate values to understand power, he merely interpreted it as is. He regarded power as less mythical and more related to everyday practices and actions. Hence, he considered alliances, strategies and networks as central in his conception of power. Machiavelli writes about what *power does* and Hobbes about what *power is* or should be. For Hobbes power becomes rationalized and manifested in its *locatedness* – in the sovereign, the agent. For Machiavelli power is significant in the way it manifests itself in shaping and reshaping *relations* in everyday practice – power as strategic force relations.

Before considering the work of Foucault and Clegg in more detail, it may be useful to refer briefly to some recent contributions on power as *located* and how some of these ideas have been used by authors in information systems and thus outline the mainstream approach to issues of power in information systems.

Dahl's Pluralistic View of Power

Dahl's (1961) conception of power is a pluralist, as opposed to an elitist interpretation. Pluralists consider power as distributed amongst people. Unlike elitists, Dahl (1957) did not study the *structure* of power. His theory states that power is not located in the structure of the organization but is located in people (as agents). Dahl's propositions on power could be summed up in the following way:

- Power is conceived of as a relationship between actors (individuals, groups, roles, nation states, etc.)
- He introduces a nomenclature which states: "an A has power over a B."
- A's power over B will have a domain, source or base, conceptualized in terms of resources open to exploitation by A. Some examples of resources for Dahl's conception are: distribution of cash, popularity, control of jobs, and control of information sources.
- A's power has some scope and range.

Dahl's work can be criticized for not considering any historical context. In this sense, Dahl's work can be considered as behaviourist. Dahl's work is a continuation of Hobbes' mechanistic approach to power that considers a *causal* relation between discrete agents. Thus, an agent is considered an intentional being; some thing that causes another thing to act in a particular way. For Dahl (1968) the difference between having power and exercising power is that having power does not require a manifest intentionality, though it is an essential requirement for its exercise. But what if acts, as was argued by Heidegger, are not, in general, intentional? Furthermore, this conception does not resolve the relationship between norms and behaviour. For example, when cars stop in front of a red light, this is not because the traffic light has some innate power, but because of drivers are following laws and norms that dictate what constitutes good driving. This implies sanctions that are probably seen as just by society as a whole and, quite possibly, by an errant driver as well. Dahl's focus is on power as manifested in social relationships and his power framework is not sufficient to provide a comprehensive analysis of this situation. The notion of norms as instruments of power will arise again when Foucault's concept of disciplinary power is explored.

From an information systems perspective, Markus (1983) and Franz (1984) both saw the issue of power exercised through information systems, or through computer centres within organizations, as of concern. These structures were mainly viewed as powerful for two reasons: firstly, they equated information with power; secondly, because computerized systems and information centres appeared to hold central positions in organizations. The Markus and Franz analyses are based on Dahl's concept of power in the form of contingency and on resource dependency theory (Hickson *et al.*, 1971; Pfeffer, 1981). The idea of information as power assumes that information is a resource that can be located. What is, or is not, information, however, depends on what are, or are not, legitimate norms in the first place. This issue will be taken up again in later discussion. The work of Markus, although limited, was important for bringing into focus the notion that information systems, and particularly computerized information systems, were affecting power relations.

Lukes' Three Dimensions of Power

Lukes (1974) introduced a three dimension model for analysing power. The first dimension implies an intentional agency theory; the second dimension includes the notion of mobilising bias and non-decision making; the third dimension of power includes people's interests.

The first dimension of power could be called episodic power. Episodic power is best defined by the following statement: "A gets B to do something" and the earlier critique of Dahl again applies. The second dimension incorporates the mobilization of bias or non-behaviour, for example, the professor who attends a meeting and decides *not* to make a proposal. This argument was discussed in the chapter on the involved manager, in the discussion of thrownness. The third dimension is introduced by Lukes in his definition of power. Lukes defines power as: "A exercises power over B when A affects B in a manner contrary to B's interests" (Lukes, 1974).

This definition raises the question of how to identify B's real interests without incurring moral relativism. For Barbalet (1987) Lukes' conception of power is substantially flawed: "If to be subject of power is to have one's real interest contravened, and if real interests can be identified only outside a subordination to power, then it is impossible ever to determine whether one is subjected to power, except when it ceases to matter." Furthermore, Lukes' work invokes the important social science debate between agency and structure. Are actions determined by culture, social group, gender or race? Or, are actions more dependent on our will and responsibility? This point will arise again in the next section which discusses the work of Giddens.

Using Lukes' conception of power Markus and Bjorn-Anderson (1987) expressed concern about how information systems professionals exercised power over users. Their framework has been criticized (Bloomfield, 1992) for separating user values from technical issues, as the difference between technical and ethical values is not that apparent. For example, in a discussion, users might try to score a point by citing a technical issue; however, their real reason might be that the system contradicts their values. The insights derived from this work were that the exercise of power not only involves computers and information systems, but also involves the selection of methods and formulation of policies. However, it concentrates only on the relationship of users and developers and it does not include the wider organizational context.

Giddens

Giddens (1984) aims to solve the problem of agency and structure, mentioned above. In doing so, Giddens proposes the idea of the duality of structure. Giddens opposes functionalist approaches to power. He argues particularly against the work of Parsons who conceived of power as a zero-sum game. For Giddens, Parsons overly concentrates on the economic and production aspects of power disregarding conflict. To illustrate, Parsons proposes the analogy of power with money. Parsons suggests that power, like money, circulates amongst people in different arenas. Giddens observes that Parsons' work is concerned mainly with the creation of order (the sociology of regulation) disregarding conflict. In order to incorporate conflict within the study of power, Giddens defines power as, "The capacity to achieve outcomes". Giddens makes the point that there is a two-way relationship between power and human agency. Human agency is intrinsic to power and without power there is no human agency.

The concept of the duality of structure, which is proposed by Giddens, as a way to solve the problem of structure and agency in power relationships, comprises two sets of concepts, structure and social systems. Structure is constituted by rules and resources. In the example of the traffic light, the rules are the laws regulating driving which enable and constrain the practice of driving. Social systems are defined by the regularities of social action; these actions do not have structures, but do have structural properties. Structures are brought about in social practices in a process called instantiation. Dominance and power relationships are, then, an effect of instantiation.

Clegg (1989) criticizes Giddens' proposal in two ways. First he opposes the idea that structures only exist through instantiation, because in this manner they do not reflect enduring relations. The second point is against Giddens' interpretative ontology, which denies the regularity principle in human agency. According to Giddens, individual motives are irreducible; however, action and motivation cannot escape from power.

In the field of information systems Walsham (1993) suggests a framework, derived from structuration theory, for the understanding of the organizational change that is associated with computer-based information systems. His framework consists of four elements: content, social context, social process and the linkage context and process. This framework offers links between the organizational environment and the processes within the organization. The limitation of this approach, which is recognized by Walsham, is that it is very difficult to apply because of the complex and abstract nature of structuration theory. Information systems, Walsham claims, are power instruments because they have embedded rules. This analysis is not very helpful since it does not shed light on the relationship between technology and power. An analytical framework is needed that describes how the interpretation of these rules is carried out, and who controls it. Monteiro and Hanseth (1995) also point out the limitations of structuration theory. Its weakness, they claim, consists in not explaining clearly the relationship between social aspects of organizations and information systems. For them the applications of structuration theory, particularly those by Walsham and Orlikowski (1992), are not specific enough in respect of information systems. They do not identify how interests are inscribed in information systems, and how technology makes social relations stable (Latour, 1991).

In order to make the language of power more specific, and hence useful for this analysis, the works of Michel Foucault and Stewart Clegg will be discussed in some detail. Foucault argues that power is contingent, diffused and becomes material in the micro-physics of everyday activity. Clegg, through his circuits of power framework, provides a very specific language on how to visualize and think through the material nature of power in everyday relations in organizations.

The aim of the rest of this chapter is to provide an introduction to the work of Foucault, Clegg and Callon; to situate it within the particular context of managers and their information systems; and to introduce, explain and justify the use of the concepts of translation and obligatory passage points. These tools will be used in the next chapter to help understand and draw a new picture of the manager in action in-the-world apparently making decisions based on information systems. It is not possible to understand and be able to use this equipment without follow-ing, in some detail, the work of Foucault, Clegg and Callon, and the rest of this chapter may need to be read more than once to gain a sufficient understanding. The case study of the London Ambulance Service, which follows the description of the theory, shows an application of the theory which is intended to assist in the process of making it ready-at-hand.

Foucault and power as force relations

The most common characteristics of post-structuralism are:
- its emphasis on language and the praxis of discourse;
- practices of linguistic signification;
- the relational nature of all totalities; and
- the marginalization of the individual as the seat of reason.

Post-structuralism stands against sovereign power. Foucault (1977b) claims that the ideology of sovereign power has dominated academic studies for 300 years, since the *Leviathan* was written. To free social scientists from this concept, Foucault proposes "To cut off the King's head in political theory". This is an invitation to abandon cause and effect metaphors and the idea of a power generating *centre* which is pervasive in the sovereign framework and which takes the form of a dominant ideology in Marxist analyses.

Foucault conceives of power as a technique which achieves its strategic effect through its disciplinary character. Two ideas are central in Fou-cault's concept of power: disciplinary power and bio-power. Disciplinary power is a form of surveillance that was initiated in such social institutions as prisons and asylums. Foucault considers the historical context of the evolution of power practices. He concentrates on how punishment was shifted from physical power to a more institutionalized, disciplined punishment. Bio-power is oriented to control both human bodies and bodies of people in general, whereas disciplinary power is aimed at particular individuals or groups. One example of bio-power might be the discourse that establishes what a normal sexuality should be. For Foucault the archetypal form of disciplinary power is Bentham's panopticon. This was a tower that was able to offer a total vision of an area to those in the tower without the possibility of being spotted by those under surveillance. This was most closely realized in Victorian prison design where the wings housing the prisoners radiate from a central tower from where the warders can observe all activities. With these characteristics power could be regularized, routinized and secured through norms. Foucault attempts to liberate us from the idea of sovereignty. He invites us to see power not only in work-places, but in other sites and practices. The idea of disciplinary power also suggests the extension of agency to organizations.

On the nature of power

Power is "a relation between forces, or rather every relation between forces is a power relation" (Deluze, 1986, p.70). Power does not have an independent objective being. It is in the network, or grid, of forces that power emerges. Its "condition of possibility ... is the moving substrate of force relations which, by virtue of their inequality, constantly engender states of power" (Foucault, 1980, p.93). Force here is no more than the "capacity to act or be acted upon, a capacity to effect and be effected" (Patton, 1989, p.93). However, this force that defines the power relation-ship is not an act directly and immediately upon the *other* (the one 'over' whom power is exercised). Instead "it acts upon their actions: an action upon action, on existing actions or on those which may arise in the present or the future" (Foucault, 1983, p.220). It is thus not a relationship of violence for "violence acts upon a body or upon things [directly]". For it to be a power relationship it requires that the *other* be thoroughly recognized and maintained to the very end as a person who acts, a force; and that, faced with a relationship of power, a whole field of responses, reactions, results, and possible inventions may open up. Thus, power is the total structure of actions brought to bear upon possible actions; it incites, it induces, it seduces, it makes easier or more difficult; in the extreme it constrains or forbids absolutely; nevertheless, *power is always a way of acting upon an acting subject*, or acting subjects, by virtue of their acting or being capable of action. It is a set of actions upon other actions; force upon counter-force; power upon resistance.

Thus, every relation is always already a power relation. In acting, a manager acts (by deed, decision, or speech act) to effect, in order to bring about change. As roles, and the contexts of roles, change this capacity to act changes and shifts. Power is never one-dimensional; it is the one-dimensional analysis of power that neglects the network notion of power. My capacity to act is always *mediated* by the multiplicity of other relations (connections) which I am already immersed in. Thus the question, "to act or not to act?", is never a simple one. Since every act will *always* also restructure or reconstitute the whole grid of power relations. A practical example may help clarify this. I have certain expert knowledge about a particular technology (say, mainframe operating systems) which places me in a relationship of power with the staff in the application development department. However, I must now evaluate the feasibility of moving applications to a client-server environment, then my acts will always be mediated by this already given relationship and by the numerous other grids, within which I am already predisposed in a particular manner. I am already tied to a pre-existing set of commitments and interests that I cannot escape or ignore. The idea of an interest-free, commitment-free, rational decision or action is a chimera.

The power relationship is an *agonistic*[2] relationship between centres of force. In this agonistic relationship, there are acts and counter-acts (resistance). These engender relationships of power and resistance that are dynamic and local. Theses acts and counter-acts draw upon local discourses and micro-practices that are contingent, even arbitrary, and do not possess any essential *telos*, any inherent purpose. Although the individual acts are intentional, power, as such, is non-subjective and ateleological. Locally a manager may direct her actions towards explicit outcomes, but these actions may combine into other actions (her own and others') in ways that she may never have foreseen or may never have agreed to. This analysis of power shows the unpredictable and contingent nature of typical corporate situations. It is this that makes the manager's world fragmented and *ad hoc* as was described by Mintzberg (1980) in his study of managers. There is always a local and *emerging* logic that may make what seemed rational previously to now look irrational and vice versa. It is also clear that there is no one person able to 'put their arms around it'. There is no one person who 'knows it all'.

Power networks are "simultaneously local, unstable and diffuse, do not emanate from a central point or unique locus of sovereignty, but at each moment move from one point to another, in a field of forces, making inflections, resistances, twists and turns, when one changes direction, or retraces one's steps, this is why they are not 'localized' at any given moment" (Deluze, 1986, p.73). At every moment the manager, every person for that matter, looks at what forces are at her disposal to get the obvious next step to be one that will serve the interests she is concerned with. She cannot predict them since they are mobile and continually changing. She will draw on them as they arise.

---

2. As this term is used by Foucault, there is no direct English equivalent. It has the sense of persistent struggle, contingent, always changing, always dynamic, fleeting.

Power never flows from grand strategies *per se*; power is too mobile and unstable for this. Power relations get shaped in the moment and may disappear in a moment. For example, power may suddenly and unexpectedly emerge in a normal day-to-day discussion. In a conversation with a colleague over some matter a manager may make some trivial comment. The colleague, not listening properly, (in terms of hermeneutic analysis applying prejudice uncritically or terminating the hermeneutic circle prematurely) may make an interpretation that favours the manager's interest. Later at a meeting the colleague supports her – based on his interpretation of what he thought she said – to the point that her proposal is accepted. He may later discover that he had misunderstood (re-enters the hermeneutic circle) her but at *that* moment in *that* meeting his support created a power relation that enabled her to act. These dynamic or mobile loci of power that emerge are not some sort of transcendent identity, *they are both medium and outcome* of force relations. There is no primordial identity, only practices and operating mechanisms. Thus, "there is no State, only state control, and the same holds for all other cases"(Foucault, 1977b).

The dynamics of power must be understood and be analysed as a chain that transverses and circulates in such a manner that it cannot be localized. Power "is employed and exercised through a net-like organization. And not only do individuals circulate between its threads; they are always in the position of simultaneously undergoing and exercising power... In other words, individuals are the vehicles of power, not its points of application" (Foucault, 1977a, p.97). Every time the manager acts, he acts in response to power (resistance) and in accordance with force. It is this notion of power that is the basis of the argument of this book. There is no place outside of power where any individual can stand to 'hold all the strings'. Every act, every communication by every person in the organization *is already in* power and simultaneously *reconfigures* power; sometimes in a minute way and sometimes in a big way.

This discussion on power can be summarized in the following propositions or theses on power (Deluze, 1986; Dreyfus & Rabinow, 1983; Foucault, 1980):

- Power is not something that is "acquired, seized, or shared. It is not a commodity, a position, a prize, or a plot"; it is the operation of non-egalitarian and mobile relations of force. It manifests in the materiality of everyday at the level of the micro-practices, "the political technologies in which our practices are formed" (Foucault, 1980). It cannot be localized as it is simultaneously local, unstable and diffuse and does not emanate from a central point or identity.

- Power relations are not superstructural, in a position of exteriority with respect to other relationships (economic, knowledge, sexual or communicative), but are immanent in these relationships. It is through them that power becomes material. It is bundles of these relationships that constitute individuals, institutions and societies. Thus, these communicative, knowledge, sexual and economic relationships are simultaneously conditions for, and outcomes of, power.

- Power is not essentially repressive. It plays a directly productive role; it comes from below; it is multidirectional, operating from the top down and also from the bottom up. "It passes through the hands of the mastered no less than through the hands of the masters" (Foucault, 1977b). At every level of society, every individual and institution is both medium for, and outcome of, the force relations. "What makes power hold good, what makes it accepted, is simply the fact that it doesn't only weigh on us as a force that says no, but that it traverses and produces things, it induces pleasure, forms of knowledge, produces discourse" (Foucault, 1977a, p.119).

- Power relations are intentional, but the intentionality is not that of any individual or subject. Every force is exercised with a series of aims and objectives. The "logic is clear, the aims decipherable, and yet it is often the case that no one is there to have invented them" (Foucault, 1977b). The local tactics may link together and combine into overall strategies that create the illusion of "grand design" but are in fact outcomes of very local contingent actions.

- Resistance is integral to power. Action implies actions of the *other*; acts imply counter acts. The "existence of power relationships depends on a multiplicity of points of resistance which are present everywhere in the power network. Resistances are the odd term in relations of power; they are inscribed in the latter and irreducible opposite" (Philp, 1983, p.35). As with power, resistance does not have a single source or identity from which it emanates, or a set of unified principles that drive it; it is local, dispersed and diffused. Only occasionally will it flow together in some, seemingly unified, spontaneous revolt.

This discussion of power is in stark contrast with, what Foucault calls, the juridical conception of power, equivalent to sovereign power, which can be summarized as follows:

- power is possessed (for instance, by individuals in the state of nature, by a class, by the people);

- power flows from a centralized source from the top to the bottom (for instance, law, the economy, the state); and
- power is primarily repressive in its exercise (a prohibition backed by sanctions).

Foucault argues that this, the commonplace, notion of power (akin to Marxist, Freudian and liberal views and dominant in management literature) is very limited and is of little use in understanding much of what constitutes the *everyday how* of power in modern society. It functions only to mask the material nature of disciplinary power that emerges through the meticulous rituals of power in everyday institutional life. As such the liberal, Marxist and Freudian critiques of power as essentially repressive contribute to the *unobserved* spread of disciplinary power in modern society. In the *Two Lectures* Foucault (1977a) argues that disciplinary power has overtaken juridical power as the dominant form of power in modern society. In fact, it was a fundamental instrument in the constitution of the modern industrial and capitalistic state. It facilitated the emergence of the normalized, efficient and rational society of the modern nation state. Free from the absolute rule of the sovereign, it apparently became a civilized society of individual liberty and expression. This is the very illusion that masks the pervasive spread of real domination. To understand this, the relationship between power and knowledge needs to be made explicit.

Power and knowledge

Another radical insight that Foucault's analysis provides is into the relationship between power and knowledge. Knowledge, as Foucault conceives it, is intimately related to the notion of disciplinary power. Knowledge "cannot exist except through relations of power, and power makes possible and produces 'regimes of truth'. Power structures a domain of knowledge at the same time that inquiry isolates areas as objects of knowledge, making them targets for the deployment of strategies of power" (Hiley, 1984, p.200). This does not mean that power is knowledge or that knowledge is power; they imply one another, they are co-constitutive. Foucault does not use the terms 'knowledge' and 'truth' in a traditional sense. Knowledge for Foucault is not a set of universally true statements, "the ensemble of truths which are to be discovered and accepted." There is no knowledge in some general ideal or abstract sense at all. Knowledge is something of this world, it is that, "which one can speak in a discursive practice." This thesis of knowledge as produced through power implies that the traditional view, that knowledge or truth can only exist where the effects of power are suspended, should be abandoned. We should "admit rather ... that there is no power relation without the correlative constitution of a field of knowledge, nor any knowledge that does not presuppose and constitute at the same time power relations" (Foucault, 1977b).

The linking of power and knowledge is through discourse as instrument and effect of power. Power by means of discourse gives rise to *regimes of truth*. Truth, being knowledge that is held to be true, is produced in discontinuous, unstable and mobile political discourses that function as the "general politics of truth." Each institution or society has its "regime of truth, its 'general politics' of truth: that is, the types of discourse which it accepts and makes function as true; the mechanisms and instances which enable one to distinguish true and false statements, the means by which each is sanctioned; the techniques and procedures accorded value in the acquisition of truth; the states of those who are charged with saying what counts as true" (Foucault, 1977b, p.131). "Truth is linked in a circular relation with systems of power which it induces and which extend it" (p.133). Power, thus, structures discourse in a discontinuous and diffused manner. Owing to the non-egalitarian and diffused nature of the relationship, such discourse gives rise to a particular regime of truth. A specific regime of truth shapes a particular domain of knowledge which, in turn, may produce a new configuration of power relations.

Following *Discipline and Punish* this power-knowledge-discourse relationship could be viewed as:

- Power – the formation of disciplinary power through the institution of discipline. Discipline is enacted by the meticulous control of time (prison, school and army regimented time schedules, time and motion studies in the factory) and space (use of architecture such as the panopticon in prison, classrooms, barracks, and production lines in the factory). The creation of disciplined bodies (docile bodies) that come into step with the control of time and space is achieved through complete and sustained surveillance. Standardization becomes a measure of the success of the power relation.

- Knowledge – the objects (isolated by the observation or surveillance) now become classified, categorized and tabulated according to the standard or norm. For every deviation thus created (criminal or criminally inclined, under-achiever or over-achiever, pervert, homo-sexual, neurotic) a set of treatments is developed. This gives rise to a whole set of disciplines such as criminology, educational psychology, psycho-sexology and psychiatry.

- Discourse – in the professional examination, power (drawing on the techniques of time/space ordering and surveillance) and knowledge are applied to the individual in a precise and meticulous manner. Case studies are carefully documented and compared with the population. They are absorbed in the scientific and institutional discourses to improve knowledge and expand the techniques of discipline.

Thus "power never ceases its interrogation, its inquisition, its registration of truth: it institutionalizes, professionalizes, and rewards its pursuit. In the last analysis we must produce truth as we must produce wealth. In the end we are judged, condemned, classified, determined in our undertakings, destined to a certain mode of living and dying, as a function of the true discourses which are the bearers of the specific effects of power" (Foucault, 1977b, p.105). It is clear that the rise of disciplinary power required by the industrialized capitalist state co-constituted the human sciences (as would be expected given the power–knowledge relationship). This is why Foucault calls them "dubious sciences" as they must "take account of those human activities which make possible their own disciplines...[as such they]...cannot account for their own possibility, legitimacy, and access to their objects because the practices which make objectification possible fall out of their range of investigation" (Dreyfus & Rabinow, 1983, p.163).

The question that may be asked at this point is how do organizations (agents) succeed in stabilizing relations of power in order to provide a reasonably stable basis for predictable action? This question will be dealt with later in this chapter in the discussion of circuits of power.

Power and the subject

Foucault is most well known for his genealogy of power and knowledge but this was not the focus of his work. It was "not to analyse the phenomena of power ... [instead] to create a history of the different modes by which, in our culture, human beings are made subjects... [I]t is not power, but the subject, which is the general theme of my research" [Foucault, 1983 #89, p.209).

For Foucault the subject, the individual, is not "some sort of elementary nucleus, a primitive atom, a malleable and inert material on which power comes to fasten or against which it happens to strike, and in so doing subdues or crushes individuals. In fact, it [the subject] is already one of the prime effects of power that certain bodies, certain gestures, certain discourses, certain desires, come to be identified and constituted as individuals.... The individual which power has constituted is at the same time its vehicle" (Foucault, 1977b, p.93). The notion of the subject as 'free agent', as an autonomous and sovereign subject must be abandoned. The transparency created by the panopticon effect leads to the internalization of the individual. In his self-surveillance the individual cultivates a self-consciousness. He continually articulates his most private experiences as if emanating from the depth of his 'soul'. This articulation places himself (or rather his 'self') in discourse. As he confesses his self-knowledge of 'who he really is' he becomes subjected and subjectified (power and knowledge are in a circular relationship). He inscribes himself on his 'self'. This ritual of self-reflection under the 'gaze' of the disciplinary society constitutes the subject as medium and effect of his own subjection. Foucault expresses it as follows: "this form of power [disciplinary power] applies itself to the immediate everyday life which categorizes the individual, marks him by his own individuality, attaches him to his own identity, imposes a law of truth on him which he must recognize and which others have to recognize in him. It is a form of power which makes individual subjects" (quoted in Dreyfus & Rabinow, 1983, p.212).

The next section investigates the other conceptual frame of power that could develop an account of how power expresses its material form in everyday relationships.

Clegg and circuits of power

In his book *Frameworks of Power*, Clegg (1989) carefully analyses how social science has considered the concept of power. He discusses different frameworks and concepts in order to introduce his framework of circuits of power, which he boldly claims includes most of the insights proposed by previous social scientists. His principal contention, in line with Foucault, is that power is a relational concept. Power is something that cannot be owned and the exercise of power will depend on relations between agents. Such relations sustain, maintain or transform power relations which can be analysed by applying his framework of *circuits of power*.

Clegg's framework explains power relationships independently of the particular circumstances of organizations or their structure. The application of the framework may lead to a complete political appraisal of an organization. The framework considers power as circulating in three different circuits:

- the episodic circuit,
- the social integration circuit,
- the system integration circuit.

The three are linked by obligatory passage points as shown in Figure 5.1.

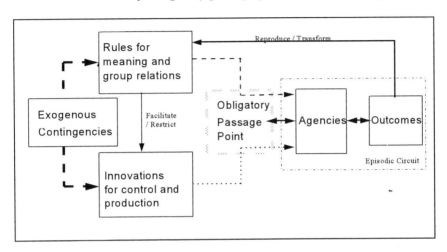

Figure 5.1: The circuits of power framework
(adapted from Clegg, 1989, Figure 8.1)

The episodic circuit of power

The *episodic circuit of power* is the most evident of the circuits because it leads directly to tangible outcomes (A gets B to do something). This circuit has been the focus of many researchers and practitioners of information systems (Lucas, 1984; Saunders & Scamell, 1986). Power is manifested here by agents being capable of controlling resources and establishing alliances to produce their intended outcomes. Agents, in this approach, do not have to be human; agents can be groups, organizations, animals or machines representing human actors, *inscribed* with their interests (Callon, 1986).

This circuit consists of agencies, resources and outcomes. It is in this circuit that agents struggle to control resources. The arrows pointing to the right stand for agents acting to achieve their desired outcomes, while the left-pointing arrows denote resistance. Those agents successfully controlling resources will be those with a stronger power base. The power base of agents is given by the circuits of social and system integration, which will be discussed later. The outcome of any exercise of power will be actions. To analyse this circuit, it is necessary to identify and describe the intended outcome, which should be described in terms of actions. It is important to identify those agents that would execute the outcome as well as those that would benefit. Finally, the circuit will be complete when the resources required to achieve the outcomes are identified.

Organizations that succeed in implementing change are those that are able to arrange their circuits of power in such a way that agents will be capable of achieving their projected outcomes. Looking at the circuit of episodic power is not enough to understand how organizations achieve this desirable state. Organizational change through, for example, information systems will affect organizations in two ways. Information systems will both affect the way jobs are performed and change the organizational norms, meanings and group membership. The former concerns the circuit of system integration and the latter the circuit of social integration. Furthermore, change in either of these circuits should be fixed in *obligatory passage points*, which will be discussed later.

The circuit of social integration

Clegg (1989) defines *social integration* in terms of the relation between rules of meaning and of membership; these rules can be formal or informal. The analysis of the *circuit of social integration* will identify the legitimate and illegitimate dimensions of power within the organization. The recognition of the illegitimate dimension of power, or its "dark side" (Hirschheim & Klein, 1994), is fundamental in performing a complete political appraisal of an organization.

One of the reasons why information systems do not achieve their designers' and clients' goals is the lack of fit between the new meanings, arising from the information system, and the prevailing organizational rules and norms. In any organization tension will arise owing to the lack of fit between the institutional order and its material condition. The material condition is constituted by technology, techniques and methods of production; the core institutional order will be integrated by the values, beliefs and norms already institutionalized in the organization. Where there is this lack of fit, the material conditions will engender social relationships and practices that can threaten the organization's continued existence (Lockwood, 1964, p.252). The consolidation of these social relationships and practices will depend on the extent to which managers are able to cope with the tendencies towards disintegration within the organization. The circuit of social integration comprises the norms, rules and meanings that give identity to particular groups and allows their integration. The realization of this circuit will allow analysts and developers to incorporate in the system those characteristics required to make it fit in the organization at the time of encoding.

The circuit of system integration

System integration is defined by Lockwood (1964) in terms of the material conditions, the "technological means of control over the physical and social environment and the skills associated with these means". Besides the material means of production, Lockwood includes in system integration the material means of organization and also violence. In short, system integration is constituted by techniques of production and discipline. System integration deals with facilitative power because the material conditions of production might empower or disempower agencies in their productive activities. Clegg stresses that the concepts of production and discipline cannot be separated. The *circuit of system integration* is the major source of change in the circuits of power framework, particularly when the material conditions of production are altered. System integration, as a result of new techniques of discipline and production, is a potent source of transformation and tension; hence its relevance to this study. It implies that there can be new agencies and new obligatory passage points that the circuit of social integration might find difficult to resolve (Clegg, 1989). That is why the introduction of computer based information systems will always be contentious. Success in implementation will depend greatly on the managerial ability to translate the new rules and norms, implied by the system, into pieces of discourse that other members of the organization can understand and accept as ready-to-hand. This could explain why participative methods for developing information systems might overcome resistance to implementation more easily than other methods. User participation can be understood, therefore, as a process through which the translation of the new rules and meanings is accomplished during the analysis and design stages of the development rather than at the moment of implementation. This way participative methodologies integrate user interests and meanings into the system during its development.

Obligatory passage points

Although the term *obligatory passage point* may sound strange, such points are the crux of the circuits of power analysis. Whenever an innovation is introduced in an organization, it creates new meanings and, therefore, disturbs the circuits of social and system integration. The new meanings are fixed in an obligatory passage point, which, in this case is a rhetorical device that presents the solution to the problem in terms of the resources of the agent proposing it. Obligatory passage points allow the formation of alliances and control over the resources that agents need to achieve their outcomes.

The concept of an obligatory passage point was developed within *the sociology of translation* and *actor network theory*. These ideas were developed by the French sociologists Michel Callon (1986) and Bruno Latour (1991). These theories attempt to provide a complete picture of power relationships: "understanding what sociologists generally call power relationships means describing the way in which actors are defined, associated and simultaneously obliged to remain faithful to their alliances" (Callon, 1986, p.224). There are four *moments of translation*: problematization, *intéressement*, enrolment and mobilization. Callon (1986) explains these moments, in detail, in an outstanding study of a Breton fishing community enlisting the help of scientists to overcome a depletion in stocks of scallops; a study that well repays reading.

The first moment is *problematization*, or how to become indispensable. Problematization is when one actor, given a problem, presents the solution to that problem in terms of his resources, by use of rhetoric. In this way an actor begins to define an obligatory passage point. Following a successful problematization, the group of actors experiencing the problem must be convinced that the only way to resolve their problem is by traversing the proposed obligatory passage point. The second moment is *intéressement*. After the identities of the actors and the obligatory passage point have been defined, the group of actors experiencing the problem must be isolated. This isolation consists in impeding other possible alliances, or interferences, that might challenge the legitimacy of the proposed obligatory passage point and conversely engaging the members of the group in the confirmation of the selected obligatory passage point. If the *intéressement* is successful it will confirm the validity of the problematization and the alliances. The third moment is *enrolment*. During this step the alliances are consolidated through bargaining and mutual concessions. The fourth and final step is the *mobilization* of the allies, consisting of determining the legitimacy of the spokesperson. This mobilization implies that actors will become spokespersons for the groups that they can now claim to represent. The movement between each step is called displacement and requires discourse; power is exercised each time displacement occurs.

The discussion of the work of Foucault in the earlier section can now be interpreted in a broader context. The micro-physics of power as materialized through techniques of discipline will seek to translate intentions towards stabilising obligatory passage points. The circuit of system integration is fundamental for understanding power relationships in information systems, not only because it provides an analytical tool for the way technology affects power relations, but also because it helps us to understand the way information systems can be shaped by power.

The works of Foucault, Clegg and Callon have provided a solid conceptual basis for understanding power as a network of relations. In order to make this framework more explicit, it will be used to analyse the notable information systems failure at the London Ambulance Service.

The London Ambulance Service Computer Aided Dispatch system

During October and November, 1992, the London Ambulance Service (LAS) launched its Computer Aided Dispatch information system (CAD). On 29 October news broke that the system had collapsed and, allegedly as a consequence, twenty people had died (Beynon-Davies, 1993). The system was reinstalled but, a week later, the system crashed again. The system was abandoned, the previous manual procedures were reinstated and the LAS Chief Executive announced his resignation. The British government reacted by ordering an independent inquiry. It has been argued that the LAS managers introduced CAD to change the organizational culture and to improve the overall performance of the service (Robinson, 1994). This is what makes the history of CAD a relevant example for this discussion.

CAD was introduced in a context of financial and performance problems and of poor industrial relations. By the time that CAD was conceived, in the early 1990s, the British government wanted to transform the National Health Service (NHS) into an internal market. If this transformation were to be successful, then the NHS would be characterized by more efficient and competitive services and operations. A new top management team was appointed to LAS in 1990 and was put under pressure to improve performance and reduce costs (Hougham, 1995). Information technology and computerized information systems were considered by the new LAS management to be techniques and strategies that would solve their problems and the decision to develop CAD was taken. In June 1991, Systems Options successfully bid £1.1m for the contract for the system; substantially less than the £7.5m bid by a British Telecom subsidiary (Beynon-Davies, 1993). Systems Options was a very small company without previous experience in developing systems of this magnitude, they only entered the tendering process at the behest of Apricot, who wished to supply the hardware for the project and wanted a software partner. Hougham (1995) argues that their lack of experience in project management was one of the main reasons for the collapse of the system. Going for the cheapest offer was also criticized by the report of the inquiry. Nevertheless, if the system had worked, LAS managers would have been praised for saving public money. LAS managers were entitled to believe that by selecting the least expensive of the bids they were doing their job of reducing costs and improving efficiency.

The episodic circuit of power

This circuit focuses on the relationship between resources and outcomes. The new system was expected to improve the performance of the service, to reduce operational costs and to change the culture of the organization. There were concerns about the quality of the service before the development of the system. A survey conducted in 1992 by the National Union of Public Employees, the largest trade union in LAS, revealed that only 13% of their members thought that they were providing a good service. The target time, according to British standards, from the moment an ambulance is requested to the moment it should arrive is 14 minutes. LAS was very far from matching this standard. It was thought by LAS managers that the introduction of a computerized system might produce a more efficient dispatching system that would result, eventually, in reaching this standard.

Looking exclusively at the episodic circuit of power, in the context of CAD, shows a strong management position, based on numerous resources for decision making, which should have been sufficient to produce a successful information system. This assumption is supported by two theories of power in organizations: contingency (Hickson *et al.*, 1971) and resource dependency (Pfeffer, 1981). Contingency theory holds that power concentrates in centrality, the capacity of decision making; whereas resource dependency theory relates power to control over resources. In the LAS managers had the power identified by these theories; they had financial resources and had wide authority to make decisions, but they did not succeed in implementing the system. Neither of these theories considers circuits of system and social integration and the requirement to fix them in a successful obligatory passage point. Consideration of these elements will illustrate the difference between an analysis based upon circuits of power and the analyses provided by more mainstream theories.

The circuit of social integration

This circuit deals with rules of meaning and membership. CAD influenced the way employees interpreted management style.. The autocratic style of the new LAS management and their emphasis on technological spending were opposed by the LAS trades unions. They wanted, instead, more training and new vehicles as well as more participation in the process of decision making (ALA, 1991). Managers, instead of stopping and reflecting, responded to this view by pushing ahead with CAD without union participation. Tension arose because the workforce interpreted these moves as a way of undermining trade unions and concentrating decision making on top management.

If employees interpreted the system as a threat to their identity and the existence of their organizations, managers interpreted staff attitudes, actions and statements as a lack of collaboration and as resistance, which increased the pressure on managers. Managers outflanked what they perceived as resistance by employing their resources, money and authority for decision making. The new system reinforced the worsening industrial relations. Employees' attitudes may have only confirmed the managers' belief that the staff were the problem in LAS.

It this context it seems as if the new Chief Executive viewed the implementation of the CAD as an obligatory passage point that could be used, successfully, to translate staff behaviour in line with the demands for improved efficiency and effectiveness. The efficiency of the existing manual procedures depended on a whole series of human decisions and judgements for which the rules were tacit and located in the lived experience of the control assistants, resource allocators, despatchers and ambulance crews. In such an environment these staff members could outflank any attempt to translate their intentions and actions to improve efficiency. This is done by simply translating the demands back to their domain of tacit knowledge. For example they might respond: "we cannot do this or that because the system (the set of rules which only we know) does not work that way" (Page, 1993 #217, #3116). In a climate of bad industrial relations, this type of outflanking was probably deployed quite often. Hence, since the staff had almost exclusive access to the operational rules of work, management had very little hope of effecting the changes that the NHS management required. However, making CAD an obligatory passage point encodes a new set of rules accessible to management and allows them to define and control the norms for each rule (times for response, allocation, and so forth).

The new information system did not buttress social integration in LAS. The new rules stemming from the new tasks were not translated successfully into the system and, perhaps more importantly, the introduction of the system exacerbated relations between management and workers. It is very unlikely in an organization where social integration is very low or characterized by conflict, that an information system – particularly if is interpreted as being a weapon of one group against another – can be consolidated and stabilized. In the case of LAS, the system required full collaboration and contributions from the workforce in order to be successful. Developing information systems calls for not only technical skills but political ones as well.

The circuit of system integration

This circuit concentrates on techniques of control, discipline and production. The major effect on control and discipline arose from discretion being taken away from the ambulance controllers and programmed into the new information system. Ambulances no longer responded to the judgement of controllers but to the calculations and orders produced by CAD. In short, CAD, in the eyes of the new top management, could become the universal gaze that would discipline the staff to conform. For them, it could become the new basis of truth in the organization. Work would be judged as good or bad because the system 'said' so. However, the management underestimated the complexity of the, mostly tacit, rules of operation and the level of auto-correction by the staff.

Most of the staff, in the process of call taking, resource allocation and dispatching, compensated for the human and technical errors in the manual system by auto-correcting. Hence, the manual system was very fault tolerant. However CAD, being automated, depended on perfect information for its success (Page *et al.*, 1993, (3024-8, 4008)). The extent of this problem was not obvious because the operators themselves were probably not aware of the degree to which the rules of the system were ready-at-hand (tacit) and hence auto-corrected (#3022 and 3046). Because the staff were not involved in the writing of the requirements specification, this tacit knowledge was not articulated and hence the system was assumed to be much simpler than it actually was (#3011). The unwilling-ness of the staff to participate could also be interpreted in a different manner. They may have realized that, if CAD were successful, it would make the rules of the game transparent and would therefore put a powerful tool for system integration in the hands of the managers; they may have realized, at least implicitly, the panoptic possibilities of CAD.

The very tight timetable is seen, by many, as one of the major reasons for the system's failure (#3035/6). However, the management were aware that the timetable was obviously unrealistic. The Chief Executive had a report from Arthur Andersen that indicated the enormous risks associated with the timetable (#3036). There were also doubts raised by other bidders about the technical feasibility of some components of the project (#3058). The development process and testing were plagued by problems (these were even documented in audits). In spite of this the decision was taken to push ahead. The inquiry concluded that most staff and managers "saw deadlines set by top level management as ... not to be challenged" (#6020). At a simple level of analysis, this could be construed as being due to the pressure that the new management were under to get LAS right. However, a more careful analysis interprets it as an effort to outflank the staff in two ways. Firstly, the new system (with the automated and transparent rules) must be put in place *before* the staff could implement counter-programmes to resist CAD becoming an obligatory passage point. Secondly, by swiftly swapping the tacit rules for the automated rules, the staff would be put in a position of ignorance that could be used as a basis for new translations. The cogency of this interpretation is enhanced because the management decided to go for direct cut-over, the full implementation in one phase, in spite of many obvious problems (evidenced in audits and minutes of meetings). "This was seen to be the only way in which the planned improvements in resource activation performance could be achieved" (#3099). Or, to state it differently, this was the only way they could completely outflank the staff; prevent them from inventing ways to keep exclusive access to some subset of the rules; and, in so doing, define the obligatory passage point.

There are also various other counter counter-programmes (presumably all justified and legitimized by management under the heading of efficiency) that seemed to indicate that the management wanted to create CAD as an obligatory passage point.

- The insistence on a paperless system. Was this to prevent a manual system being developed around CAD and hence outflanking CAD?
- The breaking up of the old, area based, teams and grouping them all into one London-wide team. Was this for efficiency or for easier translation?
- The changing of the layout of the control room. New environment, new rules, new truth?
- Inadequate training done long before implementation on a system that was still being designed and that was changing all the time.

As with all accounts of systems failure, each stage is capable of inter-pretation as either conspiracy or 'cock-up'. However, each action results from an interplay of power relations which scrambles the intents of the agents and produces outcomes at variance with the purposes each actor may identify, either at the time or later.

The interpretation presented here, in terms of fields of force relations and networks of power, has more explanatory power than the efficiency rationale presented for many of the actions of both management and staff. The system, in the way it was developed, was intended to function as the mass innovation of techniques of production and discipline.

The staff were not passive in the face of this attempt to translate behaviour, or discipline. They sabotaged the input to the system (#3111). They created a discourse of failure by continually talking about the system as a failure. Fortunately for them, the system had major technical difficult-ies which reduced the level of resistance required by them. However, their resistance may have been caused, or at least increased, by their realization of the technical deficiencies. This sense of the deficiencies may have emanated from their strong sense of the required in-order-tos get the job done.

Obligatory Passage Points

In the present case CAD was the most evident and important obligatory passage point. CAD was an obligatory passage point linking and translat-ing such different actors as: management, market ideas, efficiency expectations, staff expertise, users, systems analysts and patients. If all these actors were translated successfully and their associations remained stable, then the obligatory passage point might be considered successful.

If all actors had remained faithful to their inscriptions in the information system then management would have achieved their objectives. For example:

- The political atmosphere promoted by the British government pushing the NHS to be transformed in an internal market would have been represented in a system developed to aim at efficiency.
- The internal market ideology would have been translated into techniques and strategies enacted by the managers of LAS.
- Staff expertise would have been inscribed in the system in the form of rules for allocation and dispatch of ambulances.
- Users of the system would have been translated into CAD through training programmes.

These translations were represented in the way system developers expected users to operate the system; Mike Smith, Systems Director of LAS, stated that the failure of the system was because users did not follow the computer system instructions (*Daily Telegraph*). LAS managers considered information technology to be fundamental in achieving the efficiency goals set when they were appointed. This stance implies the belief that technology is a black box that can safely be left to expert technicians. System analysts were supposed to translate technology into the system in such a way that technology would do what it was told. In this sense systems analysts were allegedly the representatives of inform-ation technology. The second failure, on 4 November 1992, was the result of a mistake: a programmer forgot to activate a routine that would manage the memory of the system. Thus, designers and developers, the very representatives of technology, were 'betrayed' by technology itself. Poor translation also involved ambulance callers; one of the reasons given for the failure of the system was the excessive number of exceptional phone calls. Ambulance requests did not transit the obligatory passage point in the way anticipated. During that infamous night of October in 1992, LAS headquarters were flooded with calls and collapsed under the weight of 600 repeat phone calls from people still waiting for ambulances.

From this discussion it might be concluded that the translation of the actors in CAD, the obligatory passage point, failed. This might explain why, despite management having the power in terms of money and decision making, they failed to achieve their desired outcomes. Recalling Foucault's claim that power can be recognized in actions, successful outcomes through the use of technology can only be achieved by successful processes of translations. Successful translation will depend on how faithful actors are towards their alliances. Some of the highlights of the development of the circuits of power in LAS are summarized in Table 5.1.

The case of LAS shows that circuits of power are contingent and unstable. It also shows that there is no simple way to predict the *ontogenesis* of a network of power. Local contingencies may create opportunities for outflanking and shift the obligatory passage points in ways never intended by the actors in the play.

Conclusions and implications

Managers are not autonomous rational agents that merely receive pre-packaged information to utilize in decision making. Even the notion of decision making is heavy with the idea of an autonomous rational agent.

Table 5.1: Summary of the translations at LAS

	Force relation	Circuit of power and obligatory passage point
1.	Appoint new management. LAS is inefficient and ineffective and needs to be reformed	Episodic – give new top management decision making power and resources
2.	Industrial relations bad, easy enrolment not possible	Manual CAC system is a de facto OPP
3.	New management cuts middle management by 20% and launches CAD	Episodic – employ decision making and resources (create CAD as OPP?)
4.	Inscription through CAD will ensure discipline. CAD will become new basis of organizational truth	Social and system integration - CAD could define rules, meanings and discipline
5.	Staff resist and try to outflank system by not co-operating	Social integration – attempt to keep manual system as OPP
6.	Tacit knowledge and complexity stays hidden to team writing the requirements specification	Social integration – staff and unions articulate an 'us and them' discourse
7.	Apricot translates SO expertise and wins bid	Social integration
8.	SO cannot translate requirement into technical artefacts within the aggressive time-frame	System integration fails
9.	Staff try to outflank CAD as OPP by creating a discourse of failure	Social integration – control meaning attached to the CAD project
10.	Management enforces one phase implementation in last bid to inscribe discipline and establish CAD as OPP	For CAD to be OPP it must be a 'big bang' project
11.	CAD systems collapses and operations revert to the manual system – re-established as OPP	Social and system integration fails
12.	Chief Executive fails in organizational reform programme and resigns	Manual system reverts to OPP. Remains management's problem

This is an ahistorical linear model of information and decision making that is of very limited use, if any. Managers are reflexive agents who continually strive to make sense of their environment. However this sense-making cannot be isolated from the other relations that co-constitute it.

Managers are always already in the net of power; they cannot escape it. As Foucault argued above, the manager, as a manager, is already one of the prime effects of power. The manager can never get out of or distance herself from the circular grid of power. This is part of being-in-the-world.

To rise above power is a useless abstraction. Hence, research programmes and development efforts in decision support systems that postulate a neutral, rational and localized agent as their prototype of a decision maker are bound to fail.

Representations, once decontextualized, could be used as rhetorical devices to create obligatory passage points. In a game where the rules are also part of the game, anything is possible. There is no such thing as one correct interpretation. Information used on one level for sense-making could be used strategically on another level as a device for creating obligatory passage points.

Managers should not try to locate their information system. It does not have a location. Information has the potential to emerge momentarily in unexpected events and situations. Those who understand information are continually open to its possibilities; even in seemingly non-sense. Non-sense in this moment can become sense in a next. This is the frustration of those who desire to design a computerized information system.

A manager can never do, or decide, just one thing. This just one thing rationality assumes a closed linear causality, something like: to make decision **A** would achieve **B** as the desired result. This argument assumes that there is a direct, historically independent, causal link between, and only between, **A** and **B**. However, due to the *network and circular* nature of power every decision-in-action may have many unintended and unpredictable effects, **C**, **D** and **E**. There will be not only first-order, but also second- and third- and fourth-order, effects as the whole system mediates and shifts to (re-)establish power and informational relations. Some of these incidental effects may be beneficial, some may not be, but there is no way of knowing in advance. These effects may even re-constitute the regime of interpretation; and, in so doing, change the validity of the interpretation of the 'facts' upon which the decision-in-action was made in the first place. Clearly, simplistic ahistorical notions of actions and decisions are not sufficient to help the manager in-the-world to understand the dynamic and contingent nature of information in the organization.

These are just some conclusions that can be drawn; however, they are sufficient to show that conventional functional thinking will not solve any of the major problems of information, and its management, in organizations. New thinking and a fresh perspective are necessary to attain a more sophisticated view of this unfolding reality. Such thinking should be based on *circular logic* of autopoiesis and circuits of power rather than the traditional either/or logic used since Aristotle.

References

ALA (1991), 'London Ambulances: A Service in Crisis', London, ALA : Association of London Authorities.

Barbalet, J.M. (1987), 'Power, Structural Resources and Agency', *Perspectives in Social Theory*, 8, 1-24.

Beynon-Davies, P. (1993), 'The London Ambulance Service's Computerized Dispatch System: A Case Study in Information Systems Failure', Pontypridd, University of Glamorgan.

Bloomfield, B.P., and Best, A. (1992), 'Management Consultants: Systems Development, Power and the Translation of Problems', *The Sociological Review*, 40, 3, 533-560.

Burrell, G. and Morgan, G. (1979), *Sociological Paradigms and Organizational Analysis*, Portsmouth, New Hampshire, Heinemann.

Callon, M. (1986), 'Some Elements of a Sociology of Translation: Domestification of the Scallops and the Fishermen of St Brieuc Bay', in Law, J. (ed.), *Power, Action and Belief: A New Sociology of Knowledge?*, London, Routledge and Kegan Paul.

Clegg, S.R. (1989), *Frameworks of Power*, London, Sage Publications Ltd.

Dahl, R.A. (1957), 'The Concept of Power', *Behavioural Science*, 2, 201-205.

Dahl, R.A. (1961), *Who Governs? Democracy and Power in an American City*, New Haven, Yale University Press.

Dahl, R.A. (1968), 'Power', *International Encyclopaedia of the Social Sciences*, 405-415.

Deluze, G. (1986), *Foucault*, Minneapolis, University of Minnesota Press.

Dreyfus, H.L. and Rabinow, P. (1983), *Michel Foucault: Beyond Structuralism and Hermeneutics* (2nd Edition), Chicago, The University of Chicago Press.

Foucault, M. (1977a), 'Truth and Power', in Gordon, C. (ed.), *Power / Knowledge: Selected Interviews & Other Writings 1972-1977*, New York, Pantheon Books.

Foucault, M. (1977b), 'Two Lectures', in Gordon, C. (ed.), *Power / Knowledge: Selected Interviews & Other Writings 1972-1977*, New York, Pantheon Books.

Foucault, M. (1980), *The History of Sexuality; Volume I: An Introduction*, New York, Vintage Books.

Foucault, M. (1983), 'The Subject and Power', in Dreyfus, H.L. and Rabinow, P. (eds), *Michel Foucault: Beyond Structuralism and Hermeneutics*, Chicago, The University of Chicago Press.

Franz, C.R. and Robey, D. (1984), 'An Investigation of User-led System Design: Rational and Political perspectives', *Communications of the ACM*, 27, 12, 1202-1209.

Giddens, A. (1984), *The Constitution of Society*, Berkeley, University of California Press.

Hickson, D.J., Higgins, C.R., Less, C.A., Schneck, R.E. and Pennings, J.M.A. (1971), 'A Strategic Contingencies Theory of Intraorganizational power', *Administrative Science Quarterly*, 16, 2, 216-229.

Hiley, D.R. (1984), 'Foucault and the Analysis of Power: Political Engagement without Liberal Hope or Comfort', *Praxis International*, 4, 2, 200.

Hirschheim, R. and Klein, H. (1994), 'Realizing Emancipatory Principles in Information Systems Development: The Case for ETHICS', *MIS Quarterly*, 18, 1, 83-109.

Hobbes, T. (1962), *Leviathan*, London, Collier-Macmillan.

Hougham, M.G. (1995), 'London Ambulance Service', Henley, London, Henley Management College.

Latour, B. (1991), 'Technology is society made durable', in Law, J. (ed.), *A Sociology of Monsters: Essays on Power, Technology and Domination*, London, Routledge.

Lockwood, D. (1964), 'Social Integration and System Integration', in Zollschan, C.K. and Hirsch, W. (eds), *Explorations in Social Change*, London, Routledge & Kegan Paul.

Lucas, H.C. (1984), 'Organizational Power and the Information Services department', *Communications of the ACM*, 27, 1, 1218-1226.

Lukes, S. (1974), *Power: A Radical View*, London, Macmillan.

Machiavelli, N. (1958), *The Prince*, London, Everyman.

Markus, M.L. (1983), 'Power, politics, and MIS implementation', *Communications of the ACM*, 26, 6, 430-444.

Markus, M.L. and Bjorn Andersen, N. (1987), 'Power over users: Its exercise by system professionals', *Communications of the ACM*, 30, 6, 498-504.

Mintzberg, H. (1980), *The Nature of Managerial Work*, Englewood Cliffs, New Jersey, Prentice Hall Inc.

Monteiro, E., and Hanseth, O. (1995), 'Social Shaping of Information Infrastructure: On Being Specific About the Technology', in Orlikowski, W.J., Walsham, G., Jones, M.R. and DeGross, J.I. (eds), *Information Technology and Changes in Organizational Work*, London, Chapman & Hall.

Nietzsche, F. (1967), *The Will to Power*, New York, Vintage Books.

Orlikowski, W. (1992), 'The Duality of Technology: Rethinking the Concept of Technology in Organizations', *Organization Science*, 3, 3, 398-427.

Page, D., Williams, P. and Boyd, D. (1993), 'Report of the Public Inquiry into the London Ambulance Service', London, HMSO.

Patton, P. (1989), 'Taylor and Foucault on Power and Freedom', *Political Studies*, 37, 274.

Pfeffer, J. (1981), *Power in organizations*, Pitman , Marshfield, Mass.

Philp, M. (1983), 'Foucault on Power: A Problem in Radical Translation,', *Political Theory*, 11, 1, 35.

Robinson, B. (1994), ' .. And Treat Those Two Imposters Just The Same': Analysing Systems Failure as a Social Process', University of Salford., Information Technology Institute.

Saunders, C.S. and Scamell, R.W. (1986), 'Organizational Power and the Information Services Department: A Re-examination', *Communications of the ACM*, 29, 2, 142-147.

Walsham, G. (1993), 'Reading the Organization: Metaphors and Information Management', *Journal of Information Systems*, 3, 33-46.

6 Management information: knowing, explaining and arguing

Introduction

> *One needs organized information for feedback. One needs reports and figures. **But** unless one builds one's feedback around direct exposure to reality – unless one disciplines oneself to go out and look – one condemns oneself to a sterile dogmatism and with it to ineffectiveness.*
>
> **Peter Drucker**

In this chapter the ideas of the preceding chapters will be brought together to create a basis for reflecting on management information. The chapter will start with a brief review of some of the current concepts of management information. It will show that the current archetype of management information is merely a combination of the traditional first-order cybernetics concepts of management (the Taylorist dualism) and the traditional techno-functional paradigm of information and that these concepts are very limited in their potential for providing insight into the involved nature of management information in-the-world. This will be followed by an outline of an alternative framework for management information drawing on the modes of being of the involved manger that were discussed in Chapter 2. This framework will indicate that management information is a far richer and more implicit concept than suggested by the current techno-functionalist thinking.

Some conceptions of management information

The concept of management information is, after thirty years of management information systems, still without substance and a lack of fundamental thinking persists. Although there are countless texts on management information systems, very little has been said about management information as a phenomenon in-the-world. There was management information before there were computers. However, the discussion of this very important aspect of management and organization only emerged, as a defined and discrete topic, after the advent of computing technology and almost exclusively as a spin-off from this technology.

It is distressing to take up a book on management information systems and see how little new and fundamental thinking is present. In spite of this, Thierauf (1987) claims: "Since their inception over two decades ago, management information systems have reached maturity." If Thierauf is saying that the current framework for understanding management information systems has been exhausted and is producing no new insights, then his claim has much merit. It must, however, be doubted that this is what he is saying. He may in fact be implying that the concepts and principles embodied in the current, but vaguely defined, orthodoxy have 'come of age', or that they have proved themselves to be valid, true and useful. If so, his comments are far more open to challenge.

The first step in developing this discussion will be to isolate and review the key concepts that embody the current theory of management information. A set of such concepts is given in most texts on management information systems as the basic fundamental truths for the understanding of management information and thus for management information systems.

Management information and management activities

Management information supports the traditional management activities or processes, as defined by Fayol (see Fayol, 1949). Management information must support the manager in executing the management activities effectively and efficiently. The two activities that are of particular import for management information systems are decision-making and control.

Management information and decisions

Management information supports decisions (Burch & Grudnitski, 1989; Davis & Olsen, 1985; Schultheis & Summer, 1989; Simon, 1977; Thierauf, 1987). All management activities imply decisions:

- *Planning involves decisions.* Planning is problem solving by means of decisions, e.g. what activities should be attempted in the future and what are the trade-offs for each alternative?
- *Organising involves decisions.* What structure is needed? How must activities be grouped for optimal functioning? Who should report to whom?
- *Staffing involves decisions.* What type of skills are needed? Who should be placed in what position? What should a person in a specific position be paid?
- *Controlling involves decisions.* What is an acceptable level of performance? When must performance be reported? What must be reported?

The management information system must support decisions. If decisions are effectively supported, management will be successful (based on the model of Simon, 1977). To know what information a manager needs is to identify the decisions he makes on a regular basis and to analyse them to see what information he requires to make these decisions.

Management information and management level

Management information is dependent on management level (Thierauf, 1987). Using Anthony's (1965) model of planning and control systems, Gorry and Scott Morton (1971) characterized management information by management levels, as set out in Table 6.1. This model has become one of the cornerstones of current theory and is used by most authors who write about management information systems.

Management information and operational information

In this paradigm management information is produced by processing transaction data (Ahituv & Neumann, 1990). The management information system extracts data from the operational or transaction processing systems and processes it to provide management information. Thus management information is seen to be one step higher, or more refined, than transaction information. Management information is produced by producing summaries, trends and exception reports from raw operational or transactional data. A management information system acts as a filter that traps the essence of that which management is interested in (management by exception).

Table 6.1: Management information characteristics

(Adapted from Gorry & Scott Morton 1971)

Characteristics of Information	Level of Management		
	Operational	*Middle*	*Strategic*
Source	Largely internal	←----→	Largely external
Scope	Well defined Narrow	←----→	General Wide
Level of aggregation	Detailed	←----→	Aggregate
Time horizon	Historic	←----→	Future orientated
Currency	Highly current	←----→	Almost obsolete
Required accuracy	High	←----→	Low
Frequency of use	Frequent	←----→	Very infrequent
Structure	Structured	←----→	Very unstructured

Management information and problem-solving

Management information must support problem solving (Thierauf, 1987). Management involves a series of problems that need solving and the management information system must support the manager in identifying and solving these problems (or generating solutions). Thus the problem solving process and the problem domain of a manager must be analysed and understood in order to develop a management information system.

Thus management information (within this paradigm) can be summarized as follows:

> *Management information* is essential information filtered from the transaction processing systems or primary activities and processed (or structured) by the management information system in such a manner as to support management (in an appropriate manner for each level of management) in identifying and solving problems or making decisions that will ensure the efficient and effective management of the organization.

Current definitions of management information systems

A review of some of the current definitions of management information systems shows how these concepts are reflected in contemporary management literature:

A management information system is an integrated, user-machine system for providing information to support operations, management, and decision-making functions in an organization (Davis & Olsen, 1985, p.6).

The objective of an MIS is to provide information for decision making on planning, initiating, organizing, and controlling the operations of the sub-systems of the firm and to provide a synergistic organization in the process (Murdick, 1990, p.3).

Effective management information systems allow the decision maker (i.e. the manager) to combine his or her subjective experience with computerized objective output to produce meaningful information for decision making. They make use of interactive processing whereby query capabilities can be used to obtain desired information for decision making. When appropriate, they utilize mathematical models for problem finding and problem solving. From an overall standpoint, effective management information systems stress a broad perspective by allowing a conversational mode between the decision maker and the computer throughout the entire problem-finding and problem-solving processes (Thierauf, 1987, p.22).

Management information systems provide information that is useful in making decisions. This information is designed to support effective planning and control of business activities. Information that is provided by a management information system is often produced from data that are aggregated, summarized, and presented in such a way as to be of value to managers for decision making purposes (Schultheis, 1989 #57, p.55).

These definitions of management information systems clearly reflect the current theory of management information. This book attempts a total redefinition of the concepts of management and information, so to use these current conceptions as a starting point would be of little value. They are only valuable for the current project to the degree that they clearly reflect the current state of thinking about management information. However the ideas seem to make sense and many system developers are utilising them to construct systems, so the next step is to see the problems that such thinking creates.

A critique of the current management information archetype

Current thinking is completely coherent within its assumptions. This is why it seems to make so much sense, and what provides the basis for its, almost automatic, legitimacy. A critique of the current view should therefore concentrate on its implicit assumptions. There are many assumptions that could be singled out for criticism; however, this analysis will concentrate on two. First, there is the implicit acceptance of the Taylorist dualism and, second, there is the acceptance of decision making as the *a priori* basis of most, if not all, management action. As will be seen the second assumption flows logically from the first.

The Taylorist dualism, with its separation of thinking from doing, created the legitimacy for an all-pervasive system of data capturing and filtering (surveillance). In Chapter 4 it was demonstrated that the Taylorist dualism would always lead to a control paradox, where any gain in control of the management system is counter balanced by the loss of control in the environment. Furthermore, drawing on Heidegger and Varela, it was shown that this dualism is a reductionist mode of thinking and doing that always already assumes being-in-the-world: there is no understanding *out*-of-the-world. The manager for whom the management information system is designed, unless involved, is severed from the being-in. As a result the information will not make sense, since it requires an *involvement whole*. The best that the Taylorist manager can do is to interpret the information, work out its possibilities, in terms of the management form of life – implying an insurmountable strangeness. Autopoietically, decontextualized inputs will remain perturbation (noise) that may or may not influence the manager's actions. Therefore any framework for management information, to be of significance, should start with being-in-the-world, with the involved manager.

The dualism of Descartes inspire the enlightened, modern mind, including Taylor, to separate thinking from doing and intention from action. In this separation the thinking subject was created; that epitome of the rational being, the thinking manager. The emergence of the rational thinking manager, through the dualism, made *decision making* the central management activity. Since the manager is supposed to be the thinking brain receiving signals from the nervous (information) system and reacting with a calculated response that prompts the body (the managed, the doers) to action, the manager must utilize the data in thinking (in making rational decisions). If, however, the brain does not think (in the sense of manipulating representations of the world), as argued by Maturana and

Varela (1987), and corroborated by Heidegger and Wittgenstein's analysis, then the whole notion of decision making loses it automatic legitimacy.

Wittgenstein (1956) argues that "[t]hinking is not an incorporeal process which lends life and sense to speaking, and which it would be possible to detach from speaking" (#339). He comes to this conclusion by enquiring about the language of thinking. If we think in a silent, private language, how would we know whether we are translating our thoughts correctly from the private thinking language to our spoken language? If, as he argues, we do not possess a private language, then thinking can, at most, be characterized as silent speaking. Further, if, as argued in Chapter 3, speaking is itself tied to forms of life, then thinking receives its sense from the humans *doing things together* in everyday life. We think in speaking, we speak in doing: the separation of thinking and doing is illusory. Heidegger (1968) also makes this point in the following passage: "And only when a man speaks, does he think – not the other way around, as metaphysics still believes. Every motion of the hand in every one of its works carries itself through the element of thinking, every bearing of the hand bears itself in that element. All the work of the hand is rooted in thinking" (p.16). When we speak we do not explain our thoughts, our speaking is our thoughts. We know our thinking only to the degree that we speak it and do it. We should not become seduced by the *grammatical custom* behind the Descartes dualism, as Nietzsche (1967) explains:

'There is thinking: therefore there is something that thinks': this is the upshot of all Descartes' argumentation. But that means positing as 'true a priori' our belief in the concept of substance – that when there is thought there has to be something 'that thinks' is simply a formulation of a grammatical custom that adds a doer to every deed. (#484)

If we do not think, how do we know what to do – what 'causes' our actions? The argument of Heidegger, that our involvement in-the-world implies that we always already know what to do, was set out in Chapter 2. Decisions are always already present next steps in an involvement whole that already makes sense: an involvement whole that is unthought. Decisions *are* actions that flow from our being-in-the-world. It is not necessary to posit a thinker, or an intention, for every act; this is only a grammatical custom, not the way the world *is*. Isenberg (1984) in his study of senior managers also confirms this point: "Since managers often 'know' what is right before they can analyse and explain it, they frequently act first and think later. Thinking is inextricably tied to action ... Managers develop thought about their companies and organizations not by analysing a problematic situation and then acting, but by thinking and acting in close concert" (p. 89). Even the seemingly explicit decisions, such as those made by committees, parliaments and management boards, are either: *post facto* rationalizations that reify what was already sensible in the involvement whole; or power play, i.e. they are attempts to translate actions and so stabilize obligatory passage points to implement what is known (in the involvement).

This discussion could lead to the conclusion that a useful framework for understanding management information should include both the dimensions of the involved manager (being-in-the-world) and the political manager (organizational politics). The next section reflects on management information based on the ideas developed in the preceding chapters. The goal is not to define *the* theory that will replace all other theories – as was argued in Chapter 1, theory is not the issue. Rather, the goal is to expand understanding and make it more subtle and varied. The days of the grand narrative are over (Lyotard, 1986).

Management information defined

First, it must be said that definitions are always very limiting, and often confusing, things. Definitions, in general, have the sort of decontextualized nature that the whole spirit of this book is trying to argue against. To a degree, the whole movement to define anything and everything is a sign of the extent of the atomistic positivist influence. A definition must never be seen as an end in itself, it is always merely a starting point; it is impossible to capture the full meaning and situated richness of a concept in a single definition. The whole discussion of a concept must be seen as a definition, as an ever infinite unfolding of the concept. It is the development of knowledge through ever increasing and subtle variations (distinctions) of a central notion (distinction). In this light, a starting point for a definition of management information could be:

> *Management information is management understanding in-the-world, in-order-to get the job done.*

An expansion and discussion of each of the components necessary for this statement can lead to the main concepts that constitute the new paradigm of management information.

Management information is management understanding. Management information is not an objective entity that exists outside the manager. It is not something that could be pointed to, or held in the hand, in order to say, "Here is management information". Management information is the *understanding* that emerges from sense-making in-the-world. This understanding is not a matter of having a accurate picture of the facts, for everything is always already interpretation (Foucault, 1977). Understanding is the situated appropriation of communicative acts (be they reports, conversations, signals signs or whatever) that is available to the manager in-the-world. Understanding is a know-how-to that draws upon the sense and significance located in the always already present involvement whole. If the manager understands, then the manager knows how to act and so on. Therefore decisions and action do not flow from understanding, requiring that the manager must first understand and then act; decisions and action are the reification of understanding, which is a primordial already present know-how.

Management understanding is autopoietic. The autopoietic process, analytically, consists of two sub-processes: distinction making (internal coherence) and distinction relating (structural coupling). Distinction making is the process of establishing difference. It is a tacit process based on doing or using and it is unthought. In doing or in using, ever increasing, ever more subtle, distinctions emerge as the knowing that is also a doing. Since these distinctions are shaped in the available world they are only known as part of a doing. They must be languaged for them to become part of the social language. In doing things together as part of a form-of-life, the structural coupling with other autopoietic systems, other individuals, is maintained through languaging.

Management information is in-the-world. Management understanding is always already present in the network of power. It is therefore simultaneously local, unstable and diffuse. Understanding is located in the doing of everyday as part of the manager's involvement in the world.

Management information is an in-order-to get the job done. Management information comprises perturbations in the maintenance of internal coherence (understanding). Managers do not execute plans; their primordial mode of existence is getting the job done. Management information must be located in this getting the job done. No single information text will determine this insight; in getting the job done, the manager will draw on whatever is available.

Management information, as articulated here, is a much richer concept than was suggested by earlier paradigms. The question arises as to what happened to decision-making and problem-solving, which play such a prominent role in the current management information paradigm. The answer is quite simple: decision-making and problem-solving are observer viewpoints, they are an outside view of the dance of internal relations. If the world becomes occurrent then, in detached contemplation, the manager may be involved in explicit decision-making and problem-solving. However, these intentional acts will *always* presume a tacit understanding that emerges from their being-in-the-world. Managers in-the-world do not make decisions or solve problems. Managers are *in* decisions as part of getting the job done. They are the obvious, sensible, next steps that are not thought out; they are just done.

Some interpretations of management information

Management information, as described above, has many dimensions which could be expanded on. In order to explore further and situate the concept, it may be useful to list some other potential interpretations of this notion of management information.

Management information is always already understanding. If the data that the manager receives is not located and appropriated (has not become available) as know-how in getting the job done then the act of informing has not happened. Such data (reports) will only be occurrent objects in front of the manager. To be informed, is to be-in (involved) in an involvement whole in which the report is always already significant. This is why understanding (information) is always already located in-the-world; it is being-in-the-world.

Management information is part of doing. Management information can never, nor in any way, be abstracted from the context of doing. Information is not the transfer of meaning 'packets' from the operations (doing) to the management (thinking). We dwell in understanding as we dwell in our world. We always already understand our world before we point at it (talk, report, etc. about it). We do not point at it because we come to understand it.

Management information is always already located; it is contextual, historical and perspectual. Like information, management information cannot be severed from its context. There is no such thing as understanding from the outside. Meaning is always already located within the involvement whole. This is why Wittgenstein argued that we cannot transfer language from one language-game to another, or from one form of life to another. It must be appropriated within its culture, tradition and communicative context. Thus, management information is always already located. We understand each other because we already share a history, a context and a perspective – a form of life. There cannot be any sense of an ahistorical transfer of understanding from the world of operations to the world of management. At best these communications will become perturbations that may, in an indeterminable way, influence the world of the other. It seems therefore that management information that is severed from its locality can, at most, be noise.

Management information exists in-the-world of the manager. Management information is an available tool, the know-how of decisions and action in the fragmented and erratic world of the manager. Management information does not come in neat packets of understanding that wait for the manager at predefined points. Management information may become available in coping, in any doing, often unexpected, at inappropriate times and in less than ideal forms.

Management information is never complete. Managers in the management situation are constantly working out the possibilities of (appropriating and reappropriating) the data they are confronted with. They are always already in the hermeneutic circle, always interpreting, always striving for room for manoeuvre. As comportments shift new possibilities open up. There is no final context, no final for-the-sake-of-which; the job is never completed.

Management information can never be located in time and space. Management information can never be located as a series of perturbations, as available know-how, in the network of power. Analysis of information needs, as is done in traditional systems analysis, may itself reconfigure the network of power, may generate a whole series of perturbations, may help the analyst document an understanding of the manager's world, but cannot succeed in locating management information needs.

If management information refers to all these things, how can its operation be described? What is the best way to think it through in the world of the involved manager? It is not even clear whether these are appropriate questions to ask. Nevertheless, if management information is real (and at least most managers would agree that they have some empirical experiences to believe that it is) then this paradigm must enable some sort of description of these phenomena. From this brief discussion its should be clear that these are not simple questions; yet they need to be raised and answers attempted.

The management information system

To speak of a management information system is to run the risk of objectifying that which has been taken apart and questioned so radically throughout this book. The approach will be to try to elucidate and locate the management information system in-the-world of the involved manager. However, it may be impossible and also undesirable to try to integrate all the arguments and discussion of the previous chapters into one coherent picture. The attempt will be to try to create some sort of a frame that can assist the thinking through of management information in a broader context.

It therefore seems most reasonable to try to understand management information in terms of the three modes of being of the manager in-the-world that were outlined in Chapter 2. If the analysis in that chapter was correct then this is the world within which management information must function.

The analysis, which is illustrated in Table 6.2, will outline the nature of information as understanding in each of these three modes and will also try to illuminate the role of traditional representation-based information systems.

Table 6.2: Management information in the three modes of being

Mode of Being	Mode of Understanding	Managers Stance	Role of Information System
Available	Know-how [doing/using]	Always already knows. World is familiar	Not applicable
Unavailable	Interpretation [explaining]	Startled Involved deliberation	Hermeneutic appropriation Sense making
Occurrent	Discourse [arguing]	Intentional action Translation and enrolment	Evidence and truth making (OPP)

Management information as available: know-how

Management information in its most primordial sense is always already available. It is available because the manager is in-the-world. The manager is involved in the daily doing and using. In the available world, the manager always already knows the 'what' and the 'how' of the daily getting-the-job-done; this is the world of *manus*-ment. However, if the manager is not involved in-the-world but is distanced from it then management information becomes unavailable or occurrent. In the available world there is no need for representation. Representation or objectification only comes into play in the event of a distancing (or breakdown). If the manager's understanding flows from intimate structural coupling with the environment, breakdowns in doing ought to be the exception and not the rule.

Understanding as know-how implies that the manager does not explicitly attend to things such as decision making and problem solving. In the available world decisions and problem solving are obvious next moves in the involvement whole. They always already make sense – they are available.

The preceding description can only be true if the manager is involved in the 'doing of the job'. This affirms the importance of the notion of at-handness of the *manus*-ment task. It also affirms the argument in Chapter 4 that the only way to absorb variety is to eliminate the notion of externally located control, to collapse the Taylorist dualism. In such situations of localized self-control the need for representation is dramatically reduced or even eliminated (Louw, 1996). In such a *manus* environment fairly simple formal management information systems would be anticipated, as seems to be true for knowledge work environments such as consulting firms, research institutes and universities.

In this available mode of managing and understanding, actions do not flow from decisions, plans and intentions. Rather, decisions often follow action as *post hoc* rationalizations and articulations of already present know-how. Decisions and actions become available as logical options that open up as part of being-in-the-world. The manager always already knows what to do, unless, of course, there is a radical shift in the environment that dislocates the structural coupling and produces a breakdown in the interaction. If the involvement is interrupted, actions, intentions and objects may enter the focal awareness as unavailable – in need of some form of explicit attention.

Management information as unavailable: interpretation

It was argued in Chapter 2 that management information is, or comes into being as a process of appropriation; appropriation directed at making explicit the already present understanding. It would be wise to call this appropriation *hermeneutic* so as not to lose the essential character of what is suggested. This appropriation becomes necessary when the structural coupling with the environment becomes dislocated; the manager, as it were, becomes *distanced*. The already present sense, in the involvement whole, is lost. Understanding, in this mode, is momentarily unavailable due to a malfunction or breakdown. Startled, yet still involved in the world, the manager now seeks to reclaim the sensible whole of the involvement (coherence) by means of hermeneutic interpretation. The tacit way to realize this interpretation is through hermeneutic appropriation.

As was argued in Chapter 3, this appropriation is not to throw a meaning over some naked thing that is present-at-hand for the manager. The thing (report, text, conversation, etc.) that is encountered in the manager's concernful dealing with things, already possesses a reference that is implicitly contained in the manager's co-understanding of the world and thus can be articulated by interpretation. It is only because of this already available world that interpretation makes sense in the first place.

Hermeneutic appropriation

In the discussion that follows the word 'text' will often be used to keep the discussion at a more general level. In each case the notion of 'text' can be substituted by any one, or more, of many things including: a computer generated report, a human generated report, an informal discussion, a passing comment, a notice on a board, a letter, an e-mail message, a document on the internet, a chat in the bar after work, a report on television, a bodily gesture, a directed action by someone. In each case these objects may leap forward in moments of unavailableness due to breakdown and will be in need of interpretation; coherence is lost and is in need of attention.

To start this discussion, it will be useful to remember the concept of appropriation as was outlined in Chapter 3. Appropriation is the concept which is suitable for the actualization of meaning as addressed to someone *in*volved in-the-world. Appropriation is not something we receive or arrive at. It is the working out of possibilities already understood. It is the rendering coherent of a network of references (in-order-tos) that were momentarily lost in the situation of malfunction or breakdown. For example, a manager is walking through the factory discussing the production progress with the production supervisor. The explanations of the supervisor and the empirical data she observes are coherent and sensible; in short she understands the current state of affairs. Then she notices something odd (non-sensible), the referential whole breaks and a specific object (maybe a piece of machined casting) jumps into the focal awareness – she is startled. There seems to be a problem with the casting (it does not make sense). This dislocation in the referential whole needs to be made coherent again. She enquires about it from the fitter. She is not satisfied with the answer and requests the engineering drawing to look at. This drawing does not provide her with *additional information* of what is already understood; rather, she is trying to take apart the 'in-order-tos' that she already understands – the machine and its context of use for which the machined component is a part. After inspecting the drawing she realizes that the design has been altered and that the part is correctly machined. With this interpretation (sense making or rather restoring) the referential whole is again coherent and the object, as an in-order-to, makes sense; it reverts back to the referential whole, its field of significance.

The tacit process that facilitated the interpretation of the machined part is the hermeneutic circle. The whole is the already present network of meaningful relations, part of being in-the-world of a production manager. The part is the object made visible (explicit) due to the breakdown (being non-sensible). The hermeneutic process enables it to be rendered meaningful again. It must permit the working out of the possibilities for understanding *this* object as an in-order-to in the context of a machine that is itself and in-order-to, to do something in some situation of use. Thus, the hermeneutic process must render the part coherent with the already understood referential whole.

Hermeneutic interpretation is, however, not a mode of existence to be sometimes consciously selected and sometimes not. The struggle for hermeneutic understanding in moments of unavailableness is an existential essence that we have as Dasein (Heidegger, 1962, p.200). We are always already *in* hermeneutic circles, plunged into them, as it were. Also, it is important to refrain from falling back into the idea of understanding as representation or as 'having an accurate picture of the facts'. As Dreyfus (1991) explains: "understanding as significance, allows in any specific situation an open-ended but limited range of possible activities to show up as sensible" (p.191). Hermeneutic understanding is always a know-how-to in the context of doing or using. Hermeneutic interpretation is located *in* the shared world, the background practices, of daily doing or using.

Management information as occurrent: discourse

Once the manager, as it were, steps back from the world management information becomes occurrent – an object before a subject. It may be useful, as a starting point, to compare this mode of being to the situation found in a court of law. The situation is one of complete removed-ness or severed-ness. No one, except possibly the parties directly involved in the incident before the court, *knows* what happened. The incident will have generated many texts (witnesses, forensic results, psychiatric evaluation reports, finger prints...). In this mode of management information the 'truth' must be created in the most coherent (sensible) reconstruction of the facts. Each stakeholder (judge, prosecutor, defendant) has a particular interest to defend. It is in this occurrent mode of being that information now becomes entangled in networks of power. In the organization, however, there is no judge there is only the unstable and contingent play of force relations.

In this detached discourse, actions that 'occurred' in the available mode are rationalized and explained. The information system provides what stands for evidence and this shapes the discourse. This is the world of the management meeting, in the broad sense of the word. The evidence produced (reports, documents, testimony) serve only as perturbations in the quest for a coherent picture of what is believed to be the true state of affairs. Once coherence emerges, the decisions, and actions, are obvious. There are two perspectives that could be used to understand this mode of being and the dynamics of its discourse and its ways of establishing coherence. First, there is the work of Jürgen Habermas (1979; 1984; 1987); he presents this management discourse as *communicative action* in the ideal speech situation. The second view can be linked to the notions of power which were discussed in Chapter 5.

Communicative action and rational discourse

For Habermas the only legitimate and authentic basis of social evolution and integration is *communicatively rational action*; action between actors attempting to reach understanding or rational consensus. Communication, according to Habermas, is inherently or primordially oriented toward mutual understanding. When actors speak, or rather utter statements in their discourse, they perform *speech acts* (Austin, 1962); they do not merely structure linguistically correct sentences that point to, or refer to, the world in an unambiguous way. In performing speech acts, Habermas argues, speakers always relate to three different worlds: the objective world, the social world and the subjective world. In the speech act they raise universal validity claims (about the three worlds) and proffer that these can be vindicated or redeemed (Habermas, 1979, p.2). In so far as an actor desires to participate in the process of reaching mutual understanding (rational consensus), the actor cannot but relate to these three worlds and raise (and be able to redeem) the following validity claims:

- *Comprehensibility claim.* The actor claims to be uttering something understandably.
- *Propositional or truth claim.* The actor claims to give the hearer *something* to understand, a claim about the objective world.

- *Truthfulness or sincerity claim.* The actor claims to make *himself* understandable, a claim about his subjective world.
- *Normative validity claim.* The actor claims to come to an understanding with another person, a claim about the social world.

This can be clarified through the example of a typical management meeting which has a manager being addressed by the managing director. The managing director makes the following utterance (performs the following speech act): "I see from the report (evidence) that the productivity in your department is down for the third consecutive month; what is happening in your department?" The managing director raises a number of validity claims. Firstly she, the managing director claims that the manager can fully comprehend what she is requesting, viz. an explanation of the facts in the report. Secondly, she makes the propositional claim that the manager does have the knowledge to explain the facts about low productivity in the report and ought to be able to do so. Thirdly, she claims that it is a sincere request on her behalf to understand the situation in the department and is not some covert attempt to expose the manager in some way, in order to serve some selfish agenda. And, finally, the chairman claims that it is socially acceptable and normatively right for a person in the position of the chairman and managing director of the organization to make such requests to the manager under these prevailing conditions, in this case the monthly management meeting.

Such a communicative or speech act is claimed to be valid if these claims can be vindicated should they be challenged by the other partners in the communication. Communicative rationality is achieved if the validity claims of comprehensibility, truth, sincerity and rightness are recognized, vindicated and agreed upon (implicitly or explicitly) by the participants. An agreement based on vindicated claims is what Habermas refers to as *understanding*. Actors understand a speech act when they know what makes it acceptable. Understanding is, for Habermas, the inherent *telos* of human speech (Habermas, 1984, p.287).

Normally, actors start off with a background consensus pertaining to those interpretations taken for granted among them. As soon as the consensus that the presupposition that certain validity claims are in fact satisfied, or could be vindicated, is shaken, then the actors must attempt to achieve a new definition of the situation in which all participants can share. If their attempt fails, then communicative action cannot be continued. They are confronted with the alternatives of switching to strategic action, breaking off communication, or recommencing action oriented towards reaching understanding at the level of argumentative

speech (Habermas, 1979, p.4). Argumentation is speech that thematises contested validity claims, explicitly supporting or criticising them. The communicative basis of argumentative speech is sustained through the ideal speech situation. The ideal speech situation demands, or rather presupposes, that all participants would be in an equal position to:
- raise issues by asking questions;
- give and refuse orders, to permit or prohibit actions;
- call into question the truth, correctness, appropriateness or sincerity of what is said;
- express their attitudes, feelings, concerns and doubts.

The ideal speech situation is not merely a regulative principle but an unavoidable supposition, a transcendental condition, and the anticipated normative foundation of agreement in discourse (McCarthy, 1978, p.310). If the conditions of the ideal speech situation are met then the "force of the better argument" will establish the new definition, a new set of agreed upon validity claims, of the given situation.

It is as part of argumentation, the contesting of validity claims, that management information functions in the occurrent mode. In the argumentation, facts provided by the information system get contested and contextualized. In the example of the management meeting, the manager could argue that the propositional claim, reflected in the report, that "the productivity is low" is false since the report does not take into account certain facts specific to the period involved; such facts as: that a critical piece of equipment was broken and a spare part could not be found; or that a key worker in an important section resigned and had to be replaced by a less qualified person. If these counter-claims are vindicated, the managing director would understand (agree on the new set of validity claims about) the manager's account and proceed with the meeting; if not, the managing director may put forward other requests or claims to be argued.

The notion of the ideal speech situation is obviously utopian. Nevertheless, it provides a framework for articulating the idea of understanding through argumentation as the contesting and proffering of validity claims. It is in this mode of argumentation that information functions as occurrent. Information here is merely a set of tokens or perturbations in a discourse that tries to reach some sense of coherence, a consensus about the validity claims presented in the discourse.

This, it is argued here, is this mode of functioning that Feldman and March referred to in their paper that was discussed in Chapter 2; it is the *post facto* rationalization of a reality that already *is*. It is not really a matter of deciding or solving, it is more a matter of aligning that which is articulated with the reality in the already available world.

Rational discourse and circuits of power

It could be argued that communicative action with its emancipatory ideals is not a good model for the occurrent mode of being, since it implies a particular moral viewpoint, an *ought to*, that may be divorced from the actuality of everyday life. Nietzsche (1967, p. 306) argued that even morality (the ideal of emancipation) must in the final analysis become immoral for its existence: "The victory of a moral ideal is achieved by the same 'immoral' means as every other victory: force, lies, slander, injustice." From this perspective, and from the discussion in Chapter 5, it may be concluded that every communicative act, every argument is always already *in* power. Power is always already present in every being-in. This has consequences for the management information system.

In the episodic circuit of power, management information acts as an authoritative resource to establish obligatory passage points. The formal representations, laid out in management reports, act as evidence to support arguments for certain translations to be established as obligatory passage points: "Based on this and that report, ladies and gentleman, it is self-evident that we ought to do this and that." The management information system functions as a regime of truth that defines which courses of action will be adjudged as 'right' and which as 'wrong'. It will also structure what enters the legitimate discourse and what stays outside of it: "Don't come to the meeting with a proposal if you cannot *put numbers* to it!" Therefore, the parties that control the discourse where the initial system design is specified have a powerful influence in determining what stands for truth in the organization.

The interpretations in the episodic circuit assume a set of meanings that are relatively fixed and stable. If this is not the case, the episodic circuit could be outflanked by challenging the rules of interpretation, and as such the meanings, that were used in the translations: "Yes Jo, I agree that if we interpret it in the way you are suggesting then you have a point, but there is another way to see this...". In an organization where social integration is high, only very innovative outflanking would be effective. Such out-flanking, changing the rules for interpretation, may be defended by calling upon a particular membership, or form of life: "We in production do not see things in that way...". If there is a high degree of social integration in "production" such outflanking may be successful to the point that it could change the generally accepted legitimate interpretation of certain elements of the reports and hence shift the set of translations and obligatory passage points that is possible.

Stability in social integration can only be achieved through circuits of systems integration – techniques of discipline and production (empowerment and disempowerment). The possibility of counter-interpretations appearing in the discourse could be limited through discipline. In the case of bureaucratic organizations it might be done through elaborate policy and procedure manuals. Any deviant interpretations can then be translated back to these obligatory passage points: "Yes, you have a good idea but policy A or procedure C will not allow us to do it." In a more open organization a network of alliances would have to be built up and maintained through discipline, though the forms of discipline could vary. For example: it could be professional, "As an accountant I would not expect you to do that"; it could be based on a personal relationship, "As a friend I would expect you to support me"; or it could be more coercive, "If you don't toe the line I will not recommend you for that promotion." Figure 6.1 depicts a summary of management information systems in-the-world.

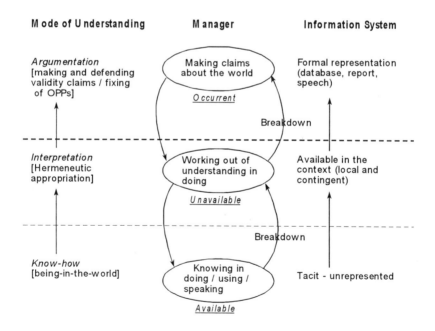

Figure 6.1: The management information system

Reflections on the framework

It is important to note that the available mode of management information, that of know-how, is the primordial one; the other modes are merely derivatives. We cannot interpret or argue about a world which we do not, in some sense, already know. Hence the most important conclusion is that the ultimate success of management information systems is not in the sophistication of the representational system, the computerized inform-ation system, but in the manager's involvement in-the-world. There is no way, as was assumed in the Taylorist dualism, to substitute representation for involvement. Once the structural coupling of the manager with the environment is severed, the know-how is lost, interpretation and argumentation become sterile and insignificant (Drucker, 1967).

A walk through the framework, again using the example of the pro-duction manager, will make these concepts more concrete, although it is not be possible to incorporate the full subtlety of all the ideas into one example. That would make the example too complex and would hide the overall picture. This example seeks a difficult compromise; to provide enough detail to make it interesting, yet not so much as to lose the overall picture.

The production manager is walking through the factory. She under-stands the factory floor, she is involved in it, it concerns her, it is her life-world. It is a continuous and significant referential whole: material in-order-to machine; machine in-order-to assemble; assemble in-order-to produce; produce for the sake of selling; selling for the sake of doing business; and so forth. Machines point to material, to operators, to production orders, to schedules, to customers, and so on. She understands this world and can interpret or make sense of anything in it; each event, each thing is tied to a whole set of references that always already make sense – it is already tied to being-in-the-world.

The production manager is on her way to the weekly management meeting. In her hand is the weekly production report. She understands it, it is embedded in her form of life called production; it is a node in a network of references that is coherent and sensible. She can use the report to change the schedule, to negotiate with the union, and so forth; she can use it because it is embedded in her life-world, the world she is always already in, not because it is a mirror of the world, a representation of the facts.

As she walks through the factory the production supervisor points out certain things he feels she should be aware of. To the outside observer they seem to think together and make decisions as they go; however, they are merely confirming the obvious next steps in the referential whole which both of them always already understand. The explanations and descriptions of the supervisor and the empirical data she observes are coherent and sensible; in short she understands.

Then she notices something odd, something non-sensible; there is a dislocation, the referential whole momentarily breaks and a specific object, a piece of machined casting, jumps into the focal awareness. There seems to be a problem with the casting, it does not make sense. She already knows this because she understands the network of in-order-tos, the parts that make up the rest of the assembly. This breakdown in the referential whole needs to be made coherent or sensible again. She enquires about it from the machine operator. She is not satisfied with the answer, it does not make sense. She requests the engineering drawing to look at. The drawing does not provide her with *additional information* of what is already understood. Rather, she is trying to take apart the in-order-tos that she already understands – the machine, the part and its context of use, the assemblage in which it would be an in-order-to. After interpreting the drawing she realizes that the design has been altered and that the part, as a component in a assembly whole, is correctly machined. With this interpretation, this sense restoring, the referential whole is again restored. The object, as an in-order-to, makes sense; it reverts back to the referential whole, its field of significance.

The production supervisor confirms that he also only became aware of the change when the customer faxed a new drawing in response to his enquiries. She is unhappy that the marketing department did not inform her of the change to the customer's specification and decides to take it up at the meeting. In the meeting she confronts the marketing manager with the evidence:

• the customer order did not refer to the change in the design;
• the delivery receipt of the castings still used the old part number;
• the new drawing that was faxed, by the customer, to the production supervisor when he discovered that the casting was different;
• the marketing report presented at the previous meeting indicated no change.

The marketing manager does not accept her validity claims that his department was negligent in failing to inform her about the change. He contests the claims by suggesting an alternative interpretation of the 'facts': it is because her production supervisor jumped the line that his sales people were not informed. He also suggests that the production supervisor should make more effort to communicate with his sales force and not liaise with the customers directly (opportunity to create the marketing department as an obligatory passage point in dealing with customers).

The production manager outflanks him by explaining that most customers prefer to deal with production directly because the sales staff are not technically qualified to deal with their requests and enquiries. The managing director agrees with her point and suggests that she may in future continue to directly deal with customers when it comes to technical detail, thus new rules are defined. The meeting continues.

The above example appear to be simple yet it contains all the elements of the three modes of understanding of a manager in-the-world: know-how in doing; reflection as part of doing; and agreement on the validity claims about the world. The purpose here is to illustrate it in simple terms so that it is clear and unambiguous. The important point is that the most primordial understanding and interaction with the world is on the level of tacit knowing (being-in-the- world of production). All other understanding (the interpretation of the drawing, the discussion with the supervisor, and the arguments in the meeting) assumes an already present know-how in-the-world in which it can be embedded.

Furthermore, it should be noted that the engineering drawing and the production report are only rendered significant by the involvement whole. They temporarily become objects of reflection in moments of breakdown or dislocation (such as the seemingly defective casting). They are then made significant through hermeneutic appropriation (the engineering drawing and discussion with supervisor) and through argumentation (the management meeting). Table 6.3 summarizes the main elements of the example.

The example demonstrates that the vast majority of, if not all, actions in-the-world and what are accounted decisions are based on an unrepresented tacit knowing. The major resource for the management information system is the pool of already present tacit knowing of the involved manager. This is not only true for those repetitive and habitual things like opening doors, walking through rooms and chatting to someone in the corridor; it is also true about so called major events. Managers in-the-world will acknowledge that in most cases where so-called big decisions were made they were already understood on a tacit level and then elaborated and justified in the occurrent mode. In most cases the formal decision making act is to convince the individual and others of the legitimacy of the tacit know-how always already present *in* the decision.

Table 6.3: The modes of management information (example)

Mode of Being	Mode of Understanding	Production manager	Information system
Available	Know-how [doing, using, speaking]	The production manager knows-how production works. It makes sense to her as part of being involved in production	Unrepresented. Walk through and speak with production supervisor
Unavailable	Interpretation [explaining]	Startled by unavailable part. Interpret engineering drawing and explanation by operator and supervisor	Engineering drawing; explanations; physical inspection of casting
Occurrent	Discourse [arguing, fixing of OPPs]	Management meeting. Validity claims, counter-claims (opportunity to fix OPP), outflanking, redefinition of the rules	Evidence: customer orders, engineering drawing, marketing report, delivery receipt

Some conclusions

Now that all the terminology is in place, it is possible to summarize the two perspectives of the relationship between the manager and the world (including information) that have emerged. This is depicted in Table 6.4 and represents the progress of the argument in providing a better understanding of what management information is.

The involved manager is always already in-the-world, completely immersed in it; always already directed in getting the job done. This being thrown into the world, this thrownness, makes much of that which the manager has available appear present as *given*; constraints that cannot be escaped, only be dealt with. For the involved manager there is no outside, on top, or privileged point of view. In being-in-this-world the manager understands this world, the manager knows-how to make sense of it and act *in* it; the manager is deeply familiar with it. However, in moments of dislocation, when this familiarity is momentarily lost, the involved manager uses information to restore sense to this already understood world by appropriating (interpreting) it. At other times, in situations of distance, the manager may create and use representations to argue about the world

so as to build alliances and translate others' actions, ideas and arguments
into local opportunities for power (or resistance).

Table 6.4: The two ontological views of the manager

	Involved Manager	**Rational Manager**
Mode of being	Available	Occurrent
Comportment	Getting the job done	Effectiveness and efficiency
Purpose of information	Sense (re)making and alliance building	Decision making and problem solving
Action imperatives	Local logic and 'bricolage'	Plan and control
	Dcing-thinking	Thinking then doing
	Opportunistic	Calculated and reasoned
Knowledge resource	Tacit knowing	Representations
Key assumptions	Thrownness	Autonomy
	Networks	Linearity

The involved manager has no faith in the big ideas, just small ideas that
get shaped locally and applied as part of getting the job done. In getting
the job done, as part of doing, the manager thinks. For the involved
manager thinking emerges from doing in a way similar to how conversations emerge from talking. The involved manager also understands
that anyone can unwittingly, at any moment, stumble into and out of
opportunities that may change the whole moves and rules of the game,
hence there can be no final moves. From the outside the involved manager
may often appear irrational; apparently not reflecting and not planning.
Nevertheless, the involved manager appears confident in doing because the
involved manager depends on intuition, gut feeling, that pool of tacit
know-how that flows from being concernfully involved in-the-world.

For the involved manager there are no simple solutions, no 'one thing'
to do, since the involved manager does not work on the basis of linear
causality. The involved manager knows that every doing, every decision,
may have as many unexpected as expected outcomes; also, that these
unexpected outcomes may even change the validity (assumptions) of the
initial act (decision).

In short, for the involved mangaer the world is an autopoietic whole, a
circular network, that defies simple solutions, formal logic, models and

theories. For the involved manager there is only coping in getting the job done. For the involved manager success is: thinking on your feet, drawing on tacit understanding, staying open to possibilities, exploiting opportunities as they arise, building alliances, covering some options and hedging others.

This is a new story, a story that is rooted in the world. Not an ought but an *is* – the always already involved manager. Thinking through some of the implications of this anti-story will be the issue for the final chapter.

References

Ahituv, N. and Neumann, S. (1990), *Principles of Information Systems for Management*, Dubuque, Wm.C. Brown Publ.

Anthony, R.N. (1965), *Planning and Control Systems: A Framework for Analysis*, Boston, Harvard University Press.

Austin, J.L. (1962), *How To Do Things With Words*, Boston, Harvard University Press.

Burch, G.C. and Grudnitski, G. (1989), *Information Systems: Theory and Practice* (5th Edition), New York, John Wiley & Sons.

Davis, G.B. and Olsen, M.H. (1985), *Management Information Systems: Conceptual Foundations, Structure and Development* (2nd Edition), London, McGraw-Hill.

Dreyfus, H.L. (1991), *Being-in-the-world: a Commentary on Heidegger's Being and time, Division I*, Cambridge, Mass, MIT Press.

Drucker, P.F. (1967), *The Effective Executive*, London, Pan Books in association with Heinemann.

Fayol, H. (1949), *General and Industrial Management*, London, Pitman Publ.

Foucault, M. (1977), 'Two Lectures', *in* Gordon, C. (ed.), *Power / Knowledge: Selected Interviews & Other Writings 1972-1977*, New York, Pantheon Books.

Gorry, G.A. and Scott Morton, M.S. (1971), 'A Framework for Management Information Systems', *Sloan Management Review*, Fall 1971, 55-70.

Habermas, J. (1979), *Communication and the Evolution of Society*, London, Heinemann Press.

Habermas, J. (1984), *The Theory of Communicative Action*, London, Heinemann Education.

Habermas, J. (1987), *The Theory of Communicative Action*, Cambridge, Polity.

Heidegger, M. (1962), *Being and time*, Oxford, Basil Blackwell.

Heidegger, M. (1968), *What is Called Thinking*, New York, Harper & Row.

Isenberg, D.J. (1984), 'How Senior Managers Think', *Harvard Business Review*, Nov-Dec 1984.

Louw, G. (1996), 'Reducing the Need for Computer-Based Information Systems in Healthcare through the Use of Self-Contained Organizational Units', in Orlikowski, W., Walsham, G., Jones, M. and De Gross, J. (eds), *Information Technology and Changes in Organizational Work*, London, Chapman & Hall.

Lyotard, J.-F. (1986), *The Postmodern Condition: A Report on Knowledge*, Manchester, Manchester University Press.

Maturana, H. and Varela, F. (1987), *The Tree of Knowledge: The Biological Roots of Human Understanding*, Boston, Shambhala.

McCarthy, T. (1978), *The Critical Theory of Jürgen Habermas.*, Cambridge, Mass., MIT Press.

Murdick, R.G.C., J.R.; Joel, E.R. (1990), *Introduction to Management Information Systems*, (2nd Edition), Columbus, Ohio, Publishing Horizons Inc.

Nietzsche, F. (1967), *The Will to Power*, New York, Vintage Books.

Schultheis, R. and Summer, M. (1989), *Management Information Systems: The Manager's View*, Homewood, Boston, Irwin.

Simon, H.A. (1977), *The New Science of Management Decision* (2nd Edition), Englewood Cliffs, N.J., Prentice Hall.

Thierauf, R.L. (1987), *Effective Management Information Systems* (2nd Edition), Columbus. Ohio., Merrill Publishing Company.

Wittgenstein, L. (1956), *Philosophical investigations*, Oxford, Basil Blackwell.

7 Implications: so what and what now?

- *Introduction*
- *The anti-anti-story*
- *The manager in-the-world*
- *Information and understanding*
- *Management and manus*
- *Power as relation*
- *Envoi*

Introduction

Teaching is even more difficult than learning. We know that; but we rarely think about it. And why is teaching more difficult than learning? Not because the teacher must have a larger store of information and have it always ready. Teaching is more difficult than learning because what teaching calls for is this: to let learn. The real teacher, in fact, lets nothing else be learned than – learning. His conduct, therefore, often produces the impression that we properly learn nothing from him, if by "learning" we now suddenly understand merely the procurement of useful information.

Martin Heidegger

In the preceding chapters I have made an effort to recast the discussion of management, the manager and information into a non-functional, non-representational paradigm: as Heidegger suggested, to return to the things themselves. This was not an easy task. The whole management language-game, management-speak, is pervaded with the ghosts of Descartes and Taylor. We have deeply rooted beliefs in words such as manage, think, understand, know, decide, information, and so forth. It is ever so easy to fall back into the old, now so seemingly obvious, terminology and notions; an orthodoxy for management thinking that was mostly articulated in the age of the Enlightenment. The effort to avoid drawing on this obvious and widely understood lexicon may have made this book rather obscure at points. Also there might still be a lot of Descartes' and Taylor's ghosts

176

hiding in the very attempts to critique them, since our own assumptions only become manifest in our doing and in our speaking or writing and thus we do not have direct access to them. Re-engineering assumptions is not a matter of merely 'rewiring' through a set of eloquent arguments. Assumptions are rooted in our being, part of our body (Polanyi, 1973). To change them may even require something akin to a religious conversion as Burrell and Morgan (1979) have argued.

I would expect a whole host of reactions and interpretations to flow from this book. From hermeneutics has come the understanding that there can be no correct or final interpretation, only individual appropriations. With this in mind I will attempt to rethink some of the implications of the arguments developed in the preceding chapters. How should we think differently if we take the view of the *involved manager*?

Obviously, the purpose of this chapter is not to outline every conclusion and every implication. If what I have said has made sense, then you, the reader, will already understand, will have some sense of a significant whole, and be able to articulate your own view. On the other hand it may be useful to enter the hermeneutic circle one more time, to contextualize again in a different format, some of the main issues at hand.

The anti-anti-story

One line of contention against the arguments put forward in this book could be that there are many, seemingly successful, management information systems out there. There also seems to be no stopping of investment in huge information systems development projects. This may, therefore, lead to the conclusion that there must be something of value in these systems; it may seem that they do work at a particular level of analysis. Yet, these systems were designed and built using the very assumptions and methods that this book calls in question – the rational manager, decision making, representations, etc. This does seem to suggest that there is something 'right' in them; that these assumptions and methods are legitimate descriptions of reality. This is a valid argument that needs to be addressed.

There are many ways to respond to this argument. A simple response could be that no-one really knows whether these systems are successful or not. The issue of information system success is so fraught with problems of definition and measurement that there is still no approach for the determination of such success that has even a moderate level of acceptance across the information systems community. It could also be argued that, irrespective of the intentions and assumptions of the original designers, the systems will always serve a certain purpose in the occurrent mode for instance: perturbations; evidence in arguments about validity claims; pieces of discourse to draw on in the micro-physics of power; or evidence to reify actions that were already based on tacit know-how. They do not serve so much to *inform* the involved manager as they serve to generate resources to facilitate the maintenance of social integration and integration – identity and structural coupling – with the rest of the system. *Hence, they are socially and politically significant but not hermeneutically significant* as was assumed in the world view of the rational manager.

This sort of argument can also be made for many other management interventions, such as business process re-engineering, total quality management and empowerment. Irrespective of the intentions of the original exponents of these ideas, and of the actual manifestations of them in different organizations, they will always be appropriated as resources in the structuring of relations of power (Bloomfield, 1992). They will serve as opportunities for creating alliances, outflanking translation attempts and renegotiation and refixing of the rules, as players attempt to fix obligatory passage points through circuits of system and social integration (Callon, 1986).

It is not that the rational manager world view is wrong and the involved manager world view is right; just as it is not that Newton's mechanics is wrong and quantum mechanics is right. Although Newton's mechanics worked well on directly observable systems, it collapsed when applied to the sub-atomic world. For the observable world, the approximations and assumptions made, mostly implicitly, by Newton's theory held good. However, later, at a different level of resolution, these approximations proved to be untenable. What was an appropriate theory on one level of resolution was not appropriate on another. In a similar way functionalism at a certain level of analysis is valid and useful. When information use and information systems are studied from an observer point of view, managers seem to make decisions and they do seem to use information in some way in this process. However, this is only an approximation that will break down once an attempt is made to understand the phenomena 'from the inside'. It is to this understanding 'from the inside' that this book is intended to contribute.

Hence, the issue is not to stop thinking about and developing systems, using the ideas of functionalism *per se*; it is rather to desist from ignoring the collapse of the, always present, approximations at another levels of analysis. It is necessary, in order to understand information and information systems in-the-world, to acknowledge the need to move to a more primal level of analysis. We need to return our thinking from whence it originated; the real world of the daily coping and doing in-the-world. This new resolution demands that that the work of Heidegger, (1962), Foucault (1977), Polanyi (1973), Gadamer (1989), Varela (1987) and others seeking to push forward the frontier of understanding the world in its world-ness, is taken seriously. Returning our understanding to the world 'as it is' does not, as functionalism would hold, require ever more empirical work. Since more empirical work will only lead to:

more observer descriptions;

more objects (data models, decisions, problem-solving, controlling) as described by subjects (managers, analysts, information systems academics);

more models in a discourse already saturated with models;

more abstractions, lifeless and devoid of context;

more representations of representations of representations...;

...

We do not need more data; we need a more primordial understanding, more thinking. Forcing the real to become an object (a representation or a model) before a subject (reason and senses); to present itself on and in our terms, will only make our science more hyper-real (Baudrillard, 1983). We need to go beyond our models and abstractions, to return to the *real-ness of the real* or the *Being of being*, as Heidegger calls it. Where exactly this will take us is not at all clear. What is clear, however, is that more of the same will just add to the confusion.

The first step to this overcoming of our representations is to change our thinking, or as Heidegger might argue, to *start thinking*. Not thinking as thinking about, but thinking as *thinking through*; as *pondering* (Heidegger, 1968). Let us then ponder some of the emerging insights that we came to in the muddling through that we attempted on our journey towards understanding management and information in-the-world.

The manager in-the-world

The manager in-the-world emerged as always already *involved* in the world. The manager's actions and 'decisions' cannot be understood by isolating them. The manager does not act or decide intentionally. Intentionally here refers to the idea that managers first have an idea in their heads and then act according to it. Thinking and doing cannot be separated as was argued, by reference to Wittgenstein and Heidegger, in Chapter 6. Decisions emerge, open up, as logical *next steps* in the involvement whole, because the manager always already knows-how in-the-world. A level of intentionality only occurs in the occurrent mode of being. This intentionality is strategic; it is directed at translating other's actions, ideas, arguments into favourable obligatory passage points. In this political play, decision making is a *staging* (Goffman, 1959) for the purpose of translating; a matter of securing alliances for actions already tacitly understood in-order-to get the job done.

In dwelling in-the-world the specific decisions and actions of the manager dissolve into the involvement whole as ready-to-hand. Managers mostly, therefore, when questioned afterwards cannot say why they have selected one specific course of action and not another; that is, accept in the sense of creating a legitimization story. If confronted they may try to reconstruct the significance or rationale for their actions, that was available in their doing, to try and explain, or construct, a rationale that lay behind them. For managers, however, the specific decision or action seemed available and significant in that it related to the toward-which, which meant, "it seemed like the right thing to do". Actions do not derive their primal rationality from detached reflection or rationalization, their rationality is in the *sense* of the involvement whole. The manager *knows* what to do or decide because the manager is always already involved in-the-world. Hence being-in-the-world is the managers most primordial sense of knowing and hence the default, and tacit, source for decision-in-action.

Information and decisions

Managers do not use data to make or manufacture decisions according to a plan, framework or model. They use data from the information system and other sources, as equipment – equipment in-order-to get the job done. However, the daily production report is not equipment as such; it is only equipment within an equipment whole. The daily production report only makes sense in its referring to other equipment such as machines, production schedules, production meetings, production targets, actual production units and the factory floor. The production manager will only make sense of the report by using it in-order-to get the job done; in-order-to produce an agenda for the production meeting; in-order-to set up targets; in-order-to develop production schedules; in-order-to negotiate with the union; and so on. In using it, the report will withdraw. Detached reflection on the report would not make it available, only as part of the involvement whole will it become significant.

In moments of dislocation, when the world is momentarily unavailable, the manager will use information to interpret the world. This information will however not give the manager *additional* understanding of the world. It will only enable the possibilities already understood by the involved manager to show up. Without the involvement whole the information will remain a set of occurrent texts and will not make sense. This is the major problem with management information systems today. As the manager's world becomes more and more occurrent or fragmented, superficial and *ad hoc* (Mintzberg, 1980), the only option available to the manager is to engage in political play *about* the world. This may be the reason why there is a rapid increase in explicit political behaviour in higher and higher levels of the hierarchy of an organization. An interesting issue is how this is effected by the process of delayering that so many organizations are experiencing?

It has been argued, and rightly so, that one of the primal functions of middle management is to act as a hermeneutic bridge to interpret the operational form of life into the boardroom form of life, to the degree that this is possible. They are in some sense involved in both forms of life. This involves the mediation of meanings to make them relatively commensurable. This management of the incommensurability of the two forms of life is one of the taxing tasks of middle management, only indirectly related to supervision or control according to the Taylor world view. Who will perform this task if this layer is removed? Is our traditional notion of the middle management role not too narrow? Will politically astute top managers be able to manage this incommensurability? Will the skilled professional also have to become more actively involved in the politics? Will this be at the expense of decision-in-action? There seem to be many issues that need thinking through.

Decisions and decision support systems

That decisions are not made but emerge as significant next steps in the involvement whole, raises questions as to the purpose of decision support systems. For the involved manager the decision support systems can, in moments of unavailability, provide a platform for interpretation, for working out the possibilities of the world already understood. This will however require that the systems will have to meet the following conditions: they will have to be available in-the-world, as part of the doing; and they must be embedded in the language and form-of-life of the involved manager. From these requirements it may be concluded that the daily conversations with the other involved members are probably a better form of decision support system than formal modelling via a computerized system. In the formal occurrent mode the decision support system will most likely be useful in providing evidence to contest validity claims; provided, of course, that they are accepted as valid evidence in the first place. Therefore it would follow *that decision support systems are politically significant but not hermeneutically significant*. The same is true for group decision support systems. They will again mostly function at the level of discourse *about the world*. This discourse may influence our know-how in doing but not in a way the we can 'know', even when we reflect on it.

It will always be doubtful what the outcome will be of using such devices as decision rooms, brain-storming tools and electronic meeting systems. All that can be said is that they can be expected to generate perturbations. Not that generating perturbations is unuseful, indeed it is essential, but it will always be ateleological. The most important and significant conclusion is that decision support systems and group decision support systems will not, in any significant way, *determine* decisions; they may provide evidence in discourse, they may also provide resources for political play, but they will not be significant for actions (decisions) in-the-world. If this is true, this calls into question the purpose and use of this information technology. Does it need to be abandoned altogether? Or, maybe it needs to be refocused. This may imply that the political role is explicitly accepted and the development efforts redirected towards this. Or, it may imply that the notion of an all-inclusive system is abandoned for a more pragmatic involved perspective of supplying ready-to-hand tools available in the involvement whole.

Representations and systems development

If managers mostly do not know, in the sense of having representations of what, and why, they do (decide) things, is there a purpose to requirement and decision analysis or any reason to do it at all? Maybe requirement analysis usefulness does not stem from the fact that the analyst can create representations – data flow diagrams or entity relationship models – from it; maybe its usefulness is in the distinctions of distinctions (language) that it (re-)creates. In trying to articulate the process to the analyst the manager begins to make explicit what she already knows tacitly. Hence, it is useful as a process of languaging in-the-world, not as a process of modelling about the world. This may be why managers frequently find the analysis process useful even though they may not use the eventual system. The question then remains whether it is worth going through the process of actually developing the computerized management information system when the value may be in the process of languaging through analysis.

If information, or rather data, does not determine decisions why develop elaborate systems for its provision at all? Data, in as much as it is available in-the-world will be mediated by the always already existing commitments or alliances. However, data may generate perturbations; data may provide evidence in contesting validity claims; and data may provide resources for political play. Therefore systems for generating represent-ations are useful, but not in terms of thinking of the manager as a system working with, and having representations, as knowing the world through representations. The involved manager knows the world before representation. We should become more realistic about what we are doing and why when building information systems. It is the line between world and representations of world that has become somewhat blurred. Keeping the *epistemological accounting* right ought to avoid a lot of confusion (Varela, 1984).

Representations, management and organization

It was argued that the level of representations needed for control is linked to the degree of Cartesian and Taylorist dualism present. Or, the greater the separation between thinking and doing the more acute the need for representations. If it is true that there is a move towards a knowledge work environment where skilled professionals manage themselves, should one expect a proportionate reduction in representations (formal information systems)? The answer to the question is not simple. The short answer is yes. The long answer is maybe not. Yes, there will be a reduced level of representations for *control*. However, the shift from the machine notion of control to the autopoietic, implies that the status of representations shift from command and control to languaging. In the autopoietic environment the emphasis is on *co-ordination* and not control. Thus, we will see, as is already apparent, a shift from management information systems to collaborative technology such as inter and intranet, computer supported co-operative work (CSCW), and so forth.

This conclusion leads to another issue that flows from the analysis. If organizations are increasingly downsized and outsourced, more and more smaller nodes working together – the so-called networked organization – what about involvement, form of life, and languaging? These notions have a sense of 'doing things *together*', in time and space. How will we communicate, and what will be the meanings of our language in this new form of organization? If most of what is shared are representations will there be any involvement whole? It seems as if such a world will only be more and more superficial, *ad hoc*, and fragmented. One could go on and on with this line of reasoning. The analysis of the involved manager suggests a challenging critique against notions such as the virtual organiz-ation, networked organizations, computer supported co-operative work, electronic meetings, and so forth. At least the analysis indicates the limits of these notions and technologies.

Information and understanding

Information is not the transformation of data; transformation is an observer point of view. Information, in its more primordial sense, is understanding in-the-world. However, this is not understanding as having an accurate picture of the facts or state of affairs, it is understanding as knowing how to. It is understanding rooted in, and made significant by, the set of commitments and involvements in which the manager is always already immersed; the involvement whole from which she speaks and towards which she is spoken. It is the endowment of meaning, not in the sense of a dictionary definition that merely points to others, but meaning as knowing how to act, what to do, in-the-world. We, as observers, can only know that someone understands if that person acts appropriately in the context of the doing. Understanding is an internal coherence that cannot be determined by any single perturbation or datum. Understanding is always mediated through the process of appropriation in-the-world.

Information and representation

Any representational systems, such as a symbolic processor like a computer, cannot provide information. It can only provide data for perturbations, for appropriation, and for talking about the world. The output of any computerized information system will only become significant in as much as it is already in-the-world. If this groundedness in-the-world is lost the data will become *hyper real*. As Baudrillard (1983, p.2) explains: "Abstraction today is no longer that of the map, the double, the mirror or the concept. Simulation is no longer that of a territory, a referential being or a substance. *It is the generation by models of a real without origin or reality: a hyper real.* The territory no longer precedes the map. Nor survives it. Henceforth, it is the map that precedes the territory – PRECESSION OF SIMULACRA – it is *the map that engenders the territory...*" (emphasis added). In the hyper-real rep-resentation, representation becomes an end in itself. This sense of information as generated by computerized information systems is already current. Taylorist managers often believe the computer generated report to be more correct (more real) than reality itself. The models in the decision support systems are more real than the opinions of others. The system is taken to be objective and real. For Taylorist managers there is a one-to-one mapping between the representations and the reality, even to the degree that the models *is* the reality. For them the computer is an objective and value-free mirror of the reality.

This hyper-real notion of information misses the heart of this discussion. There is a many-to-many mapping between the world and representations and all mappings are not equal. The computerized information system is a political artefact; through its chosen representations it is always already serving someone's interest. Access to the design process may create a powerful opportunity to structure regimes of truth in the organization. The value choices of the designers are coded into the system. The data definitions become organizational definitions. The users select from the system that which supports their validity claims, that which supports their attempts to fix obligatory passage points. To lose sight of this is to journey in the realm of the hyper real.

Management and manus

First-order cybernetics suggests that when the control system is located *outside* of the system, as in the Taylorist dualism, then a paradox emerges in that the manager cannot control the organization without paying for it in terms of the organization's ability to respond to the environment (market); the manager is part of a zero sum game. Hence, for the organization to be structurally coupled with the environment the concept of the manager as external controller must be eliminated. This opens the way for the notion of self-control. Variety can only be absorbed by locating control *in* the system. This view of management *in* the system is best captured in the root concept of management – management as *manus*, the always already present and involved hand.

In management as *manus* the Taylorist dualism is collapsed and the emphasis on, or rather the need for, representation disappears. Management shifts from being the decision making black box to the doing hand in-the-world. Management as *manus* points to the idea of treating social systems (the individuals and the organization) as autopoietic systems. As autopoietic systems their behaviours are not determined by inputs. They do not transform input (instructions, plans, goals, etc.) into actions in any determinate way. Therefore, any environment can only influence them, not determine them. The degree of the influence will depend on the sense of identity or internal coherence of the system and the intensity of the interactions with the environment.

Planning and controlling in-the-world

Planning and controlling, like decision making, is an observer perspective. Planning assumes behaviour and representations that are not *part of* the autopoietic organization. Does this mean that managers should not plan? That the whole business about strategic management is a waste of time? The utility of planning parallels that of analysis for, and the use of, information systems. Managers may get benefit from a planning process but it is not from the plans. The process of planning makes sense in two ways.

First, it is the opportunity for the participants to articulate their tacit know-how. It is a space in which to discover and to share what they already know tacitly. This may potentially be of great benefit to them and to the others participating in the process, especially when they, later, in moments of unavailableness have to interpret the world again. Second, as was argued about decision making, planning could be seen as a politically significant process and not a significant doing process. Managers plan in-order-to create opportunities and resources in-order-to translate action, ideas and arguments into obligatory passage points and not to know or determine what to do.

By shifting from the observer perspective of planning to the involved perspective, planning becomes crafting in Mintzberg's terms (1994), or tinkering as put forward by Claudio Ciborra (1994; 1996). Planning shifts from trying to find the rationally best alternative to negotiating meanings, translating actions, building alliances and fixing obligatory passage points. Planning becomes a political playing field of moves and counter-moves, where gains are small and momentary. For the involved manager the process of planning can unwittingly open opportunities that may change the moves and the rules of the game; hence, there can be no final moves.

Management, language and action

To manage social systems, from an autopoietic point of view, requires understanding of the interrelationship between three concepts, languaging, identity and structural coupling. Without identity or internal coherence the system will dissolve into the environment. Identity becomes the basis for structural coupling. Whilst maintaining identity, the system must structurally drift with the environment. If severed from the environment the system will die. The way to maintain identity and structural coupling in social systems is through languaging. Languaging is the process that binds them together.

Identity, in social systems, is a set of tacit and negotiated distinctions. These distinctions are created, and recreated in organizational languaging, in the involvement whole, in and through hermeneutic appropriation and organizational dialogue. They are not created in logos, or mission statements, or annual reports, but in the languaging of everyday practice. Only if the logos, mission statements and annual reports, make sense in the involvement whole will they function as meaningful distinctions. Maintaining the systems identity is, therefore, not a matter of labelling, it is a matter of *infusing* it with the local logic, of embedding it in the everyday work practice, the micro-physics of power.

The essence of structural coupling is *interaction*. Every minute variation in the environment must be absorbed or appropriated by the system. Hence the structure of the system will have to change, without risk to its identity. The structural drift of the system cannot be predicted since there is a co-evolution that is taking place between the organization and the environment. Languaging creates the distinctions that make social action possible; social action creates the distinctiveness that makes language possible. In human systems, there cannot be language without social action and there cannot be social action without language. It is in and through organizational dialogue and discourse that the world of work, and of play, become real. Therefore the most important task for management is to create opportunities for languaging. Strategic planning sessions, or quality circles, or customer satisfaction programmes, may used for building these. None of these initiatives or interventions, or their equivalents in other blueprints for success, works because they are right. They work because they generate an opportunity for languaging; opportunity to develop, whether by consensus or coercion, or socially agreed distinctions.

This description of languaging above is not complete. Languaging is itself always already *in* the network of power. Distinctions are not only categories for co-ordinating interaction, they are also pieces of discourse for translating action and creating obligatory passage points. By fixing distinctions, recourses for translation are created. By creating the category of unskilled worker (or executive) in the personnel administration system, a particular level of remuneration is made legitimate and can be drawn upon in translations; "we pay him that because he *is* after all an unskilled worker (or an executive)."

By creating distinctions about good or desirable outcomes (the so-called performance measures) in the organization, categories of legitimation are created, or *regimes of truth* in Foucault's terminology. Such evaluative distinctions could be extremely arbitrary, or be based on very precise measurements. In either case by making them particular sets of behaviours are set up as passages points for translations. They also become focus points for outflanking. Because they are both medium and outcome they may serve to generate a whole set of behaviours in other dimensions that effectively cancels the translation effect. The categories themselves may even become the resources that are used for the outflanking, as is the case with the "work to rule" type industrial action.

Languaging is as much a resource for power as a resource for co-ordination and co-operation. In this perspective there cannot be enduring stable points. All stability will be momentary; that is, unless power becomes pervasive through mass surveillance and discipline and the Taylorist dualism is rigorously reinstituted, as it may be in a bureaucracy. These organizations can only survive in the absence of competition. With the emergence of globalization and the increased pressure against interventions by the nation state, this would not seem to be a viable option for the future.

Power as relation

Managers are not autonomous rational agents who merely receive prepackaged information to utilize in objective and neutral decision making. Managers are always already in the net of power. They cannot escape it. Chapter 5 followed Foucault in arguing that the manager *as a manager* is already one of the prime effects of power. The manager can never 'get out' of or distance herself from the circular grid of power. This is part of being-in-the-world. To *rise above power* is a useless abstraction. Hence, research programmes and development efforts about decision support systems that postulate a neutral, rational and localized agent out-of-the-world as their prototype of a decision maker are bound to fail.

Power is not located. It may from time to time come together to create nodes of agencies that seem to be located. These nodes may however disappear as contingent factors change the rules of the game. Depending on the horizon selected, these changes may be slow or very rapid. This should, however, lead to the belief that power is located. Every point of power is simultaneously a point of resistance and power is maintained by points of resistance. There is only power and counter-power. It is in and through this play of force relations that every manager must get the job done.

Power and information

Through interpretation the manager's understanding of the world can be made explicit, be worked out. Yet, this individual understanding can only be made socially explicit if it can be translated into the actions of others. Understanding is a necessary but not a sufficient requirement for successful translation. To translate individual understanding into social action requires relations of power. When understanding enters this mode of being it becomes occurrent, representations *about* the world. The indexial nature of the relationship between the representation and the world becomes the field of political play. Nodes of power draw on the rules and techniques of discipline to fix obligatory passage points. In this occurrent and political mode information cannot be located, except for brief moments. It does not have *a* location as such. Information, as opportunities for translation, has the potential to momentarily emerge in unexpected events and situations. Non-sense in one moment can become sense in the next. It is in this mode that information has the potential to become hyper real. However, the hyper-reality will always be constrained by the ability to act in-the-world, know-how in being-in.

Envoi

It ought to be clear by now that this book is not about recipes and frameworks for successful management information systems development. This book is about thinking and learning: thinking in writing and learning in thinking. It is a leap of faith. I do not claim to have seen it all or have thought it all. I only claim to have tried very hard to think differently; to create an alternative story, that of the *involved manager*, at least as compelling as the current story of the rational manager. The book has proved nothing and I cannot write *quod erat demonstrandum*. I cannot even claim that it is entirely coherent. All I can claim is that it is an alternative story that, to me, better describes managers I know and myself as a manager. The ultimate legitimacy of this alternative story will be the degree to which it makes sense to others – and the extent to which it becomes available to others in-their-world, and that its ideas become equipment in-order-to get the job done.

References

Baudrillard, J. (1983), *Simulations*, New York, Semiotext(e).

Bloomfield, B.P., and Best, A. (1992), 'Management Consultants: Systems Development, Power and the Translation of Problems', *The Sociological Review*, 40, 3, 533-560.

Burrell, G. and Morgan, G. (1979), *Sociological Paradigms and Organizational Analysis*, Portsmouth, New Hampshire, Heinemann.

Callon, M. (1986), 'Some Elements of a Sociology of Translation: Domestification of the Scallops and the Fishermen of St Brieuc Bay', in Law, J. (ed.), *Power, Action and Belief: A New Sociology of Knowledge?*, London, Routledge and Kegan Paul.

Ciborra, C.U. (1994), 'The Grassroots of IT and Strategy', in Ciborra, C. and Jelassi, T. (eds), *Strategic Information Systems: A European Perspective*, Chichester, J. Wiley & Sons.

Ciborra, C.U. (1996), 'Improvisation and Information Technology in Organizations', *ICIS*, Cleveland

Foucault, M. (1977), 'Truth and Power', *in* Gordon, C. (ed.), *Power / Knowledge: Selected Interviews & Other Writings 1972-1977*, New York, Pantheon Books.

Gadamer, H.-G. (1989), *Truth and method* (2nd revised Edition), London, Sheed and Ward.

Goffman, E. (1959), *The Presentation of Self in Everyday life*, London, Penguin.

Heidegger, M. (1962), *Being and time*, Oxford, Basil Blackwell.

Heidegger, M. (1968), *What is Called Thinking*, New York, Harper & Row.

Maturana, H. and Varela, F. (1987), *The Tree of Knowledge: The Biological Roots of Human Understanding*, Boston, Shambhala.

Mintzberg, H. (1980), *The Nature of Managerial Work*, Englewood Cliffs, New Jersey, Prentice Hall Inc.

Mintzberg, H. (1994), 'The Fall and Rise of Strategic Planning', *Harvard Business Review*, Jan-Feb, 107-114.

Polanyi, M. (1973), *Personal Knowledge: Towards a Post-critical Philosophy* (1st pbk Edition), London, Routledge & Kegan Paul.

Varela, F. (1984), 'Two Principles for Self-Organization', in Ulrich, H. and Probst, G.J. (eds), *Self-organization and management of social systems*, Berlin, Springer-Verlag.

Selected bibliography

Ackoff, R.L. (1967), 'Management Misinformation Systems', *Management Science*, 14, 4, 147-156.

Ackoff, R.L. (1971), 'Towards a System of Systems Concepts', *Management Science*, 17, 11, 83-90.

Ackoff, R.L. (1989), 'From Data to Wisdom: Presidential Address to ISGSR', *Journal of Applied Systems Analysis*, 16, June, 3-9.

Ahituv, N. and Neumann, S. (1990), *Principles of Information Systems for Management*, Dubuque, Wm.C. Brown Publ.

ALA (1991), 'London Ambulances: A Service in Crisis', London, ALA: Association of London Authorities.

Anderson, R. (1991), 'Information and Systems', *Journal of Applied Systems Analysis*, 18, 57-60.

Anthony, R.N. (1965), *Planning and Control Systems: A Framework for Analysis*, Boston, Harvard University Press.

Argyris, C. (1977), 'Organisational Learning and Management Information Systems', *Accounting, Organisation and Society*, 2, 2, 113-123.

Argyris, C. (1993), *Knowledge for Action*, San Francisco, Jossey-Bass.

Aristotle (1962), *Nicomachean Ethics*, Indianapolis, Bobbs-Merrill Publ.

Ashby, W.R. (1957), *An Introduction to Cybernetics*, New York, John Wiley & Sons.

Austin, J.L. (1962), *How To Do Things With Words*, Boston, Harvard University Press.

Avgerou, C. and Cornford, T. (1995), 'Limitations of Information Systems Theory and Practice: A Case for Pluralism', in Falkenberg, E. (ed.), *Information Systems Concepts: Towards a consolidation of views*, London, Chapman & Hall.

Banville, C. and Landry, M. (1989), 'Can the Field of MIS be Disciplined?', *Communications of the ACM*, 32, 1, 48-60.

Barbalet, J.M. (1987), 'Power, Structural Resources and Agency', *Perspectives in Social Theory*, 8, 1-24.

Barrett, W. (1958), *The Irrational Man: A Study in Existential Philosophy*, London, Heinemann.

Bateson, G. (1972), *Steps to the Ecology of Mind*, Northvale, Jason Aronson Inc.

Baudrillard, J. (1983), *Simulations*, New York, Semiotext(e).

Beer, S. (1966), *Decision and Control*, New York, John Wiley & Sons.

Beer, S. (1985), *Diagnosing the System for Organizations*, New York, John Wiley & Sons.

Bernstein, R.J. (1983), *Beyond Objectivism and Relativism: Science, Hermeneutics and Praxis*, London, Basil Blackwell.

Bertalanffy Von, L. (1968), *General Systems Theory*, Braziller.

Beynon-Davies, P. (1993), 'The London Ambulance Service's Computerised Dispatch System: A Case Study in Information Systems Failure', Pontypridd, University of Glamorgan.

Bloomfield, B.P., & Best, A. (1992), 'Management Consultants: Systems Development, Power and the Translation of Problems', *The Sociological Review*, 40, 3, 533-560.

Bogdan, R. and Taylor, S.J. (1975), *Introduction to Qualitative Research Methods: a Phenomenological Approach to the Social Sciences*, New York, Wiley-Interscience.

Boland, R.J. (1983), 'The In-Formation of Information Systems', in Boland, R.J. and Hirschheim, R.A. (eds), *Critical Issues in Information Systems Research*, New York, John Wiley & Sons.

Boland, R.J. (1993), 'Accounting and the Interpretive Act', *Accounting, Organizations and Society*, 18, 2/3, 125-146.

Boland, R.J. and Tenkasi, R.V. (1993), 'Locating Meaning Making in Organizational Learning: The narrative basis of cognition', *Research in Organizational Change and Development*, 7, 77-103.

Burch, G.C. and Grudnitski, G. (1989), *Information Systems: Theory and Practice* (5th Edition), New York, John Wiley & Sons.

Burrell, G. and Morgan, G. (1979), *Sociological Paradigms and Organizational Analysis*, Portsmouth, New Hampshire, Heinemann.

Callon, M. (1986), 'Some Elements of a Sociology of Translation: Domestification of the Scallops and the Fishermen of St Brieuc Bay', in Law, J. (ed.), *Power, Action and Belief: A New Sociology of Knowledge?*, London, Routledge and Kegan Paul.

Callon, M. (1991), 'Techno-Economic Networks and Irreversibility', *in* Law, J. (ed.), *A Sociology of Monsters: Essays on Power, Technology and Domination*, London, Routledge.

Campbell, J. (1982), *Grammatical Man: Information, Entropy, Language and Life*, New York, Simon and Schuster.

Capra, F. (1982), *The Turning Point: Science, Society and the Rising Culture*, London, Fontana Paperbacks.

Carlson, S. (1951), *Executive Behaviour: A Study of the Work Load and Working Methods of Managing Directors*, Stockholm, Strombergs.

Churchman, C.W. (1968), *The Systems Approach*, New York, Delacorte Press.

Churchman, C.W. (1971), *The Design of Inquiring Systems: Basic Concepts of Systems and Organization*, New York, Basic Books Inc.

Ciborra, C.U. (1994), 'The Grassroots of IT and Strategy', in Ciborra, C. and Jelassi, T. (eds), *Strategic Information Systems: A European Perspective*, Chichester, J. Wiley & Sons.

Ciborra, C.U. (1996), 'Improvisation and Information Technology in Organizations', *ICIS*, Cleveland.

Clegg, S.R. (1989), *Frameworks of Power*, London, Sage Publications Ltd.

Daft, R.L. and Weick, K.E. (1984), 'Toward a Model of Organizations as Interpretation Systems', *Academy of Management Review*, 9, 2, 284-295.

Dahl, R.A. (1957), 'The Concept of Power', *Behavioural Science*, 2, 201-205.

Dahl, R.A. (1961), *Who Governs? Democracy and Power in an American City*, New Haven, Yale University Press.

Dahl, R.A. (1968), 'Power', *International Encyclopaedia of the Social Sciences*, 405-415.

Davis, G.B. (1974), *Management Information Systems: Conceptual Foundations, Structure and Development* (2nd Edition), London, McGraw-Hill.

Davis, G.B. and Olsen, M.H. (1985), *Management Information Systems: Conceptual Foundations, Structure and Development* (2nd Edition), London, McGraw-Hill.

Deluze, G. (1986), *Foucault*, Minneapolis, University of Minnesota Press.

DeProspo, E.R. (1983), *Data and Information*, Rutgers, Rutgers School of Communication, Information and Library Studies.

Derrida, J. (1982), *"Differance", Margins of Philosophy*, Chicago, University of Chicago Press.

Donnelly, J.H. and Gibson, J.L. (1990), *Fundamentals of Management*, Homewood, Boston., BPI Irwin.

Dreyfus, H.L. (1991), *Being-in-the-world: a Commentary on Heidegger's Being and time, Division I*, Cambridge, Mass, MIT Press.

Dreyfus, H.L. and Dreyfus, S.E. (1986), *Mind over Machine: The Power of Human Intuition and Expertise in the Era of the Computer* (Paperback edition, with Tom Athanasiou Edition), New York, The Free Press.

Dreyfus, H.L. and Rabinow, P. (1983), *Michel Foucault: Beyond Structuralism and Hermeneutics* (2nd Edition), Chicago, The University of Chicago Press.

Drucker, P.F. (1967), *The Effective Executive*, London, Pan Books in association with Heinemann.

Drucker, P.F. (1974), *Management: Tasks, Responsibilities and Practices*, London, Heinemann.

Drucker, P.F. (1978), *The Age of Discontinuity: Guidelines to our Changing Society*, New York, Harper and Row.

Drucker, P.F. (1978), *Post-capitalist society*, Oxford, Butterworth-Heinemann Ltd.

Drucker, P.F. (1980), *Managing in Turbulent Times*, Oxford, Butterworth-Heinemann.

Duffy, M. (1993), 'London's Embarrassing Mistake', *Journal*.

Earl, M. (1989), *Management Strategies for Information Technology*, New York, Prentice Hall (UK).

Fayol, H. (1949), *General and Industrial Management*, London, Pitman Publ.

Feldman, M.S. and March, J.G. (1981), ' Information in Organizations as Signal and Symbol', *Administrative Science Quarterly*, 26, 171-186.

Feyerabend, P. (1975), *Against Method*, London , Verso.

Feyerabend, P. (1978), *Science in a Free Society*, London , NLB.

Feyerabend, P. (1993), *Against method* (3rd Edition), London, Verso.

Flood, R.L. and Carson, E.R. (1988), *Dealing with Complexity*, New York, Plenum Press.

Flood, R.L. and Jackson, M.C. (1988), 'Cybernetics and Organization Theory: A Critical Review', *Cybernetics and Systems: An International Journal*, 19, 13-33.

Foucault, M. (1977), 'Truth and Power', in Gordon, C. (ed.), *Power / Knowledge: Selected Interviews & Other Writings 1972-1977*, New York, Pantheon Books.

Foucault, M. (1977), 'Two Lectures', in Gordon, C. (ed.), *Power / Knowledge: Selected Interviews & Other Writings 1972-1977*, New York, Pantheon Books.

Foucault, M. (1980), *The History of Sexuality; Volume I: An Introduction*, New York, Vintage Books.

Foucault, M. (1983), 'The Subject and Power', in Dreyfus, H.L. and Rabinow, P. (eds), *Michel Foucault: Beyond Structuralism and Hermeneutics*, Chicago, The University of Chicago Press.

Foucault, M. (1984), 'Nietzsche, Genealogy, History', *in* Rabinow, P. (ed.), *The Foucault Reader*, Middlesex, England, Penguin Books.

Franz, C.R. and Robey, D. (1984), 'An Investigation of User-led System Design: Rational and Political perspectives', *Communications of the ACM*, 27, 12, 1202-1209.

Gadamer, H.-G. (1989), *Truth and method* (2nd revised Edition), London, Sheed and Ward.

Gadamer, H.G. (1988), 'On the Circle of Understanding', in Connolly, J.M. and Keutner, T. (eds), *Hermeneutics vs Science? Three German Views*, Notre Dame, Indiana, University of Notre Dame Press.

Gelven, M. (1970), *A Commentary on Heidegger's "Being and Time"*, New York, Harper & Row.

Gemmill, G. and Smith, C. (1985), 'A Dissipative Structure Model of Organization Transformation', *Human Relations*, 38, 8, 751-766.

Gharajedaghi, J. and Ackoff, R.L. (1984), 'Mechanisms, Organisms and Social Systems', *Strategic Management Journal*, 5, 289-300.

Giddens, A. (1984), *The Constitution of Society*, Berkeley, University of California Press.

Giles, L. (1910), *Sun Tzu on the Art of War*, London, Luzac and Co.

Givon, T. (1989), *Mind, Code and Context: Essays in Pragmatics*, London, Lawrence Erlbaun Ass. Publ.

Gleik, J. (1987), *Chaos: Making a New Science*, London, Cardinal.

Goffman, E. (1959), *The Presentation of Self in Everyday life*, London, Penguin.

Gorry, G.A. and Scott Morton, M.S. (1971), 'A Framework for Management Information Systems', *Sloan Management Review*, Fall 1971, 55-70.

Habermas, J. (1979), *Communication and the Evolution of Society*, London, Heinemann Press.

Habermas, J. (1984), *The Theory of Communicative Action*, London, Heinemann Education.

Habermas, J. (1987), *The Theory of Communicative Action*, Cambridge, Polity.

Heidegger, M. (1962), *Being and time*, Oxford, Basil Blackwell.

Heidegger, M. (1968), *What is Called Thinking*, New York, Harper & Row.

Heidegger, M. (1971), *Poetry, Language, Thought*, New York, Harper & Row.

Heidegger, M. (1977), 'The Age of the World Picture', in Lovitt, W. (ed.), *The Question Concerning Technology and Other Essays*, New York, Harper & Row.

Heidegger, M. (1984), *The Metaphysical Foundations of Logic*, Bloomington, Indiana University Press.

Heidegger, M. (1988), *The Basic Problems of Phenomenology*, Bloomington, Indiana University Press.

Heidegger, M. (1992), *History of the Concept of Time*, Bloomington, Indiana University Press.

Hellriegel, D. and Slocum, J.W. (1989), *Management* (5th Edition), Reading Mass, Addison-Wesley.

Hickson, D.J., Higgins, C.R., Less, C.A., Schneck, R.E. and Pennings, J.M.A. (1971), 'A Strategic Contingencies Theory of Intraorganizational power', *Administrative Science Quarterly*, 16, 2, 216-229.

Hiley, D.R. (1984), 'Foucault and the Analysis of Power: Political Engagement without Liberal Hope or Comfort', *Praxis International*, 4, 2, 200.

Hirschheim, R. and Klein, H. (1994), 'Realizing Emancipatory Principles in Information Systems Development: The Case for ETHICS', *MIS Quarterly*, 18, 1, 83-109.

Hirschheim, R. and Klein, H.K. (1989), 'Four paradigms of information systems development', *Communications of the ACM*, 32, 10, 1199-1216.

Hirsh, E.D. (1976), *The Aims of Interpretation*, Chicago, The University of Chicago Press.

Hobbes, T. (1962), *Leviathan*, London, Collier-Macmillan.

Holt, D.H. (1987), *Management: Principles and Practices*, Englewood Cliffs, New Jersey, Prentice Hall International.

Hougham, M.G. (1995), 'London Ambulance Service', Henley, London, Henley Management College.

Hoy, D.C. (1978), *The Critical Circle: Literature, History and Philosophical Hermeneutics*, Berkeley, University of California Press.

Husserl, E. (1960), *Cartesian meditations: an introduction to phenomenology*, The Hague: Nijhoff, Nijhoff.

Introna, L.D. (1993), 'Information: A Hermeneutic Perspective', *The First European Conference on Information systems*, Henley-on-Thames, England.

Introna, L.D. (1994), 'Being, Technology and Progress: A Critique of InformationTechnology', in Baskerville, R., DeGross, J., Ngwenyama, O. and Smithson, S. (eds), *Transforming Organizations with Information Technology*, Amsterdam, North-Holland.

Isenberg, D.J. (1984), 'How Senior Manager Think', *Harvard Business Review*, Nov-Dec 1984.

Ives, B. and Olsen, M.H. (1984), 'User Involvement and MIS Success: A Review of Research', *Management Science*, 30, 5, 589-603.

Jantsch, E. (1980), *The Self-Organizing Universe: Scientific and Human Implications of the Emerging Paradigm of Evolution*, Oxford, Pergamon Press.

Klein, H.K. and Lyytinen, K. (1985), 'The Poverty of Scientism in Information Systems', in Mumford, E. and Hirschheim, R. (eds), *Research Methods in Information Systems*, Amsterdam, North-Holland.

Kockelmans, J.J. (1972), 'Language, Meaning, and Ek-sistence', in Kockelmans, J.J. (ed.), *On Heidegger and Language*, Evanston, Northwestern University Press.

Koontz, H. (1980), 'Commentary on the Management Theory Jungle-Nearly two Decades Later', in Koontz, H., O'Donnell, C. and Weihrich, H. (eds), *Management: A Book of Readings*, New York, McGraw-Hill Book Company.

Kreitner, R. (1989), *Management* (4th Edition), Boston, Mass., Houghton Mifflin Co.

Kuhn, T.S. (1970), *The Structure of Scientific Revolutions* (2nd Edition), Chicago, Ill., The University of Chicago Press.

Kuhn, T.S. (1977), *The Essential Tension: Selected Studies in Scientific Tradition and Change.*, Chicago, Ill., The University of Chicago Press.

Kuhn, T.S. (1977 [1964]), 'A function for thought experiments', in Kuhn, T.S. (ed.), *The essential tension: Selected studies in scientific tradition and change*, Chicago, University of Chicago Press.

Latour, B. (1991), 'Technology is society made durable', in Law, J. (ed.), *A Sociology of Monsters: Essays on Power, Technology and Domination*, Routledge, London.

Laudon, K.C. and Laudon, J.P. (1996), *Management Information Systems* (4th Edition), New York, Prentice Hall.

Lewis, C.T. and Short, C. (1879), *A Latin Dictionary: Founded on the Andrews' Edition of Freund's Latin Dictionary*, Oxford, Oxford at the Clarendon Press.

Leydesdorff, L. (1993), 'Is Society a Self-Organizing System', *Journal of Social and Evolutionary Systems*, 16, 3, 331-349.

Lockwood, D. (1964), 'Social Integration and System Integration', in Zoll-schan, C.K. and Hirsch, W. (eds), *Explorations in Social Change*, Routledge & Kegan Paul, London.

Louw, G. (1996), 'Reducing the Need fo Computer-Based Information Systems in Healthcare through the Use of Self-Contained Organizational Units', in Orlikowski, W., Walsham, G., Jones, M. and De Gross, J. (eds), *Information Technology and Changes in Organizational Work*, London, Chapman & Hall.

Lucas, H.C. (1984), 'Organizational Power and the Information Services department', *Communications of the ACM*, 27, 1, 1218-1226.

Luhmann, N. (1990), *Essays on self reference*, New York: Columbia University Press, Columbia University Press.

Lukes, S. (1974), *Power: A Radical View*, London, Macmillan.

Lyotard, J.-F. (1986), *The Postmodern Condition: A Report on Knowledge*, Manchester, Manchester University Press.

Lyytinen, K. (1986), *Information Systems Development as Social Action: Framework and critical implications*, University of Jyyvaskyla, Unpublished Ph.D. Thesis.

Machiavelli, N. (1958), *The Prince*, London, Everyman.

MacIntyre, A. (1981), *After Virtue: A Study in Moral Theory*, Notre Dame, Ind., University of Notre Dame Press.

Markus, M.L. (1983), 'Power, politics, and MIS implementation', *Communications of the ACM*, 26, 6, 430-444.

Markus, M.L. and Bjorn Andersen, N. (1987), 'Power over users: Its exercise by system professionals', *Communications of the ACM*, 30, 6, 498-504.

Maturana, H. and Varela, F. (1987), *The Tree of Knowledge: The Biological Roots of Human Understanding*, Boston, Shambhala.

Mayo, E. (1949), *The Social Problems of an Industrial Civilisation*, London, Routledge and Kegan Paul.

McCarthy, T. (1978), *The Critical Theory of Jürgen Habermas.*, Cambridge, MIT Press.

McGregor, D. (1960), *The Human Side of Enterprise*, New York, McGraw-Hill.

McGregor, D. (1966), *Leadership and Motivation*, Boston, NY, MIT Press.

McLeod, R. (1995), *Management Information Systems: A study of computer based information systems*, Englewoods Cliffs, NJ, Prentice Hall.

Mintzberg, H. (1980), *The Nature of Managerial Work*, Englewood Cliffs, New Jersey, Prentice Hall Inc.

Mintzberg, H. (1994), 'The Fall and Rise of Strategic Planning', *Harvard Business Review*, Jan-Feb, 107-114.

Monteiro, E., and Hanseth, O. (1995), 'Social Shaping of Information Infra-structure: On Being Specific About the Technology', in Orlikowski, W.J., Walsham, G., Jones, M.R. and DeGross, J.I. (eds), *Information Technology and Changes in Organizational Work*, Chapman & Hall., London.

Moravcsik, J.M.E. (1981), 'How do Words get their Meanings?', *The Journal of Philosophy*, LXXVIII, 1, 5-25.

Mumford, E. (1996), *Systems Design: Ethical Tools for Ethical Change*, Basingstoke, Macmilllan Press.

Mumford, E. and Weir, M. (1979), *Computer Systems in Work Design, The ETHICS Method*, London, Associated Business Press.

Murdick, R.G.C., J.R.; Joel, E.R. (1990), *Introduction to Management Information Systems* (2nd Edition), Columbus, Ohio., Publishing Horizons Inc.

Nietzsche, F. (1967), *The Will to Power*, New York, Vintage Books.

Nietzsche, F. (1973), *Beyond Good and Evil*, London, Penguin Books.

Nonaka, I. (1994), 'A Dynamic Theory of Organizational Knowledge Creation', *Organization Science*, 5, 1, 14-37.

Ogden, C.K. and Richards, I.A. (1927), *The Meaning of Meaning*, New York, Kegan Paul, Trench, Trubner & Co.

Okrent, M. (1988), *Heidegger's Pragmatism: Understanding, Being and the Critique of Metaphysics*, London, Cornell University Press.

Olson, D. and Courtney, J. (1992), *Decision Support Models and Expert Systems*, New York, Macmillan Publishing Company.

Orlikowski, W. (1992), 'The Duality of Technology: Rethinking the Concept of Technology in Organisations', *Organisation Science*, 3, 3, 398-427.

Orlikowski, W.J. and Gash, D.C. (1992), 'Changing frames: Understanding Technological Change in Organizations', *Center for Information Technology Research Working Paper*, Cambridge, MA, MIT Sloan School of Management.

Page, D., Williams, P. and Boyd, D. (1993), 'Report of the Public Inquiry into the London Ambulance Service', London, HMSO.

Palmer, R.E. (1969), *Hermeneutics*, Evanston, Northwestern University Press.

Patton, P. (1989), 'Taylor and Foucault on Power and Freedom', *Political Studies*, 37, 274.

Pentland, B.T. and Reuter, H. (1994), 'Organizational Routines as Grammers of Action', *Administrative Science Quarterly*, 39, 484-510.

Peters, T. and Austin, N. (1985), *A Passion for Excellence: The Leadership Difference*, Glasgow, Fontana/Collins.

Pettigrew, A.M. (1973), *The Politics of Organizational Decision-making*, London, Tavistock Publications.

Pfeffer, J. (1981), *Power in organizations*, Marshfield, Mass., Pitman.

Philp, M. (1983), 'Foucault on Power: A Problem in Radical Translation,', *Political Theory*, 11, 1, 35.

Polanyi, M. (1973), *Personal Knowledge: Towards a Post-critical Philosophy* (1st pbk Edition), London, Routledge & Kegan Paul.

Poster, M. (1990), *The Mode of Information: Poststructuralism and Social Context*, Cambridge, Polity Press.

Pratt, A.D. (1982), *The Information of Image*, New Jersey, Ablex Publ. Corp.

Prigogine, I. and Stengers, I. (1985), *Order out of Chaos*, New York, Bantam.

Ricoeur, P. (1979), *Hermeneutics & the Human Sciences*, Paris., Cambridge University Press.

Robbins, S.P. (1988), *Management: Concepts and Applications* (2nd Edition), Englewood Cliffs, N.J., Prentice Hall International.

Robinson, B. (1994), '... And Treat Those Two Imposters Just The Same': Analysing Systems Failure as a Social Process', University of Salford., Information Technology Institute.

Rorty, R. (1982), *Consequences of Pragmatism*, Minneapolis, University of Minnesota Press.

Roszak, T. (1986), *The Cult of Information*, New York, Pantheon Books.

Roszak, T. (1994), *The Cult of Information: A Neo-Luddite Treatise on High-tech, Artificial intelligence, and the True Art of Thinking* (2nd Edition), Berkeley, University of California Press.

Saunders, C.S. and Scamell, R.W. (1986), 'Organizational Power and the Information Services Department: A Reexamination', *Communications of the ACM*, 29, 2, 142-147.

Sayles, L.R. (1979), *Leadership: What Effective Managers Really Do and How They Do It*, New York, McGraw-Hill Book Company.

Scarrott, G.G. (1985), 'Information, the Life Blood of the Organization', *The Computer Journal*, 28, 3, 203-205.

Schultheis, R. and Summer, M. (1989), *Management Information Systems: The Manager's View*, Homewood, Boston, Irwin.

Senge, P.M. (1990), *The Fifth Discipline: The Art and Practice of the Learning Organization*, New York, Doubleday.

Senge, P.M. (1990), 'The Leader's New Work: Building Learning Organizations', *Sloan Management Review*, Fall 90, 7-23.

Senn, J.A. (1990), *Information Systems in Management*, Belmont, California, Wadsworth Publ.

Shannon, C.E. and Weaver, W. (1949), *The Mathematical Theory of Communication*, Urbana, University of Illinois Press.

Simon, H.A. (1977), *The New Science of Management Decision* (2nd Edition), Englewood Cliffs, N.J., Prentice Hall.

Singh, J. (1966), *Great Ideas in Information Theory, Language and Cybernetics*, New York, Dover Publications Inc.

Smith, C. and Gemmill, G. (1991), 'Change in the small group: A dissipative structure perspective', *Human Relations*, 44, 7, 697-716.

Smuts, J.C. (1987), *Holism and Evolution*, Cape Town, N & S Press.

Stamper, R. (1988), 'Pathologies of AI', *AI & Society*, 2, 1, 3-16.

Stamper, R.K. (1985), 'Information: Mystical Fluid or a Subject for Scientific Enquiry?', *The Computer Journal*, 28, 3, 195-199.

Sterba, R.L. (1976), 'The Organization and Management of the Temple Corporations in Ancient Mesopotamia', *The Academy of Management Review*, 1, 3, 16-26.

Steward, D.K. (1968), *The Psychology of Communication*, New York, Funk & Wagnalls.

Stewart, R. (1967), *Managers and Their Jobs*, London, Macmillan.

Strassman, P. (1990), *The Business Value of Computers*, New Canaan, The Information Economics Press.

Strong, E.P. (1965), *The Management of Business: An Introduction*, New York, Harper & Row.

Strumpfer, J.P. (1990), *Modes of Inquiry: Acquiring Knowledge about Complex Phenomena*, University of Stellenboch, Unpublished course notes, Author.

Taylor, F.W. (1914), *The Principles of Scientific Management*, London/New York, Harper & Row.

Taylor, F.W. (1990), 'Scientific Management', in Pugh, D.S. (ed.), *Organization Theory: Selected Readings*, London, Penguin Books.

Teubner, G. (1993), *Law as an Autopoietic System*, Oxford, Blackwell Publishers.

Teubner, G. and Febbrajo, A. (1992), *State, Law, and Economy as Autopoietic Systems: Regulation and Autonomy in a New Perspective*, Milan, Dott. A. Giuffre Editore.

Thierauf, R.L. (1987), *Effective Management Information Systems* (2nd Edition), Columbus. Ohio., Merrill Publishing Company.

Tully, C.J. (1985), 'Information, Human Activity and the Nature of Relevant Theories', *The Computer Journal*, 28, 3, 201-210.

Ulrich, H. and Probst, G.J. (1984), *Self-Organization and Management of Social Systems*.

Varela, F. (1984), 'Two Principles for Self-Organization', in Ulrich, H. and Probst, G.J. (eds), *Self-organization and management of social systems*, Berlin, Springer-Verlag.

Vickers, G.S. (1967), *Towards a Sociology of Management*, London, Chapman and Hall.

Von Foerster, H. (1984), 'Principles of Self-Organization – In a Socio-Managerial Context', in Ulrich, H. and Probst, G.J. (eds), *Self-organization and management of social systems*, Berlin, Springer-Verlag.

Von Krogh, G. and Roos, J. (1995), *Organizational Epistemology*, Basingstoke, Macmillan Press.

Walsham, G. (1993), *Interpreting Information Systems in Organisations*, Chichester, John Wiley & Sons.

Walsham, G. (1993), 'Reading the Organization: Metaphors and Information Management', *Journal of Information Systems*, 3, 33-46.

Walsham, G. (1994), 'Interpretivism in IS research: Past, present and future', Research Paper in Management Studies, Cambridge, University of Cambridge.

Ward, J., Griffiths, P. and Whitmore, P. (1990), *Strategic Planning for Information Systems*, New York, John Wiley & Sons.

Whitley, R. (1984), *The Intellectual and Social Organization of Sciences*, Oxford, Clarendon Press.

Wildavsky, A. (1983), 'Information as an Organizational Problem', *Journal of Management Studies*, 20, 1, 29-40.

Wilden, A. (1980), *System and Structure: Essays in Communication and Exchange*, Bungay, Tavistock Publications.

Winograd, T. and Flores, F. (1987), *Understanding Computers and Cognition*, Massachusetts., Addison-Wesley.

Wiseman, C. (1985), *Strategy and Computers*, New York, Dow Jones-Irwin.

Wittgenstein, L. (1956), *Philosophical investigations*, Oxford, Basil Blackwell.

Wranke, G. (1982), *Hermeneutics and the Critique of Positivism*, Boston University Graduate School, unpublished dissertation.

Wranke, G. (1987), *Gadamer: Hermeneutics, Tradition and Reason*, Cambridge, Polity Press.

Wren, D.A. (1979), *The Evolution of Management Thought* (2nd Edition), New York, John Whiley & Sons.

Wurman, R.S. (1989), *Information Anxiety: what to do when information doesn't tell you what you want to know*, New York, Bantam Books.

Zimmerman, B.J. (1993), 'Chaos & Nonequilibrium: The Flip Side of Strategic Processes', *Organization Development Journal*, 11, 1, 31-38.

Zuboff, S. (1988), *In the Age of the Smart Machine*, New York, Basic Books.

Figure and table index

Index